Praise for *Revolutionary Collective*

"A brilliant collection of essays on the revolutionary Marxist tradition, from the classics—Lenin, Trotsky, Rosa Luxemburg—up to recent authors, such as the South African poet Dennis Brutus and the French activist and philosopher Daniel Bensaïd. The essays deal both with their individual contributions and their places in collective movements. As Le Blanc persuasively argues, their ideas do not only belong to the past but are also a compass for the struggles of the present." —**Michael Löwy**, author of *The Theory of Revolution in the Young Marx*

"Paul Le Blanc tackles the thorny but inescapable problem of the 'revolutionary collective' in this valuable selection of his essays with his usual lively tone and openness to opposing views. This is a fine book for the beginner or advanced activist thinking about what we have lost and what we might recuperate." —**Paul Buhle**, coeditor of the *Encyclopedia of the American Left*

"This collection of essays crystalizes many of the themes running throughout Paul Le Blanc's life's work. Ever attentive to the reciprocal and complex relationships between individuals and broad historical forces—'history is the lives of innumerable people'—Le Blanc explores a diverse range of figures in the global tradition of socialism from below and draws out their lasting lessons for the future. The essays provide sufficient contextual explanation and clarity to be accessible to those new to this history, while supplying rich and unexpected details that will hold the interest of seasoned revolutionary Marxists. These stories of collective organization and struggle, which combine expansive scholarship with personal anecdote, will provide sustenance and hope to those seeking to understand and resist capitalism in our own calamitous present." —**Helen C. Scott**, editor of *The Essential Rosa Luxemburg*

"Paul Le Blanc provides us with a sparkling array of revolutionary portraits, illuminating the interplay of socialist movements with individual liberatory initiative." —**John Riddell**, editor of the multivolume *The Communist International in the Lenin's Time*

"Paul Le Blanc has a gift for tracing the life course of his subjects, keeping their individual face always present but putting them in a thick context of events, disputes, and organizational loyalties. This gift is particularly telling in the case of activists who may be little more than a name to many of us, including such determinedly original thinkers as Alexander Bogdanov and James Burnham. Paul certainly has his heroes but thankfully very few villains—no, not even the ex-Trotskyist turncoat James Burnham. Throughout he engages in genuine dialogue with other scholars, myself included. In all, a remarkable achievement to add to the list of Le Blanc's impressive studies of the twentieth-century Marxist Left." —**Lars T. Lih**, author of *Lenin Rediscovered*

"Is there a future for Leninism? In an outstanding assembly of essays with a bold mission, Paul Le Blanc brings a lifetime of socialist commitment to bear on the entangled affinities and conflicts within the revolutionary Marxist tradition. A dozen discrete studies, marked by a broad and deep knowledge, allow him to offer unexpected links that remind us of the promise and possibilities of the collective enterprise of social transformation." —**Alan Wald**, author of *The New York Intellectuals: The Rise and Decline of the Anti-Stalinist Left From the 1930s to the 1980s*

"A series of highly readable sketches of participants in the revolutionary movement over the last century, including such central figures as V. I. Lenin, Rosa Luxemburg, Leon Trotsky, and Antonio Gramsci. Some of the individuals portrayed remained devoted to the struggle their entire lives, while others abandoned it along the way. Nevertheless, each made contributions to revolutionary political thought and activism that are worth studying today. A central unifying theme of the book is why 'a democratic collective process is needed by revolutionary activists.'" —**Mike Taber**, editor of *Under the Socialist Banner: Resolutions of the Second International, 1889-1912*

"People do not make history as they please, but under given circumstances that have been transmitted from the past—and yet they do make history. In *Revolutionary Collective*, Paul Le Blanc gives us an overview of some of the most important revolutionary thinkers and activists of the twentieth century, people who were committed to changing those circumstances. A red thread throughout the book is an examination of the interaction between individual engagement and collective emancipation. Written in his usual erudite, intellectually generous and lucid style, Le Blanc's book is a gift to radicals today, equipping us with historical lessons and helping us to oriente ourselves for the ongoing task of changing the world." —**Alex de Jong**, co-director, International Institute for Research and Education, Amsterdam

"While socialist thought and action emphasize the necessity to overcome capitalism's innate individualism, most writing on revolutionary socialist thinkers and leaders remains centered on their individual strengths and weaknesses, sins and achievements. This volume rightly focuses our attention on common sources of inspiration, on learning through successes and failures lived and thought through in joint struggle, and on the seldom celebrated but nevertheless real value of 'unoriginal' contributions that pass on the knowledge gained by previous generations in their struggle for human liberation. Always thoughtful in his critique and generous even to those to whom he finds himself fundamentally in opposition, Paul Le Blanc draws us back toward these deep, collective sources for every attempt at socialist renewal." —**Pepijn Brandon**, Senior Researcher International Institute for Social History, Amsterdam; coeditor, *Worlds of Labour Turned Upside Down: Revolutions and Labour Relations in Global Historical Perspective*

REVOLUTIONARY COLLECTIVE

COMRADES, CRITICS, AND DYNAMICS IN THE STRUGGLE FOR SOCIALISM

Paul Le Blanc

Chicago, Illinois
Haymarket Books

Published in 2022 by
Haymarket Books
P.O. Box 180165
Chicago, IL 60618
773-583-7884
www.haymarketbooks.org
info@haymarketbooks.org

ISBN: 978-1-64259-589-5

Distributed to the trade in the US through Consortium Book Sales and
Distribution (www.cbsd.com) and internationally through Ingram Publisher
Services International (www.ingramcontent.com).

This book was published with the generous support of Lannan Foundation
and Wallace Action Fund.

Special discounts are available for bulk purchases by organizations and
institutions. Please email info@haymarketbooks.org for more information.

Cover design by Rachel Cohen.

Printed in Canada by union labor.

Library of Congress Cataloging-in-Publication data is available.

10 9 8 7 6 5 4 3 2 1

CONTENTS

PREFACE

The revolutionary Left, and the working-class movement of which it has traditionally been a vital component, have long placed considerable value on the notion of *collectivism*. This infuses the goal of its struggle: a cooperative commonwealth in which the free development of each will be the condition for the free development of all. It also infuses the struggle itself: we are sisters and brothers, we are family and comrades, an injury to one is an injury to all, solidarity forever.

In stark contrast to assertions of its detractors (and to both naïve misconceptions and damaged mentalities among some of its would-be partisans), this collectivism is the opposite of *uniformity*, whether enforced by conformist pressures or authoritarian strictures. As the young Marx emphasized more than once, human beings find in their very core a remarkable blend of strivings for freedom (self-determination), creative labor, and genuine community. This animates both the visionary ends and the activist means associated with revolutionary collectivism. A revolutionary organization, if it is to be vibrant and relevant, is dependent not only on the coming together of its members, its comrades, but also on their initiative, their creativity, their critical thinking. To suppress or somehow obliterate the individuality essential to being human negates the very life-force that gives meaning to the revolutionary project.

Exploring the revolutionary Marxist tradition has been a focal point of five decades for me as a scholar and an activist. The fruits of my labors have included *Lenin and the Revolutionary Party* (which, combined with *From Marx to Gramsci*, constitutes a bedrock for me), plus the short biography *Leon Trotsky*, three books on Rosa Luxemburg, and such studies as *A Short*

History of the U.S. Working Class, A Freedom Budget for All Americans, and *October Song: Bolshevik Triumph, Communist Tragedy 1917–1924.* The very title of the present book, *Revolutionary Collective,* highlights themes running through all these works, having to do with numerous people dynamically coming together to create a transition to a better world.

This volume includes nine essays focused on individuals associated with the revolutionary socialist movement. There are also two general surveys at the volume's beginning, and a survey of a different kind at its conclusion. The resulting collection of a dozen essays gives considerable stress to the *collective* nature of the revolutionary struggle.

The first essay provides a survey of "Lenin studies," some of which bring Vladimir Ilyich Lenin forward from the dark shadows cast by those inclined to minimize the vibrancy and subversive relevance of his life and work. The collective nature of the scholarly enterprise matches the earlier interplay of thinkers and doers in the practical political movement of which Lenin was so important an element. The second essay further explores the complexities of the collective dimension of this movement—the Bolshevik current of the Russian socialist movement.

When we turn to significant individuals related to the Bolshevik-Leninist tradition, we find their contributions inseparable from this quality of revolutionary collectivity. That is most obvious in the emphasis on Leon Trotsky's "unoriginality," even as he offers distinctive insights on realities of the later twentieth century (insights flowing from essential aspects of Marx's thought). The fourth essay surveys important though often neglected contributions (both positive and problematical) of Alexander Bogdanov, who helped shape early Bolshevism up to 1908, and whose influence continued to be felt afterward. But an understanding of the Bolshevik tradition as being inseparable from revolutionary collectivity also animates contributions offered by Georg Lukács and Antonio Gramsci, central theorists and leaders of Hungarian and Italian Communism in the 1920s (foundational figures of what has been tagged "Western Marxism"), before the tradition was corrupted by the bureaucratic-authoritarianism associated with Stalinism.

Beyond the Bolshevik tradition—but in my mind inseparable from the broader "revolutionary collective" of which it was part—are the contributions of Rosa Luxemburg. I have surveyed some of these contributions, and aspects of her life, in my recent collection *The Living Flame: The Revolutionary Passion of Rosa Luxemburg,* but this piece has been inspired by new work in helping to edit volumes two and five of her *Complete Works* (in collaboration with Peter Hudis and Helen Scott). Luxemburg brings essential qualities to the revolutionary collective—both at points of divergence and convergence with the tradition that is the focus of this volume.

Two individuals discussed in this collection decisively broke from the Bolshevik-Leninist tradition—Karl Korsch and James Burnham. There were, of course, different and no less decisive breaks that we can find with the others, the most obvious being Trotsky, who was only able to defend that tradition outside of the official Communist mainstream. But the role of practical revolutionary leader was abandoned by Lukács under the impact of Stalinism; simply to survive politically in the Communist movement (and, finally, to survive physically while living in Stalin's Russia), he made—for a time—far-reaching compromises, settling for a more contemplative life as philosopher and literary critic, although his earlier achievement (the focus of the essay here) was never entirely erased. Gramsci's role as a practical revolutionary was also broken in the same period, in this case by his arrest in fascist Italy. Nonetheless, although he died a slow death during his ten-year imprisonment, he remained vibrantly alive as a Marxist theorist through intensive labors on his *Prison Notebooks*.

Korsch approached similar tasks, although with greater internal limitations than these Hungarian and Italian contemporaries. Yet he was never able to surrender to the status quo and thereby left future revolutionaries something of value. The fact remains that, in the end, Korsch's break from Leninist perspectives left him unable to provide any clear, coherent, practical orientation for those who would engage in revolutionary socialist activism. That is even more manifest in the break effected by James Burnham, who, after a relatively brief but passionate affair with Marxism, went on to compose a devastating critique, at the same time crossing over to join the unrelenting enemies of revolution, democracy, and socialism. As he did so, he became a masterful ideologist of political conservatism, a counterrevolutionary theorist par excellence, and he literally consigned to the flames much of what he had sought as a revolutionary. With each of these "heretics" we can see efforts to make theoretical sense of the collectivities with which they had identified, and there is—in my opinion—something to learn from the results.

There are, finally, essays on two revolutionaries I personally knew. Dennis Brutus, the South African poet-activist who broke rocks with Nelson

Mandela while imprisoned on Robben Island, became a mentor to a global layer of poets and activists, inspiring many of us with his eloquence, persistence, and insights. As an exile from his homeland, he lived in Pittsburgh for several years, and we became close. Daniel Bensaïd, the dynamic French Trotskyist from the tempestuous "generation of 1968," is someone I met at international gatherings. It was only in his memoirs, however, that I really came to know the impatient young militant who helped lead audacious revolutionary assaults. He discovered—as he aged—a revolutionary patience, which pushed his theorizations far "outside the box." Brutus and Bensaïd were both powerfully influenced by the Bolshevik-Leninist tradition, and the contributions of each can help nourish future efforts to reach a better future.

And that is, in fact, the point of this collection.

The final survey at the conclusion of this volume also connects some of my personal experience with the historical sweep of the tradition whose facets I explore in this volume. It touches more directly on thoughts of "what are we to do" with insights from the past as we find ourselves amid the intersecting swirls of present and future.

Postscript at the End of an Astonishing Year

While the introduction above and the essays in this volume (aside from that on Bogdanov) were composed before the crises unfolding in 2020, their relevance seems in no way diminished by the new developments. Some of those—if we restrict ourselves to what has happened within the United States—include: the renewed challenge to the political mainstream posed by Bernie Sanders and the related rise of socialist ideas, organization, and activity; the explosive second wave of the Black Lives Matter movement; the maneuvers and right-wing mobilizations engineered by Donald Trump in an attempt to prevent his loss of the presidential election and his defeat, followed by ongoing mobilizations and maneuvers; assaults and pushback regarding women's rights; the COVID-19 pandemic; and other manifestations of our deepening global ecological crisis. My own renewed activism is reflected in further streams of writing I have done related to all these developments (perhaps some of that can become yet another book), but for me, it is all within the framework of the conceptualizations presented in this volume. We are a continuation of comrades who have gone before.

I agonized over comrades not included here, yet some can be found elsewhere. "Remembering Ruth Querio" and "The Marxism of C. L. R. James" are in my collection *Left Americana: The Radical Heart of US History* (Chicago: Haymarket Books, 2017). Two others can be found in online reflections: "Sarah Lovell: Collective Portrait of a Revolutionary," *Bulletin in Defense of Marxism*, September 1994, https://www.marxists.org/history/etol/newspape/bidom/n118-sept-1994-bom.pdf; and "Remembering George Shriver," *International Viewpoint*, May 10, 2020, http://internationalviewpoint.org/spip.php?article6581.

Of course, the vast revolutionary collective defies efforts to do it justice within the covers of books. Not only have there been so many amazing people who have been part of this collective, but its numbers continue to increase. The ever-unfolding oppression and violence inherent in global capitalism continues to generate inspiring and sometimes explosive responses of people who become convinced that a better world is possible. Convinced that such a future must be fought for, and must be won, many will seek to learn from, and thereby make contributions to, the tradition explored in these pages.

Rome/Pittsburgh, 2020/2021

ACKNOWLEDGMENTS

My deepest thanks to friends and comrades at Haymarket Books for their assistance in the creation of this volume, with a special tip of the hat to my copy editor, Trevor Perri. There are others too numerous to mention who have also been integral and intimate elements in a vast collective process that resulted in these essays, though I will mention one, who has been my beloved life partner for well over a decade, Nancy Ferrari.

"Lenin Studies: Method and Organization" first appeared in *Historical Materialism* 25, no. 4 (2017).

"Bolshevism as a Revolutionary Collective" first appeared as "Lenin and the Bolshevik Party, a Revolutionary Collective" in the online journal *Links: International Journal of Socialist Renewal,* July 10, 2018. It was one of the keynote presentations opening the International Conference on Russian and Soviet History—"The Centenary of the 1917 Russian Revolution(s)"—at Budapest's Eötvös Loránd University, May 15–16, 2017; presented in a panel on the Russian Revolution at the International Institute for Research and Education in Amsterdam, November 4, 2017; and at the fourteenth annual Historical Materialism conference in London, November 9–12, 2017.

"The Unoriginality of Leon Trotsky" first appeared as "Trotsky's Revolutionary Ideas—Originality or Continuity?" in the online journal *Links: International Journal of Socialist Renewal,* December 2, 2018.

"Learning from Bogdanov" first appeared in the online blog of *Historical Materialism,* May 1, 2020.

"Spider and Fly: The Leninist Philosophy of Georg Lukács" first appeared in *Historical Materialism* 21, no. 2 (2013).

"Antonio Gramsci and the Modern Prince" is derived from a presentation for a socialist study group more almost two decades ago and was first published in the online journal *Links: International Journal of Socialist Renewal*, December 1, 2018.

"Rosa Luxemburg and the Actuality of Revolution" was presented at the Historical Materialism Conference in London on November 9, 2019. It first appeared in the online journal *Links: International Journal of Socialist Renewal*, November 17, 2019. A small portion of it appears in the introduction of *Living Flame: The Revolutionary Passion of Rosa Luxemburg* (Chicago: Haymarket Books, 2020).

"The 'Anti-Philosophy' of Karl Korsch" first appeared in *International Socialist Review* 104 (Spring 2017).

"The Odyssey of James Burnham" is a revised version of "From Revolutionary Intellectual to Conservative Master-Thinker: The Anti-Democratic Odyssey of James Burnham," which appeared in *Left History* 3 (Spring–Summer 1995).

"Dennis Brutus: Poet as Revolutionary" first appeared as "Dennis Brutus: Poet and Revolutionary (1924–2009)" in *Critique: Journal of Socialist Theory* 38, no. 2 (May 2010).

"Revolutionary Patience: Daniel Bensaïd" first appeared in the online journal, *International Viewpoint*, May 14, 2014.

"Reflections on Coherence and Comradeship" first appeared in the online version of *Socialist Worker*, March 27, 2019.

Chapter One

LENIN STUDIES

Method and Organization

"Leninist abstraction has returned to be real because the Leninist utopia is again a desire."

—Antonio Negri[1]

The growing field of Lenin studies has been nurtured by the growth of crises and struggles in our own time. And some believe the nurturing can go both ways—that the growing number of studies can contribute to the present-day activists' efforts at developing revolutionary strategy and organization and struggle.[2]

Vladimir Ilyich Lenin and his comrades in the revolutionary Bolshevik wing of the Russian socialist movement had multiple facets and impacts. Our focus in this survey of Lenin studies will be restricted to Lenin's revolutionary method, through a critical and comparative exploration of works by Antonio Negri, Alan Shandro, and Tamás Krausz. This will leave out much of interest and value. Roland Boer's splendid research and reflection on Lenin and religion is only one example.[3] Another is August Nimtz's invaluable excavation of the centrality of electoral politics in Lenin's revolutionary strategy.[4]

Of considerable importance have been memoirs and studies of on-the-ground Bolshevik and Leninist practice from the early 1900s through the early 1920s, as well as early experience-based theorizations by sophisticated practitioners (such as Georg Lukács and Antonio Gramsci) in other countries.[5] Attention to such material—which cannot be incorporated into this

1

chapter—will enable us to connect what Lenin and other political leaders had to say with the practical work of the activists who paid attention to, and helped to shape, what was theorized, providing essential insights into past events and future possibilities. As this suggests, genuine Leninism cannot be grasped if we restrict our attention to Lenin himself. If there are to be future incarnations of a usable Leninism, they must have that quality of democratic and international collectivity.

Is It Permissible to Speak of "Leninism"?

This brings us to a terminological quibble that has recently assumed significant proportions among some scholars and activists identifying (or wrestling with whether they should identify) with Lenin's political thought and practice.

One reasonable formulation was advanced by the late revolutionary theorist Daniel Bensaïd, who commented that "the invention of 'Leninism' as a religiously mummified orthodoxy, was part of the process of bureaucratisation of the Comintern and the Soviet Union," concluding, "That's why, as far as possible, I personally avoid utilizing this 'ism.'" Yet when we look at how such prominent Bolsheviks as Gregory Zinoviev and Nikolai Bukharin characterized the nature and quality of Lenin's political thought and practice, we find formulations that differ from Stalin's.[6]

Noting that "the Russian Leninists, the Leninists of the Communist International and of the whole world are confronted by grand and important tasks" in the wake of Lenin's death, Zinoviev urged comrades to "strengthen and solidify the union between the most advanced Communists and the whole of the non-party working masses," and to "succeed with the plough of Leninism in raising new and deeper layers . . . assisting even those who have only a spark of talent," and "helping the multi-million working mass in educating itself and in raising its cultural level, in order to fit itself for the work of socialist reconstruction." Comparing the views of Marx with those of Lenin, Bukharin argued, "It is clear that Leninist Marxism represents quite a particular form of ideological education, for the simple reason that it is itself a child of a somewhat different epoch." At the same time, Bukharin added, "if we regard Marxism not as the entirety of ideas such as existed in the time of Marx," but as a distinctive tool and methodology, then "Leninism is not something that modifies or revises the method of Marxist teaching" but is "a complete return to the Marxism formulated by Marx and Engels themselves."[7]

While such formulations do not bear the marks of bureaucratic authoritarianism or mummified orthodoxy that one might be led to expect, there is truth in the way Bensaïd characterizes certain early articulations of the term *Leninism*. Serious historians such as E. H. Carr documented long ago that the term was utilized as a device to advance factional and bureaucratic agendas, in a campaign against a fabricated "Trotskyism."[8]

Sharing the skittishness regarding the terms *Leninism* and *Leninist*, Tamás Krausz reaches for something else to refer to what elsewhere he calls "Lenin's Marxism" and "Lenin's approach to Marxism" and (perhaps absent-mindedly) "the Leninist tradition of Marxism." And so we find (fortunately not often) awkward reference to "the Leninian approach to socialism" and "the Leninian legacy."[9]

Negri's solution seems preferable. Arguing "the first and greatest danger is that of entering into a debate on 'Leninism,'" he quite simply proclaims: "Leninism does not exist." He immediately modifies the proclamation by adding, "or rather, the theoretical statements contained in this term must be brought back to bear on the set of comportments and attitudes to which they refer: their correctness must be measured in the relationship between the emergence of a historical subject (the revolutionary proletariat) and the set of subversive problems that this subject is confronted with." And then, again quite simply, he makes free use of the terms *Leninism* and *Leninist* when discussing Lenin's thought and practice.[10]

Pioneers in the Field of Lenin Studies

The current phase in Lenin studies could be said to have opened in 2001, when a conference in Essen (Germany) gathered many contributors to the field (including Negri and Shandro). The conference presentations were published several years later in a volume of renewal, *Lenin Reloaded*.[11]

This added, of course, to earlier studies by E. H. Carr, Isaac Deutscher, Tamara Deutscher, Moshe Lewin, Marcel Liebman, Ernest Mandel, Ernst Fischer, Neil Harding, Tony Cliff, Ronald H. Clark, and others, as well as to what had been offered by a more critical current that included Robert C. Tucker, Christopher Read, Ralph Carter Elwood, James D. White, the early Robert Service and the older Neil Harding. There was, as well, the distinctive and extremely influential subbranch of Lenin studies represented by ex-leftist and moderate leftist, liberal, and conservative analysts guided by the sensibilities of Cold War anti-Communism. This included: Bertram D. Wolfe, Alfred G. Meyer, Robert V. Daniels, Louis Fischer, Adam Ulam, Stefan T. Possony, and Richard Pipes, with some later scholars, such as the older Robert Service, following in their wake.[12]

But outstanding among the pioneers are Lars Lih and Nadezhda Krupskaya. Their contributions deserve special attention.[13]

Within the ranks of those currently interested in Lenin, there is a significant contingent seeing Lars Lih as being pretty much the beginning and the end of any serious study of Lenin.[14] Lars himself would never make such a claim. Just as it is crucial to place Lenin in his context in order to understand the Leninism of Lenin, so should Lih be seen within the larger context of Lenin studies.

Pride of place among pioneering Lenin scholars goes to Nadezhda Krupskaya. In contrast to the rigid definition proposed by Stalin—that "Leninism is Marxism in the epoch of imperialism and of the proletarian revolution"—Krupskaya presents us with the approach and ideas and practices actually developed by Lenin during his life as a revolutionary activist, engaged in the struggle to end all oppression and exploitation through working-class democracy and socialism. This understanding of "Leninism" was of little use to a rising bureaucratic dictatorship that—out of the isolation and erosion of the Russian Revolution—sought a dogmatic ideology to help reinforce its own increasingly abusive power as it ruthlessly sought to modernize backward Russia.[15] The Stalinist evaluation of Krupskaya has been helpfully clarified by one of Stalin's closest associates, V. M. Molotov:

> Krupskaya followed Lenin all her life, before and after the Revolution. But she understood nothing about politics. Nothing. . . . In 1925 she became confused and followed Zinoviev. And Zinoviev took an anti-Leninist position. Bear in mind that it was not so simple to be a Leninist! . . . Stalin regarded her unfavorably. She turned out to be a bad communist. . . . What Lenin wrote about Stalin's rudeness [when he proposed Stalin's removal as the Communist Party's General Secretary] was not without Krupskaya's influence. . . . Stalin was irritated: "Why should I get up on my hind legs for her? To sleep with Lenin does not necessarily mean to understand Leninism!" . . . In the last analysis, no one understood Leninism better than Stalin.[16]

Krupskaya, a committed Marxist since the mid-1890s when she was in her early twenties, was not only "an active militant" throughout two decades of exile but also Lenin's "collaborator in every circumstance" (according to the esteemed historian of international socialism, Georges Haupt) and "above all the *confidante* of the founder of Bolshevism."[17]

Krupskaya's book *Reminiscences of Lenin* suffered disfigurement from having to be composed and published amid the growing intolerance and repression of the Stalin regime, yet it holds up well as an "informative and generally accurate" account of Lenin's life and thought, partisan yet relatively free from "personal acrimony or exaggerated polemics," and overall "admirably honest and detached"—as biographer Robert H. McNeal aptly describes it. Appearing in the early 1930s, before the worst and most murderous of Stalin's policies would close off the possibility of even its partially muted honesty, it is a truly courageous book. In his 1935 diary, Trotsky wrote of her in this period that she had "consistently and firmly refused to act against her conscience." An educated Marxist and experienced revolutionary, she was determined to tell as much of the truth as she was able about the development of Lenin's revolutionary perspectives, with extensive attention to his writings and activities, and to the contexts in which these evolved. Within a few years, like so many others, she felt compelled to capitulate utterly and completely and shamefully in support of Stalin's worst policies. As Haupt once put it, "there is still much that is left unsaid on the drama of her life, on the humiliation she underwent." But the memoir of her closest comrade remains as a monument to the best that she had to give over many years, and as an invaluable (in some ways unsurpassed) source on the life and thought of Lenin.[18]

Among the most significant contributions to Lenin studies in our own time, of course, have been those made by Lars Lih. Emphasizing the fundamentally democratic qualities of Lenin's political thought, and his boundless optimism regarding the capacity of the working class to bring about socialism, Lih has challenged an influential interpretation of the relationship of Lenin's thought to the Marxism of his own time. Lenin's thought is often separated from and counterposed to the variation of Marxism represented by Karl Kautsky within the German Social Democratic Party and the Socialist International (or Second International). This counterposition could take three forms:

1.   that Lenin's thought constituted a break from genuine Marxism, represented by Kautsky, with all of its democratic sensibilities and historical materialist realism;

2. that Lenin, in contrast to people like Kautsky, did not flinch from following through in the authoritarian-totalitarian potentialities inherent in the Marxism of Marx;

3. that Lenin—unlike Kautsky and many others—actually grasped and embraced the truly revolutionary essence of Marxism, and therefore was able to embark on a qualitatively different and superior political project. (This third notion has been developed in various ways by revolutionary Marxists and, in a different way, by Stalinists.)

Whatever the form or variation, this stark counterposition happens to be incompatible with the take on reality articulated by significant others. Krupskaya's reminiscences, for example, and Gregory Zinoviev's *History of the Bolshevik Party*, as well as writings of Leon Trotsky (and of some influenced by him, such as Isaac Deutscher and Ernest Mandel)—all indicate that the Marxism associated with such figures as Karl Kautsky and George Plekhanov is an integral component of the Marxism of Lenin and other early Bolsheviks. And Lars Lih helps to clinch the matter.[19]

Lenin was organically connected with the best in "the Marxism of the Second International." Referring to the 1891 Erfurt Program of the German Social Democratic Party, a document largely composed by Karl Kautsky and explicated in his classic work *The Class Struggle*, Lih suggests the term "Erfurtian Marxist" could be applied to Lenin (and others in the revolutionary wing of the world socialist movement of that time).

Diverging from Kautsky

Yet a distinction can be made between the theoretical basics of Marxism and certain vitally important strategic specifics and on-the-ground practical policy (which also have theoretical implications). It can also be shown that divergences began to unfold between Lenin's and Kautsky's parties in the years leading up to the First World War.

We find in Lenin's writings immense respect for Kautsky before the First World War, an engaged reference to one or another of his ideas, and the sense of shared theoretical framework. But there is nothing that smacks of discipleship. Lih emphasizes that Lenin was "in love" with Marx and Engels and saw them, in Lenin's words, as "the genuine article." Lenin's pre-1914 approach to Kautsky lacked such intimacy.[20]

At the same time, one finds pulls and tugs *within* Kautsky's Marxism, between activist and fatalist dynamics. The former produced greater sensitivity toward complexities of, and openness to, revolutionary possibilities, while the latter closed off possibilities and reduced reality to simpler propositions, consistent with either a dogmatic optimism or fatalistic pessimism. Kautsky's revolutionary-activist inclinations were only partially checked by elements of dogmatic fatalism up through 1909, but by 1910, even more by 1914 and 1917, his Marxism was increasingly characterized by the latter.[21]

Alan Shandro argues that, despite common ground shared with Kautsky prior to 1914, Lenin had a very particular way of conceptualizing the notion of *proletarian hegemony* (working-class predominance) in the struggle for democracy—involving "the political ability to act independently as a class and hence . . . an organized vanguard informed by Marxist theory and capable of diagnosing and acting upon significant movements in the logic of struggle." Antonio Negri makes a similar point about the necessity for a "guarantee of the independence of the proletariat as the hegemonic class of the revolutionary process," adding: "The party is both the continuity of the struggle for democracy and the condition for the unification of the proletariat and of the socialist struggle."[22]

Related to this, Tamás Krausz comments on the growing hegemony of the Bolsheviks in the workers' movement from 1912 to 1914, their successes grounded "in the Bolsheviks' aiming to connect the short-term—even daily—demands of the workers with prospects for the 'proletarian dictatorship.'" Legal work and reform struggles were integrated into a revolutionary approach to winning political power for the working class. The notion of hegemony, emphasized by Shandro and Negri, resulted in an organizational orientation enabling the Bolsheviks, as Krausz notes, to edge out moderate Menshevik competitors—gaining control of trade unions and cooperatives, surging in subscriptions to Bolshevik as opposed to Menshevik newspapers, and finally in electing more working-class delegates to parliament. Such developments from 1912 to 1914 would have powerful repercussions in 1917.[23]

One need not agree with all that is presented in these new studies to conclude that there are rich deposits of theory and insight in the approach, ideas, and practices developed by Lenin in the course of his life as a revolutionary activist.

Leninist Method

With an appeal for us to "return to Lenin," Antonio Negri's *Factory of Strategy: 33 Lessons on Lenin* provides an exploration of the context and logic of Lenin's theorizations. The book was developed decades before his widely read works coauthored with Michael Hardt—*Empire, Multitude,* and *Commonwealth.* Published in Italy during the 1970s, *Factory of Strategy* reflects discussion and debates on the Italian Left of that time, as activists and intellectuals associated with workerist-autonomist currents confronted, and sought to forge a dynamic left alternative to, an increasingly reformist mass Communist Party.[24]

It is significant that Negri, more than four decades later and in a very different context, believes the book has continued relevance. He stresses: "Clearly there can be times when Lenin's discourse is summed up and valued, but as the outcome of a confrontation, not as a premise." This corresponds to the view of Tamás Krausz, who tells us in *Reconstructing Lenin* that "the Leninist tradition of Marxism is the only one that has offered, at least for a time, an alternative to capitalism," that "in a search for alternatives, the discontented keep running into 'Lenin's Marxism' at every turn," and that "the legacy of the primacy of Lenin's Marxism is not a thing of the past." Alan Shandro, in his *Lenin and the Logic of Hegemony,* joins the chorus with more rarified vocabulary when he tells us: "Lenin's politico-strategic logic of the struggle for hegemony yields insights useful for thinking about the constitution of a proletarian-popular community through the struggles of an irreducible plurality of political actors."[25]

Each of these writers recognizes that Lenin's time is qualitatively different from our own in quite important ways. "A historically adequate interpretation of Lenin's Marxism—in Marxist terms—must begin," Krausz tells us, "with the recognition that Lenin's legacy is essentially a specific, practical application of Marx's *theory of social formation*" in a specific moment in history, and that "Lenin's political and theoretical legacy, as a historical variant of Marxism, is unique and unrepeatable."[26] The mass left-wing working-class movements, powerfully influenced by revolutionary theories of Marx and others, and essential components of the political scene in the time of Lenin, have faded. Negri tells us: "The composition of the contemporary working class in struggle and the composition of the entire proletariat have nothing whatsoever to do with the composition of the proletariat of the early twentieth century." Dramatically insisting that "we are a planet away from Lenin's issues," he explains:

The working class we struggle in . . . has been turned into mass by the capitalist mode of production itself, transformed by the technological changes introduced by capital in order to combat those Leninist "vanguards" and beat their overbearing and victorious organized isolation; the composition of the class we struggle in is entirely different. Today's mass worker turns her deskilling, which capital imposed on her as a sign of a new isolation, into the unity of all abstract labor; it transforms the interchangeability of her tasks into chances of general mobility across sectors and territories, *and so on.*[27]

Krausz, drawing from the later writings of the aging Georg Lukács, also pushes in this direction—but he goes further, into Lenin's own time, suggesting that "Lenin was unable to identify the economic features of the 'latest' stage of capitalist development, the transformation of the workers' movements in the 'developed countries,'" which—he suggests—resulted in the unanticipated isolation of the Russian Revolution. Unlike Negri, Krausz seems to believe there were deeper socioeconomic reasons for the Western European working classes' failure to follow the example set by the revolutionary workers of Russia. Yet he offers no comparative examination of the specifics of labor process and working conditions, living conditions, cultures and subcultures, and the consciousness the working classes of Russia and other countries. Nor are such considerations (the possibility of revolutionary incapacity within Western European working classes) entertained by Shandro—and, as will be suggested below, there may be grounds to justify his disinclination to do so.[28]

Whatever their differences with each other, Krausz and Shandro fully agree with Negri that revolutionary activists must seriously engage with Lenin if they hope to move forward in replacing destructive capitalist tyranny with life-affirming socialist democracy. He insists that "by looking into the Leninist relation between tactical strategy and organization to verify in a particular class composition (as correctly interpreted by Lenin) the general laws it identifies," it will be possible to "put these laws to the test of practical criticism." This is a process of "recognizing the shifts, leaps, and discontinuity that workers' theory is forced to confront," and in his opinion "there are no other ways of linking our thought to Lenin's today."[29] Understanding the methodology Lenin utilized in his context, Negri insists, sheds light on what we must do in our own.

Garbling Lenin—or Sharpening the Knife?

Negri's *Factory of Strategy* is sometimes so closely reasoned as to allow no sunlight between its complex layers of analysis. In his explanation and defense of Lenin's thought, Negri employs conceptualizations and vocabulary that seem so specialized as to cause (one imagines) Lenin himself to vigorously scratch what hair was left on his head with extreme perplexity.

According to this philosopher-activist, Lenin's revolutionary political thought has a very particular trajectory—from Marx's analysis in *Capital* (related to Russian specificities), which logically extends to a specific theory of organization, which in turn logically culminates in a theory of revolution, including the strategy and tactics of insurrection. This in itself may seem a rather bizarre mix-up. One would think there should first be an analysis of society and how it should be altered, followed by the development of strategy on how to bring about such change, and only then the development of an organization capable of carrying out that strategy for social change.

What's worse, we are presented with what seems a topsy-turvy set of terms. It seems it is good to be *sectarian*, while avoiding *codism*, with a *working class* that leads the *proletariat* (aren't they synonyms?), culminating in a *revolution from above* (this is projected as good and necessary) that *burns* one's previous work, all in the name of Leninism, and somehow this will lead not to a multiple train wreck, but instead to communism, a society of the free and the equal.

If one approaches this work with patience and attention, however, and with some knowledge of Lenin's actual writings (this was, after all, a set of lectures designed to accompany the reading of such texts by groups of activists), what might seem a hopeless chaos assumes a more interesting focus. One is reminded of a story Krupskaya tells:

> Vladimir Ilyich and I were once reminded of a simile used by Lev Tolstoy. He was going along and saw from afar a man squatting and waving his arms about in a ridiculous way; a madman, he thought, but when he drew nearer, he saw it to be a man sharpening a knife on the kerb. The same thing happens in theoretical disputes. From the outside it seems a sheer waste of time, but when you go into the matter more deeply you see that it is a momentous issue.[30]

Sifting through the rarified terminology brings us closer to the sharpening of the theoretical scalpel. There are, of course, different uses of terminology among various Marxists—for example, the word *ideology*, which for Lenin and others is simply a neutral reference to a set of ideas or belief system helping one make sense of reality, which means Marxism itself is an ideological perspective. But many (including Negri) define the term quite differently as conveying a *false or distorted* understanding of reality, to which Marxist science should be counterposed. Making the complex, important point that the notion of ceaseless change and development is built into the methodology of Marxism and into its analysis of the most dynamic of all economic systems, capitalism, Negri emphasizes discontinuity as being essential both to the nature of capitalism and the working class, concluding with the potentially baffling comment that "the discontinuity of Marxism is a negation of ideology."[31]

There are other words that Negri seems to use in peculiar ways that are not so easily resolved, most seriously when he discusses "the political composition of the *working class* and the *proletariat* in Russia." Utilizing the two italicized synonyms might seem redundant, but consider this sentence: "Where the *working class* was distinct within the vanguard of the *proletariat*, the externality of the process of organization and the need to impose the recomposition of the proletariat from above amounted to a need and desire for a theoretical isolation of the vanguard from the process of masses in conditions of emergency."[32]

There is more than one complication in the sentence—but it is clear that the two (again) italicized words are not meant to be synonymous. Given the lack of clarification within the text, one must guess at the meaning of this unusual distinction. Is *proletariat* (derived from its usage in ancient Rome) referring to the impoverished masses in general? Does it include landless and poor peasants and the degraded urban poor? Does *working class* refer "only to industrial labor," which "excludes all other laboring classes" (as Negri indicates in his later *Multitude*)? If these things (or something like them) are the case, then this and other sentences in the text would make sense, corresponding to on-the-ground realities in tsarist Russia, and would become politically useful. *The industrial working class must play the leading role in rallying the masses of the Russian people, but it must also maintain political independence, not becoming submerged in the great impoverished mass.* Negri explains: "This leadership is the hegemony of the interests of the working class in its specificity, which must initially be represented by the independence of organization, and is here shown to be an ability to actualize this dialectical shift, to dominate the series of democratic stages in the most radical deepening of the revolutionary process, in the withering-away of the state, in the destruction of the machine of power that has been built around wage labor."[33]

There are simpler mysteries that can be solved through a close reading of Negri's text. At a certain point he is critical of certain Marxists in the Second International because, for them, "Marxism was not a sectarian standpoint," whereas "the originality of Lenin's reading of Marxism" involves the "grasp of its determinate existence as a sectarian judgment." A common definition of the term *sectarian* connotes divisively placing the outlooks and needs of one's small religious or political group ahead of everything else, stilting one's relationship with the rest of humanity and reality, and (in regard to would-be "Marxist" sectarians) doing this at the expense of the actual, living struggles and movements of the workers and the oppressed. But Negri's usage of the term is quite different, connoting bias and partisanship for the working class and the class struggle. As he explains:

> Throughout the civilized world the teachings of Marx evoke the utmost hostility and hatred of all bourgeois science (both official and liberal), which regards Marxism as a kind of 'pernicious sect.' And no other attitude is to be expected, for there can be no 'impartial' social science in a society based on class struggle. In one way or another, all official and liberal science *defends* wage-slavery, whereas Marxism has declared a relentless war on that slavery.[34]

At the same time, he keeps warning against something that is translated as "codism"—and it takes several pages before he refers to this in the same clarifying breath as "a static conception of reality." This appears to be akin to dogmatism—although *codismo* in Italian refers to "tailing" or "tail-ending," in left-wing parlance, indicating following uncritically behind. Related to the resistance to such things, we are confronted with this odd sentence: "Each single objective, when reached and consolidated, must be burned by the revolutionary party." The thought is repeated: "The political decision of the vanguard of the organized proletariat posits and then burns each single moment of the development that contains the struggles." He links this with a persistent conceptualization of permanent revolution—for example, he asserts, "the notion of the democratic-bourgeois dictatorship of the proletariat, a fundamental concept from the standpoint of permanent revolution, is located in this framework," and again:

Lenin states that Marxists recognize the actual need for a state, and thus for a dictatorship in the particular phases that the revolution goes through; they especially recognize where the contents of the struggle, needs and power of the masses can only produce a bourgeois-democratic determination of the contents of the revolutionary process. However, all of this must constantly be burned and overcome: the permanent revolution is the goal of communists.[35]

This connotes a dialectical process of building up one phase of the revolutionary struggle, which can make possible (but only through "burning" or fueling or being consumed and transcended by) the next phase of revolutionary struggle—a succession of revolutionary moments necessarily succeeding each other.[36]

Yet another odd insistence comes from Negri with the assertion that "we have come to appreciate the significance of the revolution from above so strongly advocated by Lenin." Such revolutionary Marxists as Lenin were known for their enthusiastic support for "from-the-bottom-up" revolutionary democracy. But Negri's "revolution from above" formulation (which Lenin himself never employed) refers—in part—to notions that are consistent with revolutionary-democratic perspectives. It involves the question of *leadership*, of "the organizational ability of the working class to lead" the revolutionary struggle of society's broader layers of the impoverished "proletariat" (to use Negri's particular conceptualization), and "the organizational ability to set into motion the mechanisms of the permanent revolution at each moment," and "the subjective ability of the class vanguard to be the point of the diamond, an effective military force to lead this process" of revolutionary insurrection.[37]

This relates to Negri's understanding of Lenin's theorization of the interplay between spontaneity and organization. He sees in Lenin "an exaltation of spontaneity that is not occasional but permanent and systematic," a notion that workers' spontaneity will always be at the basis of revolutionary social democracy and its process of organization." At the same time, "even at the spontaneous level and in economic struggle, the working class fights directly against the overall power structure that confronts it, and the moment of this insurgence is absolutely fundamental to the genesis, and thus the organizational development, of social democracy." Working-class hegemony in the struggle for human liberation can crystalize only to the extent that experienced and thoughtful working-class activists who work together, vanguard elements of the working class, are able to provide leadership to the larger and broader struggles—utilizing their skills and understanding to help advance the spontaneous upsurge, but also to propose a path forward and to win increasing numbers of people to embark upon that path. Negri tells us, "Lenin never forgets that the refusal to submit to spontaneity is not a negation of spontaneity. Quite the opposite: the refusal to submit to spontaneity emerges, affirms itself, and consolidates when spontaneity is at its highest." He concludes: "The main problem today is one of organization, or the ability to channel the movement toward the full consciousness of its power."[38]

Distinctive Elements in Lenin's Approach

Compelling as Negri's reasoning is, questions can be raised. Not all of the questions, however, necessarily hold up as criticisms. Some force us into clarifications.

For example, are all the closely reasoned explications of Lenin's thought applicable only to him? Could not the same type of elaborate exegeses, or in some cases precisely the same points, be articulated in regard to Karl Marx, Karl Kautsky, or Rosa Luxemburg? In regard to Marx, the answer is obviously yes (as Negri himself demonstrates at various points in this text), although Lenin is credited with brilliantly applying Marx's approach to unique turn-of-the-century specifics of the Russian socio-economic reality. Kautsky and Luxemburg are—unlike Marx—largely absent from this text, but that "gap" is easily explained. Negri is focused on Lenin's actual writings, and unlike Marx, they were not the central reference points in those writings. The same can be said for each of these figures: they are disciples of Marx, not of each other. Kautsky is fifteen years older than Lenin and Luxemburg, and of the three he was the first to engage with what Marx and Engels offered. Both Lenin and Luxemburg respected him, and his work certainly influenced them, but the two younger revolutionaries went on to forge their own paths.

The fact that Negri can sustain his analysis in a close reading of a quite significant range of Lenin's writings suggests a multifaceted and multilayered intensity inherent in Lenin. The thoughtful, often excellent, analyses and theorizations offered in the writings of Karl Kautsky would necessarily yield a quite different exegeses than that which Negri is able to construct around the writings of Lenin, at least in part because Lenin is developing his thought in a different context. More than this, the realities of which he is a part, and the role he plays within his own party—in contrast to what is the case with Kautsky—would naturally pull his conceptualizations in a somewhat different direction.

Negri's comments on Lenin's orientation dovetail with Alan Shandro's contribution. Shandro sees Lenin's distinctive contributions to Marxism flowing from the way he approached issues of *spontaneity* and *hegemony*. We need to unpack this in order to grasp the thrust of his analysis. Conceptualizations common to an "orthodox Marxist" perspective can be found, Shandro shows us, in writings of the young Lenin, the young Leon Trotsky, the young Rosa Luxemburg, and others taught and mentored by such eminent theorists as Kautsky and Plekhanov. But beginning in the early 1900s, he argues, Lenin felt increasingly compelled to develop a more complex and dynamic view that moved beyond conceptions embraced by Kautsky. (Shandro misses the fact that others—particularly Luxemburg and Trotsky—were, each in their own way, also moving beyond what Shandro calls the "matter of fact didacticism" of so-called orthodox Marxism.) For Lenin, Shandro asserts, this was generated by three crises: (1) challenges posed by the rise of strong reformist and Economist currents within the socialist movement, (2) challenges of the 1905 revolutionary upsurge, and (3) challenges posed by the First World War.

In treading this ground, Shandro takes issue with certain influential interpretations of Lenin's thought. According to Marcel Liebman and Tony Cliff, the 1905 upsurge caused Lenin to reject an allegedly "elitist" element inherent in his earlier thinking, and Shandro joins with Lars Lih in demolishing this view.[39] Another influential interpretation, given special stress by Raya Dunayevskaya and Kevin Anderson, has to do with Lenin's study of the dialectical philosophy of Hegel during the First World War, which is said to have generated a veritable revolution in his own thought, reflected in all subsequent writings.[40] While he does not dismiss the importance of Lenin's philosophical clarifications, Shandro sees the so-called "Hegelian epiphany" as seriously overstated. The three historical moments of challenge force Lenin to deepen and develop his Marxism, not to fundamentally revise it.

Instead, Shandro insists that—far from a "break"—there is a *fundamental continuity* in the development of Lenin's thought, stretching from *What Is to Be Done?* (1902) and *One Step Forward, Two Steps Back* (1904) to *Two Tactics of Social-Democracy in the Democratic Revolution* (1905) to *Imperialism,* the *Highest Stage of Capitalism* (1916) and *The State and Revolution* (1917) to *The Proletarian Revolution and the Renegade Kautsky* (1918). He does not provide a full discussion of these crucial texts, his purpose being to trace within them a distinctive approach to questions of spontaneity and proletarian hegemony. One can certainly find the notion of proletarian hegemony in the theorizations of Kautsky, Plekhanov, and the Mensheviks, but there are different twists that one can give to this notion—and the Leninist twist, he argues, facilitated ever-greater (and necessary) debate within the Russian Social Democratic Labor Party. This centered on the configuration of class alliances, with Lenin's strategy crystallizing around a "worker-peasant alliance" which (in the opinion of Menshevik Raphael Abramovitch) replaced "an analytical Marxian outlook" with "romantic utopianism," seeking "to make a bourgeois revolution without the bourgeoisie, against the bourgeoisie."[41] This approach, Shandro argues, enabled Lenin to develop a far more nuanced and effective revolutionary politics. It also generated early unease and then bitter opposition among those influenced by the traditional orientation (the "unilinear historical logic," as Shandro terms it) Lenin was moving beyond.

This connects with points made in *Reconstructing Lenin*. Not seeking to create an independent "*ism* within Marxism," Krausz tells us, what Lenin did was to "rediscover, reenergize, and deepen elements of the Marxist tradition that mainstream European social democracy was intent on burying." In the process of doing this, he observes, Lenin "contributed many original ideas to the theoretical reconstruction of revolutionary action and movement in opposition to reformist social democratic tendencies." Rule by the people over their collective economic life, and the free development of each and every person, brought about through revolutionary struggles of the world's laboring majorities, constituted the animating vision of Marx—"the *conscious human activity to transform society*" and "the self-movement and self-creation of history through social classes and individuals." As Negri puts it, "Marx and Lenin's definition of our task of destruction of the state for communism will only be given within the recognition of a newly recomposed strategic project, and in a subsequent cycle of international workers' struggles."[42]

In Lenin's last five years of life, this inspiring future development was blocked (and was turned into its opposite) by two calamities. First, the failure of revolutions in other lands left Russia isolated in its own economic backwardness. Second, horrific tidal waves of violence, in large measure generated by powerful forces that feared and hated this "strategic project," came down upon revolutionary Russia with incredible force. The postrevolution breakdown of Lenin's "stateless communism" orientation, crucially important to any consideration of the Leninist tradition, is discussed by Shandro, Krausz, and Negri.[43] The scope of our exploration here, however, covers the greater portion of Lenin's life—the more than two decades preceding the post-1917 calamities. Leninist partisans argue that the calamities can be traced to the failure of revolutionaries outside of Russia to develop something akin to the organizational weapon and strategic orientation which Lenin and his Bolshevik comrades were able to forge in those decades.

Democracy was "one of the cornerstones of his political concept prior to 1917," Krausz emphasizes, buttressing Lenin's "critique of bourgeois democracy and bourgeois approaches to democracy with the economic and social dimensions of democracy—demonstrating the oppressive functions of the bourgeois system aligned with his critique of capitalism," and with revolutionary political solutions through which "bourgeois democracy in turn becomes plebian democracy and then a *workers' democracy* (semistate)," with an increasingly just and democratic society ultimately giving way to a stateless communism. Krausz concludes that "Lenin's topicality resides in the fact that he transformed his own historical experiences into a set of theoretical concepts that undermine and destroy any justifications for bourgeois society and, in spite of the contradictions involved, he provides tools for those who still think of the possibility of another, more humane world." Negri emphasizes the same point, that Lenin's "organizational project is developed with allusions to the contents of communism and to the issue of the withering-away of the state, which becomes a key issue sustained throughout the whole of the revolutionary process."[44]

Moving beyond the norms of Social Democracy caused political ruptures, particularly with the Menshevik wing of the Russian Social Democracy hewing more closely to orientations developed by Plekhanov and Kautsky. It also meant a revolutionary break with what represented—for many—the "common wisdom" among Marxists in the early twentieth century. Consider Angelica Balabanoff's recollection of Lenin's articulation of his "April Theses" of 1917: "One sentence in the speech he delivered that evening was to recur to me many times in the months that followed, as it has many times since: 'Unless the Russian Revolution develops into a second and successful Paris Commune, reaction and war will suffocate it.'" She goes on to explain:

I had been trained, like most Marxists, to expect the social revolution to be inaugurated in one of the highly industrialized, vanguard countries, and at the time Lenin's analysis of Russian events seemed to me almost utopian. Later, after I had returned to Russia itself, I was to accept this analysis completely. I have never doubted since that if the revolutionaries—including many Mensheviks and Left Social Revolutionaries—had not convinced the peasants, workers, and soldiers of the need for a more far-reaching, socialist revolution in Russia, Tsarism or some similar form of autocracy would have been restored.[45]

Alfred Rosmer shared similar recollections. Lenin was seen as having drifted "outside the stream of orthodox Marxism," with some scoffing that that his perspectives of 1917 were not Marxist but "Blanquism with *sauce tartare*." Rosmer recalls that French syndicalists and anarchists such as himself found Lenin's Marxism to be "a pleasant revelation," which they liked "sauce and all." Won to Lenin's outlook, Rosmer concludes that it was, in fact, well-grounded in the texts of Marx and Engels, representing, in contrast to "Plekhanov and Kautsky who have gone off the rails" (as Lenin put it), a genuine and truly "undistorted Marxism."[46] These are points that Shandro and Krausz insist upon, and that Negri hammers home in his lectures.

Logic and History

We have noted that Negri's study—like the others we are examining here—does not contend that Lenin's *State and Revolution* represents a fundamental break from his earlier approach, but instead insists on a continuity of Lenin's thought from the early 1900s down through 1917. Unlike the others, however, he presents us with an intriguing logical cascade that he attributes to Lenin.

His compelling yet unconventional analysis provides the basis for a specific conceptualization corresponding with the autonomist Marxism with which Negri has been closely associated (holding that the organizational specifics of Leninism may be correct for Lenin's own specific context, but not for our own). Negri insists that the starting point is "Lenin's reading of Marx," specifically "a reading and critical analysis of Karl Marx's *Capital*," and "his approach to the theory of organization [is] derived from a theory of capital." In turn, "the question of the program ... proceeds from a theory of organization to a theory of revolution."[47]

All of this relates to the very title of Negri's book, *Factory of Strategy*, which also connects to controversial assertions of Lenin in *One Step Forward, Two Steps Back*—that, drawing from Marx's analysis in *Capital*, one must distinguish between "the factory as a means of exploitation (discipline based on fear and starvation) and the factory as a means of organization (discipline based on collective work united by the conditions of a technically highly developed form of production). The discipline and organization that come so hard to the bourgeois intellectual are very easily acquired by the proletariat just because of this factory 'schooling.'" Negri blends this with an ongoing, insistent, reasonable emphasis on the specificities of the Russian social formation under tsarism, which are profoundly different from our own.[48]

This comes through powerfully in one of the book's central passages, where Negri insists that "this concept of the party and organization as a factory is adequate to the actual level at which the project of Leninist organization develops, reproducing the technical and political composition of the proletariat." The organization

> develops by making itself adequate to an ideology of organized labor typical of the large factory and of the class vanguard in Russia, also taking into account the internal and determinate characteristic of the shift we have described, where in fact capital and the organization of the factory are a formidable step forward in the formation and consolidation of an industrial proletariat as a material vanguard of the struggle.

In Lenin's argument, Negri tells us, "we find an application of some of the fundamental criteria of historical materialism, from which Lenin's definition of the party grasps a level of class composition in an absolutely correct manner." He argues that "the factory is able to form a conscious vanguard, exalting the organizational moment and providing the conditions for emancipation, in a way that is all the more clear as the exploitation that a backward society such as Russia is subjected to gets deeper." He concludes: "For this reason, Lenin's adherence to an overall situation of the Russian proletariat and to the definition of the levers that will destroy this system determines that conception of the party."[49]

One suspects, however, that aspects of Leninist organization may be more prosaic than Negri allows, that there are some basic elements of organizational purpose and logic which transcend Russian specifics and the logic of *Capital*. Workers, like all people, do not telepathically think with one mind, nor do all share an equal amount of political experience, theoretical knowledge, revolutionary commitments, and organizational skills. Those—a relative few—who do have these qualities can be considered *cadres*, who are essential for the organization of any social movement and social struggle. This generalization applies beyond the realities of the factory and social relations in tsarist Russia. It can be found, Negri himself shows us, in *What Is to Be Done?*, among other Lenin texts: "no revolutionary movement can endure without a stable organization of leaders [or cadres] that maintains continuity.... Such an organization must consist chiefly of people professionally engaged in revolutionary activity."[50]

The purpose of the Communist International was to create parties with such cadres outside of Russia, in countries throughout the world, all of which lacked the specificities of the Russian "determinate situation" or social formation. Yet Negri comments starkly that "the Leninist party never had anything to do with the kind of communist party of the Third International and the communist reformism it produced."[51]

Negri is at his weakest when he discusses the Communist International. In contrast to his close reading of Lenin's writings, here we find sweeping generalizations with no documentation. He smudges together the period of the Third International in the time of Lenin (ignoring the rich experience and hard-won lessons of these initial years) with the period of Stalinist domination, and in this latter period he conflates the phase of ultra-leftist and rigid "Bolshevization" with that of the reformist Peoples Front.[52] It is all a negative blur.

"It was typical of the process of Bolshevization to try to impose a series of firm precepts on all parties that referred to themselves as part of the Bolshevik revolution," he tells us. This "cut some vanguards off at the legs and made it impossible for them to make themselves adequate to the particular situations they were meant to intervene in." He cites the Communist Party of the United States as "the extreme example," whose experienced class-struggle cadres were "castrated" by "an incredibly slavish repetition of the model" of Bolshevization. He asserts that this resulted in "the exclusion of African-American members from the organization (in the name of a politics of nationality that repeated something that might have been valid in Russia, even though in the United States class unity was given and blacks and whites worked on the same assembly line)."[53]

The only source cited for this badly garbled account is Theodore Draper's 1960 study *American Communism and Soviet Russia*, with no details or even page numbers. Some of the leading participants who resisted the Stalinist variant of "Bolshevization" afflicting the US Communist Party in the period of 1924–1929 (and were expelled for such resistance) tell a qualitatively different story. Although representing divergent oppositions, they are in basic agreement that the early years of relations with the Communist International were positive and helpful. This is also true in regard to dealing with the African American struggle and the initial in-gathering of black cadres, a fact corroborated by a number of capable historians in a number of recent studies.[54]

Between 1987 and 2015, John Riddell and teams of collaborators produced a remarkable English-language resource—the proceedings of the first four congresses of the Communist International, held from 1919 to 1922, in the time of, and with the full participation of, Lenin. This invaluable contribution to Lenin studies presents us with the excitement and powerful energy of a diverse and articulate accumulation of revolutionaries, some exuberantly young and fresh to the struggle and others having considerable political experience, seeking to learn from and apply to their own homelands the lessons of the Bolshevik Revolution, wrestling with striking similarities and differences, discussing and sometimes debating numerous matters of importance with Lenin and other prominent Bolshevik leaders.[55]

The Organization Question and the Communist International

In the more than 2,000 pages of the just-published proceedings of the 1921 and 1922 world congresses, we find speeches, reports, debates, resolutions, motions, and countermotions on an incredible range of topics. Some of what is said is foolish, and some of what is said is profound. Significant and illuminating attention is given to the matters we have been considering here.

There is little in the proceedings from Comintern world congresses of 1921 and 1922 that conform to dismissive characterizations advanced by all-too-many scholars, including Negri. One can certainly point to the disastrous "March Action" of 1921 in Germany, in which adventuristic Comintern representatives, in grand authoritarian style, played a decisive role in pushing some less experienced German Communists into ultra-left and destructive efforts, riding roughshod over more responsible leaders such as Paul Levi and Clara Zetkin. This caused Levi to break decisively with the Comintern. It is clear from Riddell's volumes, however, that there were sharp differences in the Communist International around this, with Lenin and Trotsky relentlessly criticizing the "March Action," a putsch attempt that was, if anything, in stark contradiction to "the Russian model." Far from seeking to "break" the more responsible German leaders, Lenin consulted closely with Zetkin and sought to repair Levi's status—thwarted not only by Levi's own angry refusal, but also by the need to compromise with the angry younger leaders of the German Communist Party. This deference to a majority in the German Communist leadership actually reflects democratic, rather than bureaucratic, tendencies in the early Comintern (even though Lenin agreed with Levi's critique of what the hotheads had done).[56]

Nor does Negri's notion of the Leninist party as uniquely Russia-specific find corroboration with what Lenin had to say. Embedded in the early Comintern proceedings are a rich array of materials, directly from Lenin and his comrades, on the creation of revolutionary parties outside of the Russian context, culminating in the 1921 theses, "The Organizational Structure of the Communist Parties, the Methods and Content of Their Work."[57] From background materials presented in one of many useful appendices, we can see that the theses were shaped, in part, with Lenin's very active input and were put forward in the Comintern's Third Congress at Lenin's insistence.[58]

Far from a dogmatic effort to impose "the Russian model" on all Communist parties, there is an insistence on relative national autonomy:

> There is no immutable, absolutely correct structure for Communist parties. The conditions of proletarian class struggle are variable and subject to a process of constant change. In line with these changes, the organization of the proletarian vanguard must also constantly seek appropriate forms. Similarly, the organization of each party must conform to the historically determined features of its country.[59]

And then there is this insistence on leadership and authority being rooted in flexibility and in close contact with the actual working class and its struggles: "To lead the revolutionary class struggle, the Communist Party and its leading bodies must combine great striking power with great capacity to adjust to the changing conditions of struggle. Successful leadership also requires close ties *with the proletarian masses*. Without such ties, the leaders will not *lead* them but at best only follow along after."[60]

This insistence on engagement with the real, everyday struggles of the working class is a major point stressed in the document:

Communists make an enormous *mistake by pointing to the Communist program or the armed struggle as excuses for passivity, scorn, or even hostility to workers' current struggles for* small improvements in their working conditions. No matter how small and modest the demands may be that the workers now pose for struggle against the capitalists, this is never cause for the Communists to stand aloof from the struggle. Of course, our agitation should not give the impression that we Communists blindly instigate unwise strikes or other rash actions. However, among the workers in struggle, the Communists should always earn the reputation of being their most competent comrades-in-arms.[61]

One of the most important aspects of the document is its warning against the very type of centralism that has all-too-often been put forward as "Leninism":

Democratic centralism in a Communist Party should be a true synthesis and fusion of centralism and proletarian democracy. This fusion can be achieved only on the foundation of constant and common activity and struggle by the entire party.

In a Communist Party, centralization should not be formal or mechanical. It should relate to Communist activity, that is, to the formation of a strong, agile, and also flexible leadership.

A formal or mechanical centralization would concentrate "power" in the hands of the Party bureaucracy, lording it over the other members and the revolutionary proletarian masses which are outside the party.[62]

The resolution criticizes the lack of genuine (as opposed to "formal") democracy, a deficiency common in the parties of the Second International. It tells us:

In the organizations of the old, non-revolutionary workers' movement, a pervasive dualism developed, similar to that of the bourgeois state, between the "bureaucracy" and the "people." Under the paralyzing influence of the bourgeois environment, functionaries became estranged from members, a vibrant collaboration was replaced by the mere forms of democracy, and the organizations became split between active functionaries and passive masses. Even the revolutionary workers' movement cannot avoid being influenced to some degree by the formalism and dualism of the bourgeois environment.[63]

Warnings against the wrong kind of centralism are repeated more than once: "Optimal centralization of party activity is not aided by dividing up the party leadership schematically into a hierarchy with many different levels arrayed one above the other." Instead, democratically elected committees in working-class districts and regions should guide the work of the organization in those localities, suggesting a high degree of relative autonomy within the organization. This is projected as a way of providing political leadership in a manner ensuring that close contact is maintained between it and the broad masses of Party members in the various locales.[64]

Not only did Lenin help to shape the theses, he also defended them after they were adopted. This comes through clearly in his comments at the Fourth World Congress of the Communist International in 1922. He took some time to speak critically of the organizational resolution he had helped to draft and have adopted at the 1921 Congress. His complaint was that it was "too Russian"—in part because "it is so long that nobody but a Russian would read it." As Max Eastman reported, Lenin "continued to laugh a little at the memory of that remark after he had begun to say something else" (according to a footnote by Riddell).[65] While it has become a commonplace to interpret that comment as a rejection of an alleged dogmatism in the organizational theses, the "something else" that Lenin went on to express is the opposite of rejection.

Having already insisted that "the resolution is an excellent one," he emphasized: "the resolution is excellently drafted; I am prepared to subscribe to every one of its fifty or more points." The problem was not with the content but with the inability of the non-Russian comrades to absorb the points being made, because "we have not learnt how to present our Russian experience to foreigners." And so "foreign comrades have endorsed it without reading and understanding it." Far from denouncing and repudiating the resolution, Lenin said: "That resolution must be carried out. It cannot be carried out overnight, that is absolutely impossible." He repeated that "the resolution is too Russian, it reflects the Russian experience. That is why it is quite unintelligible to foreigners, and they cannot be content with hanging it in a corner like an icon and praying to it." Far from urging that the resolution therefore be overturned, he concluded that it must be studied and explained carefully, because the foreign comrades "must assimilate part of the Russian experience." He stressed that "the most important thing we must do in the period we are entering is to study," and that the foreign comrades "must study in a special sense, in order that they may really understand the organization, structure, method, and content of revolutionary work. If they do that, I am sure the prospects of the world revolution will be not only good, but excellent."[66]

What Lenin sought to convey regarding the organization, structure, method, and content of revolutionary work is captured, in various ways, in the volumes under review, regardless of differences one might have with one or another interpretive detail. Well worth considering, for example, is Tamás Krausz's discussion of the oft-distorted notion of the *revolutionary vanguard party*:

> The party as vanguard meant simply that the organization must find roots as part of the social class and incorporate all progressive and revolutionary elements (that is, "those who are first to mount the barricades") as mentioned in the *Communist Manifesto*. This description of vanguard, of course, has no real kinship with the structure that came about in a later period, the bureaucratic embodiment of the "Stalinist state party," in spite of the fact that the latter kept referring to Lenin and its so-called origins in 1903.

In discussing what is often seen as a hallmark of Leninism, he provides a rich characterization of genuinely revolutionary politics, worth quoting at length:

> The concept of democratic centralism as the "law" of party bureaucracy was a product of a later historical period—the combination of power, pragmatism, and a messianic "future expectation." It is easy enough to define the basic concept of democratic centralism: democracy in reaching decisions and unity in implementing them. The difficulty resides only in how to apply this basic principle to small propaganda groups that do not have an organic relationship with the working class. That is, groups whose constituencies are not created from among the most class-conscious members of this class through a hard-fought process of selection. The Russian Social Democratic Party, and later the Bolshevik Party, benefited from real feedback thanks to its close relations with its *social base*. The [Russian] Social Democratic Party, at least *potentially*, was a real mass party from the beginning. It had an ideology and an organization chart [organizational structure?], for example, that were recognized by politically conscious members of the working class in 1905 and 1917 as valid expressions of their politics.[67]

This corresponds to the Communist International's organizational theses of 1921 and to what Lenin defended in 1922. Essential qualities of the revolutionary party that Lenin and his comrades developed in tsarist Russia were seen to be generally applicable (and adaptable) on a global scale.

Longing and Commitment

Anyone sifting through such historical artifacts—the political thought and practice of Lenin and his contemporary comrades—in what were for Lenin our own far-future realities (on what Negri suggests is a different planet from Lenin's) may be struck by their seeming applicability in the present day.

But activists who are so inclined face immense challenges. "Obviously establishing the party is quite different from longing for it!" Negri tells us.[68] We face dramatically evolved realities of capitalism, the fading of the organized mass socialist workers movement on a global scale, the absence of the kind of revolutionary party Lenin had to work with. Self-satisfied sects can afford to spout Lenin quotes while denouncing all others on their end of the spectrum for not measuring up (which often amounts to denouncing reality for being inadequate).

For activists who are truly committed to changing the world for the better, not some imaginary rhetorical world but the actual world in which we live, the immense challenges remain. The studies explored here, and the Leninist tradition to which they pertain, will certainly be a resource for those who remain true to that commitment.

Chapter Two

BOLSHEVISM AS A REVOLUTIONARY COLLECTIVE

The Russian Revolution of 1917 clearly reveals the complexities of Bolshevism, and of Lenin's Bolshevik party, as a revolutionary collective. In fact, there is a convergence of complexities related to several different factors I would like to touch on in these remarks. These include party structures, personalities, and outlooks.

One set of complexities involves the organizational conceptions that animated Bolshevism, involving democratic centralism, an interplay of democracy and cohesion, as well as an interplay of centralized leadership and significant local, on-the-ground autonomy. Another involves the pulls and tugs of the diverse and vibrant personalities among the Bolsheviks—particularly at the leadership level. Experienced and articulate individuals powerfully influencing the thinking and actions of a layer involving hundreds and thousands of Bolshevik activists, who in turn influenced the thinking and actions of thousands and millions of workers, sailors, soldiers, peasants, intellectuals, and others. Yet another subset of complexities involves the employment of a relatively complex ideology (Marxism), which in itself is open to divergent interpretations, and which can be applied in different and sometimes contradictory ways to political, social, and economic realities that are *themselves* complex and ever-changing. There is also a complexity in the ongoing tension between those leaders engaged in developing and adapting Marxist *theory* on the one hand, and the practical on-the-ground organizers on the other—and among these practical organizers, we can perceive tensions between those whose primary focus is to maintain the organizational structures and cohesion of Bolshevism, and others whose primary focus is to influence and lead mass struggles and mass movements. We could go on and on with this—defining further complexities within each of the complexities.

The point is that we cannot really understand the Bolshevik Revolution of 1917 with conventional but simplistic conceptualizations, which focus on a heroic Lenin (or an evil genius Lenin) leading an abstract entity—"The Party," or "Party-and-Soviets"—to take political power. There is no doubt that Lenin's role in history merits a focused study of who he was and what he thought, wrote, said, and did. But Lenin cannot be understood as the personification of the Bolshevik party. What he thought and wrote and said and did cannot be comprehended if we abstract these things, and the man himself, from those who were his comrades. If we fail to understand Bolshevism as a revolutionary collective that was an integral part of a broader working-class movement, and as a vibrant and complex and living entity, we will not be able to comprehend the actualities either of Lenin or of the Russian Revolution.

This comes into a better focus if we engage with some of the historical specifics. Let us begin with "the Word"—Marxist theory and analysis as developed by the Bolsheviks—before we move on to the flesh and the bone (the personalities and the structure) of the Bolshevik party.

The theoretical orientation of Marxism was grounded in a dialectical and materialist and humanistic methodology, one that viewed history as being shaped by economic development and class struggle. It saw an increasingly dominant capitalism as immensely productive and dynamically creative, but also as compulsively expansive and exploitative, and as a violently destructive global system. Yet capitalism was proletarianizing more and more people in society and throughout the world, creating an ever-growing working class of people dependent on the sale of their labor-power. Such laboring people *potentially* would have the need, the will, the consciousness, and the power necessary for effectively challenging the oppressiveness of capitalism and replacing it with the humanistic economic democracy of socialism.[1]

Of course, Marxism is far more complex than this, with more than one interpretation being possible, and more than one way of applying this complex and sophisticated approach to the specifics of late-nineteenth and early-twentieth-century Russia. Marxists in Russia generally agreed that the country's small but growing working-class was the hope for the future in both challenging the tsarist autocracy and helping to overthrow it in what they termed a "bourgeois-democratic revolution." The development of capitalism after this democratic revolution would, most agreed, create the preconditions for a socialist revolution. But there were disagreements over how this working-class scenario would relate to the peasant majority. Marxists in the Menshevik faction argued that the peasants were too backward-looking to be a reliable ally and that the obvious partner in overthrowing tsarism would be procapitalist liberals. The Bolsheviks led by Lenin insisted that the principle of working-class hegemony would be most consistent with a worker-peasant alliance for a democratic revolution. Menshevik spokesman Raphael Abramovitch was not the only one to scoff that this added up to "a bourgeois revolution without the bourgeoisie, against the bourgeoisie, by means of a dictatorship of the proletariat over the bourgeoisie"—but Lenin and his comrades called for a revolution that would culminate in what they termed "a revolutionary democratic dictatorship of the proletariat and the peasantry."[2]

We should linger over an ambiguity in Lenin's position, as articulated in 1905. On the one hand, he was inclined to agree that the democratic revolution must usher in capitalist economic development in order to establish the wealth and productivity and a working-class majority that would make socialism possible. In his polemic *Two Tactics of Social Democracy in the Democratic Revolution*, Lenin argued that because the democratic revolution was, in fact, a "*bourgeois*-democratic revolution," it would "for the first time, really clear the ground for a wide and rapid . . . development of capitalism," and would, "for the first time, make it possible for the bourgeoisie to rule as a class."[3]

On the other hand, Lenin seemed to leave open the possibility that some variant of Trotsky's "permanent revolution" scenario might be possible— that (as Lenin put it in his article "Social Democracy's Attitude Toward the Peasant Movement") "from the democratic revolution we shall at once, and precisely in accordance with the measure of our strength, the strength of the class-conscious and organized proletariat, begin to pass to the socialist revolution. We stand for uninterrupted revolution. We shall not stop half-way."[4]

This openness to the possibility of the democratic revolution flowing into the socialist revolution expanded with the explosion of the First World War. As Lenin emphasized time and again, this was a war "waged 'for the sake of the profits of the capitalists' and 'the ambitions of dynasties' on the basis of the imperialist, predatory policy of the great powers," and that it must be opposed with "the tactics of revolutionary struggle by the workers on an international scale against their governments, the tactics of proletarian revolution. . . . Socialists must . . . take advantage of the governments' embarrassments and the anger of the masses, caused by the war, for the socialist revolution."[5]

According to his companion Krupskaya, during the war Lenin "spoke a lot about the questions that occupied his mind, about the role of democracy," arriving at "a very clear and definite view of the relationship between economics and politics in the epoch of struggle for socialism." Krupskaya elaborated:

> The role of democracy in the struggle for socialism could not be ignored. "Socialism is impossible without democracy in two respects," Vladimir Ilyich wrote . . . "1. The proletariat cannot carry out a socialist revolution unless it has prepared for it by a struggle for democracy; 2. Victorious socialism cannot maintain its victory and bring humanity to the time when the state will wither away unless democracy is fully achieved."
>
> These words of Lenin's were soon fully borne out by events in Russia. The February Revolution of 1917 and the subsequent struggle for democracy prepared the way for the October Revolution. The constant broadening and strengthening of the Soviets, of the Soviet system, tends to reorganize democracy itself and to steadily give greater depth of meaning to this concept.[6]

Krupskaya went on to quote at length from one of Lenin's war-time polemics:

> We must *combine* the revolutionary struggle against capitalism with a revolutionary program and tactics in respect of *all* democratic demands, including a republic, a militia, election of government officials by the people, equal rights for women, self-determination of nations, etc. So long as capitalism exists all these demands are capable of realization only as an exception, and in incomplete, distorted form. Basing ourselves on democracy as already achieved, and showing up its deficiency under capitalism, we demand the overthrow of capitalism and expropriation of the bourgeoisie as an essential basis both for abolishing the poverty of the masses and for *fully and thoroughly* implementing *all* democratic transformations. Some of those transformations will be started before the overthrow of the bourgeoisie, others *in the course of* this overthrow, and still others after it. The social revolution is not a single battle but an epoch of a series of battles on all and every problem of economic and democratic transformations, whose completion will be effected only with the expropriation of

the bourgeoisie. It is for the sake of this ultimate goal that we must formulate *every one* of our democratic demands in a consistently revolutionary manner.[7]

To sum up Lenin's orientation: The revolutionary party must interweave socialism with working-class consciousness and struggles, it must emphasize struggle for full democracy as the pathway to socialism, and it should press for working-class hegemony, predominance, in the struggle for a democratic revolution—with no confidence in procapitalist liberals. Related to this was the distinctive Bolshevik perspective of a worker-peasant alliance in the struggle against tsarism. The antibourgeois orientation was further intensified with the eruption of the First World War, as opposition to the imperialist war was accompanied by an intensified revolutionary internationalism and class struggle thrust. The heightened concern to interweave struggles for democracy and socialism, and the conviction that the conflict would facilitate the spread of socialist revolution in various countries, strengthened the inclination to consider the possibilities of "uninterrupted revolution" in Russia.

Much of this orientation was the collective product and property of the Bolsheviks as they evolved from 1905 to 1917 and was shared (sometimes with significant nuances of difference) among various comrades. Its contours and specifics are particularly well explained by Nadezhda Krupskaya, in her *Reminiscences of Lenin*.

The crystallization of the Bolshevik political perspective of a worker-peasant alliance to push forward the democratic revolution was collective, as was the translation of that perspective into social and political action. This brings us to the organizational structures that made this so. Krupskaya emphasized that Lenin "always, as long as he lived, attached tremendous importance to Party congresses. He held the Party congress to be the highest authority, where all things personal had to be cast aside, where nothing was to be concealed, and everything was to be open and above board."

The "Draft Rules of the RSDLP," which Lenin wrote in 1903, establishes the party congress, or convention, as the "supreme organ of the Party." Composed of representatives of all units of the Russian Social Democratic Labor Party, the congress was to meet "not less than once in two years" and was to be responsible for determining party policies and perspectives and for appointing a central committee and an editorial board for the party's central organ (its newspaper). The central committee "coordinates and directs all the practical activities of the Party," while the editorial board "gives ideological guidance."

The draft rules suggest a balance between democracy and centralization. For example: "Each committee . . . organization or group recognized by the Party has charge of affairs relating specifically and exclusively to its particular locality, district or national movement, or to the special function assigned to it, being bound, however, to obey the decisions of the Central Committee." Most important, however: "All Party organizations and collegiate bodies decide their affairs by a simple majority vote."[8]

Lenin's organizational perspective could be summarized in this way:

◊ Members are activists, who agree with the basic Marxist program of the party and are committed to collectively developing and implementing the program, and who collectively control the organization as a whole.

◊ The party functions transparently and democratically, with the elective principle operating from top to bottom. All questions are decided on the basis of democratic vote, and the decisions are carried out.

◊ The highest decision-making body is the party congress, made up of democratically elected delegates.

◊ Between congresses, a central committee (elected by and answerable to the congress) ensures cohesion and coordinates work on the basis of the party program and the decisions of the congress.

◊ Local units of the party operate within the party program and decisions of the party as a whole, but within that framework they operate under the democratic control of the local membership.

It is interesting to consider the conception of the Bolshevik party which John Reed's old friend, Max Eastman, had absorbed through his studies in Soviet Russia. In his 1926 book *Marx, Lenin, and the Science of Revolution*, Eastman wrote:

> It is an organization of a kind which never existed before. It combines certain essential features of a political party, a professional association, a consecrated order, an army, a scientific society—and yet it is in no sense a sect. Instead of cherishing in its membership a sectarian psychology, it cherishes a certain relation to the predominant class forces of society as Marx defined them. And this relation was determined by Lenin, and progressively readjusted by him, with a subtlety of which Marx never dreamed.[9]

In fact, there were different personalities and personality types giving life to the Bolshevik organization. Of course, central from beginning to end was Lenin, who by most accounts combined in his person considerable warmth, humor, selflessness, zest for life, and tactical flexibility interwoven with revolutionary intransigence.[10]

Women were a minority among the Bolsheviks in patriarchal Russia. Among those who played central roles were Nadezhda Krupskaya and Alexandra Kollontai. Krupskaya, an educated Marxist and devoted revolutionary activist, deployed her considerable talents and energies in the practical work of building up and maintaining Bolshevik communications and organizational functioning. This enabled her to write her authoritative *Reminiscences of Lenin*, which surveys Lenin's development very much within the revolutionary collective that was Bolshevism. Playing a more public role, Kollontai channeled her keen intellect and passion into theorizing and organizing around the so-called "woman question"—pushing hard against male chauvinist attitudes and patterns within the revolutionary movement. Her contributions bore fruit as increasing numbers of women workers flowed into the revolutionary movement. This was an essential development. International Women's Day in 1917 helped spark the upsurge that overthrew the tsar.[11]

The two brothers-in-law Leon Trotsky and Lev Kamenev were incredibly different in multiple ways. While Kamenev was a capable speaker, writer, organizer, and political analyst, in each of these realms Trotsky could be incandescent. Kamenev was extremely sociable in ways that Trotsky could not be, yet he was also prone to be influenced by others—including political opponents—in ways that, also, Trotsky could not be. Yet Trotsky (a relative newcomer to Bolshevik ranks) had a reputation for arrogance, and his immense popularity and demonstrated ability to work with people was offset by an often-prickly personality. Kamenev's charm could often be a valuable asset—and it matched epicurean tastes that Trotsky found repellent. Trotsky's combination of energy, brilliance, and Spartan inclinations served him well as he organized the October 1917 insurrection, and also when he assumed the role of organizer and commander of the Red Army during the Russian Civil War.[12]

Gregory Zinoviev, often associated with the far steadier and more consistent Kamenev, sometimes could match Trotsky in oratory and arrogance, but like Kamenev he was one of Lenin's closest collaborators over many years. All three (Trotsky, Kamenev, Zinoviev)—at various moments, and on different issues—were also in open conflict with Lenin amid the hurly-burly of internal democracy within Bolshevism. Zinoviev's intellectual breadth and feel for revolutionary politics come through clearly in his valuable popularization *History of the Bolshevik Party*. His organizational abilities were certainly greater than those of another popular figure, the youthful and impetuous Nikolai Bukharin. Bukharin was an innovative theorist who proved more than once quite willing to challenge Lenin from the left. Both Zinoviev and Bukharin were to play important and influential roles in the Communist International that would be formed after the Russian Revolution. But in 1917 as well, although in quite different ways and from different standpoints, the influence of these two prominent Bolsheviks had significant impact.[13]

Two eminently practical organizers—not inclined to be distracted by theoretical fireworks—were Alexander Shlyapnikov and Joseph Stalin. A worker-Bolshevik par excellence, with a reputation for courageous and principled action, Shlyapnikov's strength was organizing among factory workers and in trade unions. A former divinity student, inclined to be blunt and sometimes brutal, Stalin's specialty was as an organization man devoted to building and maintaining Bolshevik structures. Shlyapnikov's qualities brought him close to Lenin's intensified revolutionary-democratic drive predominant from 1914 to 1917. With Lenin's turn to more authoritarian expedients (temporary as they were supposed to be) amid the horrific difficulties of civil war and social collapse in 1918–1921, Shlyapnikov's qualities put the two at loggerheads. With assistance from Alexandra Kollontai, Shlyapnikov formed the Workers' Opposition. Other Bolsheviks also formed oppositional groups to defend the revolutionary-democratic goals of the October Revolution. Stalin's inclinations, of course, went very much in the opposite direction—to the point of developing a bureaucratic-authoritarian apparatus that would eventually destroy the revolutionary collective that had been Bolshevism. This process unfolded with increasing velocity from the mid-1920s to mid-1930s.[14]

The cause of this degeneration was the isolation of the revolution, turned in on itself in an economically backward Russia. As Lenin explained more than once, "we are banking on the inevitability of the world revolution," and:

> We are now, as it were, in a besieged fortress, waiting for the other detachments of the world socialist revolution to come to our relief. These detachments *exist*, they are *more numerous* than ours, they are maturing, growing, gaining more strength the longer the brutalities of imperialism

continue. . . . Slowly but surely the workers are adopting communist, Bolshevik tactics and are marching towards the proletarian revolution, which alone is capable of saving dying culture and dying mankind.[15]

In the wake of the Bolshevik Revolution, then, we can see the attempt to internationalize Bolshevism, with the creation of a global revolutionary collective, or a centralized network of such collectives—the Communist International. By the time of the Second World Congress in 1920, the assembled delegates from revolutionary organizations proclaimed: "The Communist International has made the cause of Soviet Russia its own. The international proletariat will not lay down its sword until Soviet Russia is but a link in the world federation of soviet republics." Comintern President Gregory Zinoviev, optimistically suggested that "probably two or three years will be needed for the whole of Europe to become a Soviet republic." According to a retrospective account by two participant-observers (Julian Gumperz and Karl Volk), "hundreds of delegates came from all countries of the world: real labor representatives elected and re-elected a hundred times [to mass workers' organizations], revolutionaries and opportunists, workers from the factories and shrewd attorneys, terrorists and elegant Socialists from the salons of Europe."[16]

Another eyewitness, Alfred Rosmer, would recount:

> There was something intoxicating about the atmosphere of Moscow in that month of June 1920; the quiver of the armed revolution could still be felt. Among the delegates who had come from every country and every political tendency, some already knew each other, but the majority were meeting for the first time. The discussions were heated, for there was no shortage of points of disagreement, but what overrode everything was an unshakable attachment to the Revolution and to the new-born communist movement.

The history of this movement contains much that has the quality of comic opera, also much that constitutes deep and sometimes horrific tragedy, but also— despite its ultimate failure—a remarkable heroism, with lessons to be learned.[17]

Those who not only wish to understand what happened in history—but also how a world (badly in need of change for the better) might *actually* be changed—will need to wrestle with and learn from the convergence of complexities that add up to Bolshevism as a revolutionary collective.

Chapter Three

THE UNORIGINALITY OF LEON TROTSKY

I would like to begin this chapter by confessing that I consider myself a Trotskyist, just as I consider myself a Leninist and a Marxist. But I want to clarify that by repeating something that has gotten me into trouble with some friends who also identify as Trotskyists.

Early in my short biography *Leon Trotsky*, I wrote: "A key dimension of Trotsky's reputation is as a brilliantly innovative theorist." That was okay—it was what came next that was the problem:

> In looking at the ideas Trotsky put forward in his theoretical writings . . . I will be inclined to emphasize the aspects of *unoriginality* in Trotsky's thought, especially in relation to the much-vaunted theory of permanent revolution, his analysis of Stalinism, his prescriptions for defeating Hitler, and the much-misunderstood Transitional Program. All these are drawn from Marx and from revolutionary Marxists of Trotsky's own time, including the best of Second International Marxism in the period leading up to 1914, as well as the collective project of the early Third International.[1]

I will want to focus on the substance of what Trotsky had to say on such things as permanent revolution and Stalinism and so on. But first I want to take a little time unpacking this originality thing.

The Collectivity of Marxism

I think it is very unhelpful to turn Leon Trotsky into some kind of ideological icon, with a special set of theories presented under the banner of "Trotskyism," for the purpose of elevating him (and those of us who worship the icon) above the rest of humanity—or at least above everyone else on the Left. It can also lead to the fashioning of ideological measuring rods, with which we can beat those among us who seem to deviate from the master's doctrine. I think it is especially unhelpful to have a competing set of labels: there go some *Marxists*, here comes a *Leninist*, and that one over there is a *Trotskyist*, then there's a *Luxemburgist*, here's a *Gramscian*, and so on. Trotsky (and Marx and Lenin and Luxemburg and Gramsci) didn't see things that way. Trotsky considered himself a revolutionary socialist, which was the same for him as a communist—although he did believe that the whole set of Marx's ideas and way of approaching things was so impressive and valuable, that he was happy to call himself a Marxist. This is also true of such people as Luxemburg, Lenin, and Gramsci—and in my book *From Marx to Gramsci*, I seek to demonstrate that these three revolutionaries, along with Trotsky and Marx and Engels, are best understood as being close enough in methodological approach and practical political orientation to be grouped together.[2]

Trotsky had an advantage over the others though, due to the banal fact that he was able to live longer, enabling him to apply Marxist analysis to the most horrific tyrannies of the twentieth century—Stalinism and fascism (particularly fascism's most virulent form, Nazism).[3] We'll return to that shortly—but first, let's consider how Trotsky was inclined to define the term *Marxist*—especially in relation to the term *Leninist*.

One of the places Trotsky explored this was in the voluminous notes for his unfinished biography of Stalin. He noted, "Marxism is in itself a historical product and should be accepted as such. This historical Marxism includes within itself three basic elements: materialist dialectics, historical materialism, and a theoretical critique of capitalist economy." He went on to assert: "Leninism is Marxism in action, that is, theory made flesh and blood." It's not that Marx was a theorist instead of an activist—he was active in the Communist League of the late 1840s and the International Workingmen's Association (the First International) of the 1860s and early 1870s. But, according to Trotsky, "Lenin's work differs enormously from the work of Marx and his old comrades just as much as Lenin's epoch differs from that of Marx. Marx, the revolutionist, lived and died as the theoretical teacher of young parties of the proletariat and as a precursor of its future decisive struggles. Lenin led the proletariat to the conquest of power, secured victory by means of his leadership, led the first workers state in the history of humanity," through the Russian Revolution, at the same time working for the global triumph of working-class rule, especially through the Communist International.[4]

Of course, just as Marx was lucky to have what Trotsky calls "old comrades" who made essential contributions to what he thought and was able to do, so it was with Lenin—his achievements were necessarily part of a collective endeavor. His comrades were especially concentrated in a centralized organizational network within the Russian revolutionary movement, a network known as the Bolsheviks. Their revolutionary Marxist perspectives reflected the lessons and insights of accumulated experience, to which Lenin gave voice, and these, in turn, were a decisive influence within the early Communist International.[5]

Unfortunately, the forces in and around the Communist International were not successful in extending revolutionary working-class victories to other countries. The working-class regime of Soviet Russia was not only isolated in a hostile capitalist world; it was also severely damaged by a brutal civil war and devastated by multiple tidal waves of economic crisis.

In the new Soviet Republic, this generated authoritarian habits and inclinations within the apparatus of the Communist Party and Soviet state. A self-interested bureaucracy crystallized that claimed to represent the old revolutionary commitments but, in fact, was going in a very different direction. As Trotsky explained in his 1937 testimony to the Dewey Commission, at this point (back in the early 1920s) the bureaucracy initiated a campaign in which "all the old formulae of Bolshevism were named 'Trotskyist.' That was the trick. What was the genuine thing in Bolshevism is opposed to every privilege, to the oppression of the majority by the minority." Stalinists now denounced this as "the program of Trotskyism."[6]

Trotsky's Distinctiveness

Trotsky's distinctiveness is that, unlike many, he sought to remain true to the original revolutionary perspectives. In a sense he became original simply through applying old principles—as consistently and creatively as he could—to new realities. This brings us back to Marxism.

Marxism fuses a view of history, an engagement with current realities, and a strategic orientation for replacing capitalism with socialism. The dominant interpretation of history shared by Marxists of the early twentieth century went something like this: since the rise of class societies (with small, powerful upper classes of exploiters enriched by vast laboring majorities), there have been a succession of historical stages characterized by different forms of economy—ancient slave civilizations giving way to feudalism, which has given way to present-day capitalism.

The growth of capitalism was facilitated by democratic revolutions that swept away rule by kings and the power of landed nobles, making way for increasingly democratic republics and capitalist economies. The victory of the capitalists (the bourgeoisie) paves the way for the triumph of industrialization and modernization. This creates economic productivity and abundance making possible a socialist future (a thoroughly democratic society of freedom and plenty, in which there will be no upper class and no lower class). Capitalism also creates a working-class (or proletarian) majority that potentially has an *interest* in, and the *power* required for, bringing into being a socialist future.

Many Marxists consequently believed that there must first be a bourgeois-democratic revolution, followed by industrialization and modernization, before the necessary preconditions for a proletarian-socialist revolution can be created. There seemed a crying need for such a bourgeois-democratic revolution in economically "backward" Russia of the early 1900s. It was a land oppressed by the tsarist autocracy and landed nobility (to which capitalists were subordinated as junior partners), with a small working class and a large, impoverished peasantry. Many Marxists concluded they should fight for the triumph of such a bourgeois-democratic revolution, so that capitalist development could eventually create the economic and political preconditions for a working-class revolution that would eventually bring about socialism.

For some Russian Marxists (the Mensheviks, influenced by "the father of Russian Marxism," George Plekhanov), this meant building a worker-capitalist alliance to overthrow tsarism. Lenin and his Bolsheviks—profoundly skeptical of the revolutionary potential of Russia's capitalists—called instead for a radical worker-peasant alliance that would carry the antitsarist struggle to victory. But even they did not question the "orthodox" schema: first, a distinct bourgeois-democratic revolution paving the way for capitalist development; later—once conditions were ripe—a working-class revolution to bring about socialism.[7]

Yet from a Marxist point of view, this schema provides a theoretical and political puzzle. If the working class is as essential to the democratic revolution as the Mensheviks claimed, and if their direct exploiters are the capitalists with whom they are engaged in class struggle, then how can these mortal enemies be expected to link arms as comrades in a common struggle? And if—as Lenin insisted—the workers must, in fact, turn their backs on the capitalists (in alliance with the peasantry) to overthrow tsarism, what sense would it make for them in the moment of victory to turn power over to their cowardly exploiters?

"Trotsky alone [was able] to cut the gordian knot of the Marxism of the Second International," Michael Löwy has argued, "and to grasp the revolutionary possibilities that lay beyond the dogmatic construction of the democratic Russian revolution which was the unquestioned problematic of *all* other Marxist formulations." Yet scholars Richard B. Day and Daniel Gaido, in their massive documentary volume *Witnesses to Permanent Revolution*, have provided a sharp and persuasive challenge to this. "Leon Trotsky, while certainly the most famous and brilliant proponent of permanent revolution, was by no means its sole author," is how they sum it up. Among the others are Karl Kautsky, Alexander Helphand (who used the pen name Parvus), Rosa Luxemburg, David Riazanov, Franz Mehring—and, one could add, Lenin, with his formulation "uninterrupted revolution." The phrase "permanent revolution," and essential elements of the theory, can be found in works of Marx and Engels—especially in their writings of 1850. With specific reference to Russia, the conceptualization crops up in their writings of the 1870s and 1880s—for example, in the 1882 introduction to the *Communist Manifesto*.[8]

Trotsky himself insisted that his "permanent revolution" conception overlapped with perspectives of other Marxists. Some have characterized this as an effort to "minimize the originality of his conception" in order to "play down the supposedly 'heretical' nature of the theory of permanent revolution."[9] In fact, it seems Trotsky's comments were grounded less in political expediency than intellectual honesty. Far from being the unique innovation of Leon Trotsky, it is a perspective that flows naturally from the revolutionary conceptualizations inherent in the analyses and methodology of Marx himself. "Trotsky is deeply committed to one element in classical Marxism," as Isaac Deutscher has observed, "its quintessential element: permanent revolution."[10] Revolutionary-minded theorists and activists—seeking to apply such Marxism to the world around them—will naturally come up with formulations going in a "permanent revolution" direction.

Yet it was Trotsky's sparkling prose that most clearly and boldly formulated the interrelated elements of permanent revolution. Trotsky's formulation linked the struggle for democracy—the end of feudal privileges (especially redistribution of land to the peasants), freedom of expression, equal rights for all, rule by the people—with the struggle for socialism, a society in which the great majority of people would control the economic resources of society, to allow for the full and free development of all. It also linked the struggle for revolution in Russia with the cause of socialist revolution throughout the world.

Permanent Revolution

Trotsky's version of the theory of permanent revolution contained three basic points. (1) The revolutionary struggle for democracy in Russia could only be won under the leadership of the working class with support from the peasant majority. (2) This democratic revolution would begin a transitional period in Russia in which all political, social, cultural, and economic relations would continue to be in flux, leading in the direction of socialism. (3) This transition would be part of and would help to advance and must also be furthered by an international revolutionary process.

One might go further, beyond countries like Russia: *permanent revolution* has application in the capitalist heartland, not simply in the less developed periphery. Struggles for genuine democracy, struggles to end militarism and imperialist wars, struggles to defend the environment from the devastation generated by capitalism, and struggles simply to preserve the quality of life for a majority of the people cannot be secured without the working class coming to power and overturning capitalism. This means our own struggles in the here-and-now also have a "permanent revolution" dynamic. Nor can socialist victory be secured without the spread of such revolutions to other lands. Trotsky insisted on (in his words) "the permanent character of revolution as such, regardless of whether it is a backward country that is involved, which only yesterday accomplished its democratic revolution, or an old capitalist country which already has behind it a long epoch of democracy and parliamentarism." He added:

> The completion of the socialist revolution within national limits is unthinkable. . . . The socialist revolution begins on the national arena, it unfolds on the international arena, and is completed on the world arena. Thus, the socialist revolution becomes a permanent revolution in a newer and broader sense of the word; it attains completion only in the final victory of the new society on our entire planet.[11]

But, again, this is plain Marxism, not some innovative theoretical twist of Trotsky's. And he never claimed otherwise.

Analysis of Stalinist Bureaucracy

After Lenin's death, the rising bureaucratic apparatus headed by Stalin in the Communist Party and Soviet state instinctively gravitated toward a variant of "Marxism" that snapped all threads connecting the essential elements of Trotsky's formulation of permanent revolution: connections between democracy, socialism, and internationalism. Stalin advanced the notion that this so-called "socialism" (burdened by scarcity and authoritarianism, problems that would eventually fade away if all comrades did what they were told) could be created in the Soviet Union itself within a capitalist-dominated world.[12] Therefore Communist parties in other countries (required to follow the Stalinist line) were encouraged to struggle for democracy and social reforms, but they were *not* to struggle for socialist revolution. Instead, they were expected to make alliances with "progressive capitalists" and create regimes to peacefully coexist with the Soviet Union. This approach was interrupted briefly, from 1929 to 1934, by a so-called "left turn" which we will examine shortly.

As Tom Twiss documents in his fine study *Trotsky and the Problem of Soviet Bureaucracy*, Trotsky's early efforts to analyze Stalinism contained some serious misjudgments.[13] Still, early on he got much of it right. Describing in 1932 the typical functionary of the Soviet bureaucracy, "who manipulates the general line [of the Party] like a fireman his hose," Trotsky was merciless: "He eats and guzzles and procreates and grows himself a respectable potbelly. He lays down the law with a sonorous voice, handpicks from below people faithful to him, remains faithful to his superiors, prohibits others from criticizing himself, and sees in all this the gist of the general line." A few million such bureaucrats constituted the governing apparatus, he added, and a majority of them "never participated in the class struggle, which is bound up with sacrifices, self-denials, and dangers. . . . They are backed by the state power. It assures them their livelihood and raises them considerably above the surrounding masses." Using the analogy of the bureaucratization of the top layers in trade unions and working-class political parties raising themselves above the working class they claim to represent, Trotsky argued that

> the ruling and uncontrolled position of the Soviet bureaucracy is conducive to a psychology which in many ways is directly contradictory to the

psychology of a proletarian revolutionist. Its own aims and combinations in domestic as well as international politics are placed by the bureaucracy above the tasks of the revolutionary education of the masses and have no connection with the tasks of international revolution.

Trotsky's analysis is summed up with a single conceptually packed sentence:

On the foundation of the dictatorship of the proletariat—in a backward country, surrounded by capitalism—for the first time a powerful bureaucratic apparatus has been created from among the upper layers of the workers, that is raised above the masses, that lays down the law to them, that has at its disposal colossal resources, that is bound together by an inner mutual responsibility, and that intrudes into the policies of a workers' government its own interests, methods, and regulations.[14]

Far from portraying Stalinism as the product of an evil genius, Trotsky sees it as related to the more general development of a bureaucratic-conservative dynamic naturally deriving from historical circumstances, conditioned by specific economic realities. This involves an analytical methodology quite recognizable to those familiar with the approach of Karl Marx.

Fascism—What It Is, How to Fight It

Nazism, and fascism in general, are similarly analyzed by Trotsky through the employment of basic Marxist categories (and dovetailing with other Marxist analyses—for example, those of Antonio Gramsci in Italy and of Rosa Luxemburg's close comrade Clara Zetkin in Germany).[15] Before exploring Trotsky's analysis of fascism, we should note another aspect of Stalinism—its ultraleft turn of 1929–1934.

By the early 1930s, the urgency of stopping Hitler and the Nazi movement from taking power in Germany was absolutely clear to Trotsky. But such urgency was something that the mainstream of the Communist movement proved incapable of grasping. The reason can be found in the political disorientation generated by Stalinism.

Stalin's dictatorship resulted from the failure of socialist revolution to spread beyond the confines of what had been the huge and backward Russian Empire, contradicting Bolshevism's original revolutionary-internationalist expectations. The resulting authoritarian bureaucracy, which dominated not only Soviet Russia but the entire Communist International, adhered to a shallow pragmatism characteristic of such regimes. When a global economic depression began to devastate the capitalist world in 1929, such shallow pragmatism allowed revolutionary hopes to balloon among the bureaucrats, but these were expressed in a mechanistic and bureaucratic form.

A theory of three "periods" was advanced by the Stalinists: the first period (1917–1922) had been one of revolutionary upheaval, revolutionary flow; the second period (1922–1929) had been one of revolutionary ebb and capitalist restabilization; and the new *third* period opening with the Great Depression would usher in capitalist collapse and revolutionary triumph. The future belonged to the world Communist movement headed by Comrade Stalin. The greatest threat to revolutionary victory was posed not by fascists and Nazis—they were seen as foolish demagogues who would prove helpless in the face of history's revolutionary tidal wave. The real threat consisted of left-wing working-class currents that were not part of the Stalinist mainstream in the Communist movement. Such elements (whether moderate socialists or revolutionary socialists) threatened to mislead the workers, drawing them away from the true revolutionary leadership of Comrade Stalin. This meant they were, ultimately and objectively, twins of the fascists—instead of socialists, they should be considered "social-fascists."[16]

Street fighting between German Communists and Nazis became a daily routine in the early 1930s, but an alliance against the Nazis with the massive German Social Democratic Party—the so-called "social-fascists"—was unthinkable. And if Hitler's Nazis took power, in the view of Stalin's followers, the masses would soon turn against them, leading to Communist triumph: "After Hitler—our turn!" This outlook harmonized well with the fierce and brutalizing rapid industrialization and agricultural collectivization policies in the Soviet Union associated with Stalin's murderous "revolution from above" of 1928–1934.[17]

For Trotsky, the rise of Nazism could be explained by several convergent developments. Nazism's growing mass base came largely from what he viewed as "petty bourgeois" layers—farmers, shopkeepers, civil servants, white-collar employees, all of whom definitely did not want to be "proletarianized" and were becoming increasingly desperate for an alternative to the grim status quo and the deepening economic crisis. They, and some "backward" layers of the working class, were for various reasons alienated from the "Marxism" associated with both the massive German Communist Party and the even more massive Social Democratic Party, both of which were rooted in majority sectors of the country's working class. Petty bourgeois and alienated working-class elements flocked to a plebeian movement steeped in the ideological witch's brew of superpatriotic nationalism and racism prevalent in late nineteenth-and early twentieth-century Germany. Fierce anti-Semitism was blended with vague anticapitalist rhetoric. Yet the Nazis drew much material support from substantial elements within the upper classes (aristocrats, financiers, industrialists) who detested Social Democrats and trade unions and who genuinely feared the possibility, particularly with the Great Depression, of the sort of Communist revolution that had triumphed in Russia a dozen years before. The mass political movement the Nazis were building provided a counterweight and ultimately a battering ram to smash the Marxist threat.

An essential ingredient in the growth of Nazi mass appeal was the earlier and ongoing failure of the major parties of the working-class left to provide a revolutionary solution to the problems afflicting society—the Social-Democrats thanks to the reformist and opportunistic moderation of their own bureaucratic leaders, the Communists thanks initially to their woeful inexperience, later compounded by the sectarian blinders of "third period" Stalinism. Especially when left-wing organizations and parties prove ineffective, Trotsky argued, petty bourgeois layers will be vulnerable to fascist appeals, drawing the more conservative layers of the working class along with them—which is exactly what was happening in regard to the Nazi movement, as masses of Germans were attracted by Hitler's sweeping authoritarian certainties.

Trotsky called for a *united front* of Social-Democrats and Communists (including, as well, the dissident fractions of each), drawing on a conceptualization that the early Communist International had been won to—by Lenin, Trotsky himself, and others: the notion that a working class divided between reformists and revolutionaries could still defend and advance its interests through a fighting unity. A united front must be formed, and within this context the revolutionaries, as the most effective fighters, could ultimately win the adherence of a working-class majority. This dynamic played out in Russia in 1917, when the reactionary General Kornilov was defeated by united working-class action, in turn giving the Bolsheviks predominant influence in the working class. "Should the Communist Party be compelled to apply the policy of the united front, this will almost certainly make it possible to beat off the fascist attack," Trotsky argued. "In its own turn, a serious victory over fascism will clear the road for the dictatorship of the proletariat"—that is, for the working class to take political power and initiate a transition to socialism.[18]

In addition to breaking the Nazi threat and bringing a socialist transition in Germany, such a revolutionary development would likely generate similar revolutionary upsurges and transitions elsewhere and by ending the Soviet Union's isolation also help overcome the influence of Stalinism there and in the world Communist movement. In addition to pushing aside the twin tyrannies of Hitlerism and Stalinism, the question is naturally raised whether such developments might have prevented the Second World War.

United Front, Transitional Program

Of course, history took a more tragic turn. Once Hitler came to power, the Communist International ultimately zig-zagged in the opposite direction and by 1935 was calling for what some perceived as a sort of Super United Front—called the People's Front or Popular Front. Communists were now supposed to unite not only with moderate socialists but also (and especially) with liberal capitalist politicians for the purpose of creating liberal capitalist governments that would form an alliance with the Soviet Union against Hitler's Germany. Comintern spokesman George Dimitrov explained: "The toiling masses in a number of capitalist countries are faced with the necessity of making a *definite* choice, and of making it today, not between proletarian dictatorship and bourgeois democracy, but between bourgeois democracy and fascism." As historian E. H. Carr has noted, "Lenin's 'united front' had been designed to hasten the advent of the proletarian revolution," while "Dimitrov's 'popular front' was designed to keep the proletarian revolution in abeyance in order to deal with the pressing emergency of Fascism," adding: "care was taken not to ruffle the susceptibilities of those imperialist Powers whose support the Comintern was seeking to woo for the anti-Fascist front."[19]

Time after time, over the eight decades since then, revolutionary socialists have found old-time Stalinists and moderate socialists alike aggressively pushing forward that same political line. In arguing against it, Trotsky didn't devise some new theory but simply continued to apply the united front perspective guiding the Communist International under Lenin.

The insights and perspectives that Trotsky developed in his time still have resonance and value for our own time. Yet there is—in the conclusion of these remarks—a question of method that deserves attention. It is related to Trotsky's caution against devising a set of presumably "orthodox

Trotskyist" or "orthodox revolutionary" tactics to be applied "from Paris to Honolulu," as he put it. In discussions with Trotsky and others in Mexico in 1938, a seasoned US comrade (Charlie Curtiss) expressed a concern that Trotskyists from various countries, in his words, "have an extremely mechanical approach to the problems of permanent revolution." He urged that "emphasis should be placed upon the study of each concrete case, not upon abstractions only but upon each concrete case." Trotsky agreed, chiming in that "schematicism of the formula of permanent revolution can become and does become extremely dangerous to our movement in Latin America." In seeking to provide leadership in workers' struggles, he emphasized, it made no sense to "pose an abstract socialist dictatorship to the real needs and desires of the masses." Instead, revolutionaries must start from actual "daily struggles to oppose the national bourgeoisie on the basis of the workers' needs," through this approach "winning the leadership of the workers," through democratic mass struggles helping workers gain power.[20]

Related to this was Trotsky's criticism of comrades who "substitute a [seemingly revolutionary] monologue for actual political work among the masses." He expressed the same concern in various ways, at another time warning against an inclination, as he put it, to "terrorize the workers by some abstract generalities and paralyze the will toward activity." It is important to listen to and learn from others in order to be able to communicate revolutionary perspectives in a way that makes sense to people—or as Trotsky put it, revolutionary activists "should have in the first place a good ear, and only in the second place a good tongue."[21]

This connects with what Trotsky is reaching for in the *Transitional Program* of 1938. "It is necessary to help the masses in the process of the daily struggle to find the bridge between present demands and the socialist program of the revolution," he wrote. "This bridge should include a system of *transitional demands*, stemming from today's conditions and from today's consciousness of wide layers of the working class and unalterably leading to one final conclusion: the conquest of power by the proletariat."[22] Involving increasing numbers of people in actual mass struggles, in the here-and-now, for goals that seem quite reasonable to them but which come into sharp collision with the capitalist status quo—this is what helps generate revolutionary consciousness and revolutionary struggle.

"How to mobilize the greatest possible numbers; how to raise the level of consciousness through action; how to create the most effective alliance of forces for the inescapable confrontation with the ruling classes"—this was the problematic with which Trotsky wrestled in this foundational document of the Fourth International, the global network of Trotskyist organizations. More than six decades after the founding, Fourth Internationalist Daniel Bensaïd shared his own understanding: "The concept of transitional demands overcomes sterile antinomies between a reformist gradualism which believes in changing society without revolutionizing it, and a fetishism of the 'glorious day' which reduces revolution to its climactic moment, to the detriment of the patient work of organization and education."[23]

Here again, such insights are hardly unique to Trotsky. They are certainly essential to his politics, but they have also been an integral element in the methodology of revolutionary Marxism over the past 160 years, and part of the collective wisdom of the international workers' movement for even longer. They can certainly be found in Lenin and in the first four congresses of the Communist International. And they can be found in Rosa Luxemburg's earlier admonition at the dawn of the twentieth century that the uncompromising struggle for social reforms is the pathway for the working class in achieving the consciousness, the confidence, the organization, and the experience for realizing the aim of the socialist revolution.[24]

The fact remains that, along with the other aspects of the revolutionary ideas of Leon Trotsky touched on in this chapter, such challenging conceptualizations can be useful for us as we seek, today and tomorrow, to build effective struggles for freedom and socialism.

Chapter Four

LEARNING FROM BOGDANOV

The amazing Alexander A. Malinovsky is better known by his revolutionary last name, Bogdanov, which he took from his wife, Natalia Bogdanovna Korsak (herself a revolutionary as well as a nurse and a midwife). Up until now, among those who do not know the Russian language, only fragments of Bogdanov have been available. Although he was the primary target of Lenin's philosophical polemic *Materialism and Empirio-Criticism*, we have not been able to read, except for snatches and excerpts, the Bogdanov texts that provoked and responded to what Lenin had to say. The one complete work of his that has been easily accessible is a remarkable 1908 work of left-wing science fiction, *Red Star*.[1]

Born in 1873, Bogdanov was widely commemorated in the Soviet Union upon his death in 1928—for example, by Nikolai Bukharin, at the time one of the top leaders of the Russian Communist Party:

In the person of Alexander Alexandrovich we have lost a man who in terms of his encyclopedic knowledge occupied a special place not only in the Soviet Union, but was one of the most significant minds of all countries. This is one of the rarest qualities amongst revolutionaries. Bogdanov felt equally at ease in the refined atmosphere of philosophical abstraction and in concrete formulations of the theory of crises. The natural sciences, mathematics and social sciences: he was an *expert* in these fields, he could survive battles in all of these areas, and he felt "at home" in all of these spheres of human knowledge. From the theory of fireball lightning to the analysis of blood to the broadest generalizations of "Tectology"—this was the true scope of Bogdanov's theoretical interests. An economist, a sociologist, a biologist, a mathematician, a philosopher, a doctor, a revolutionary and, finally, an author of the beautiful *Red Star*—in all of these areas he was an absolutely exceptional figure in the history of our social thought. . . . The exceptional strength of his mind, his nobility of spirit, his loyalty to ideas—all these qualities entitle him to the lowering of our banners at his grave.[2]

It has seemed obvious to many of us trapped in the English language that we have been missing out on an incredibly important body of work and experience. A dramatic shift is underway. James D. White's very substantial *Red Hamlet: The Life and Ideas of Alexander Bogdanov* is part of a collective project being produced through the Historical Materialism series of Brill Publishers, with later paperback editions being put out by Haymarket Books—involving at least ten projected volumes of Bogdanov's writings. Two of these have already appeared: *The Philosophy of Living Experience* (1913), and *Empiriomonism* (1904–1906). Those interested should consult the recently constructed Alexander Bogdanov Library website.[3]

Bogdanov is not only a central figure in the history of Russian Marxism but was also coequal with Lenin in the early formation of the revolutionary socialist current known as Bolshevism. After a period of intimate cooperation in building and leading the Bolshevik faction of the Russian Social Democratic Labor Party, their falling out resulted in a fierce conflict from 1907 to 1909, with Bogdanov's version of Bolshevism seeming to be the stronger variant in the eyes of many.

The insightful revolutionary novelist Maxim Gorky wrote of Bogdanov: "He will accomplish in philosophy the same kind of revolution that Marx accomplished in political economy. . . . If he should succeed, we will witness the defeat of the remnants of bourgeois metaphysics, the disintegration of 'bourgeois soul' and the birth of a socialist soul." Bogdanov and his cothinkers were developing a variant of Marxism far more vibrant than that of the venerable George Plekhanov, "the father of Russian Marxism" to whose philosophical orientation Lenin continued to adhere. More decisively, the Bogdanovite political orientation veered far to the left of what Lenin deemed practical in the wake of the defeat of the 1905 revolutionary upsurge. "Plekhanov and Lenin, though diverging on questions of tactics, both believe in and preach historical fatalism," explained Gorky. "The other side preaches a philosophy of action. To me it is clear on whose side there is more truth."[4]

Strengths and Limitations

Gorky's appraisal describes not only his own perspective of that faraway time, but also the spirit with which White's biography is infused. The result provides immense strengths as well as serious limitations. The bulk of this volume provides a much-needed, detailed, clearly written, immensely sympathetic journey through Bogdanov's writings from the late 1890s through the 1920s.

On the other hand, we are provided with very little information on the personal dimensions of Bogdanov's story. There is passing mention but no real discussion of his parents, of his wife, of his sometime lover who gave birth to his son, of the great majority of his friends, of his colleagues, and of his revolutionary comrades. There is no critical exploration of his personality, although aspects of it come through in the generous quotations White provides from others.

There is some elementary socioeconomic, cultural, and political contextualization, although the fact that Bogdanov was a revolutionary activist necessarily squeezes out more attention to this aspect of his life. Even here, there are limitations. Bogdanov was involved with the "armed struggle" dimension of Bolshevism (which included "expropriations," or bank robberies), but there is very little information about this, for example.

Another limitation is that White, a strong and longtime adherent of what Lars Lih has termed "the textbook" interpretation of Lenin, presents him as inherently and grimly authoritarian from start to finish.[5] When aspects of Lenin's life and thought seem to go in a very different direction, White is quick to place shadows and question marks over what might place Lenin in a favorable light. He rarely gives Lenin the benefit of any doubts and generally seems pleased to give dark interpretations to what Lenin says, thinks, or does (or speculations on what Lenin conceivably might have said or thought or done). This orientation comes through clearly in a comment in the book's very weak final chapter:

> The conflict with Lenin dominates much of Bogdanov's political career. The Russian Bogdanov scholar A. L. Takhadtazhan writes that it never ceases to amaze him that a cultured and humane person such as Bogdanov should be for so many years the political associate of such a sinister character as Lenin. In other words, for Takhadtazhan the question is not what brought an end to the association between Bogdanov and Lenin, but how it could ever come about in the first place. This is a useful way to look at the question.[6]

White's reflections on the question predictably show Bogdanov to be a very good guy and Lenin to be a very, very bad guy. Nonetheless, White is a serious enough scholar to provide ample material indicating complexities that can provide alternate interpretations to his own. And whatever the limitations, they are transcended by White's primary contribution: a rich and systematic account of Bogdanov's thought.

Economics, Philosophy, Organization

Bogdanov's first major work, *A Short Course of Economic Science* (1897), provided an historically oriented exposition of Marxist economics. When it first appeared, Lenin reviewed it with enthusiasm:

> Mr. Bogdanov's book is a remarkable manifestation in our economic literature; not only is it "no superfluous" guide among a number of others (as the author "hopes" in his preface), it is by far the best of them. . . . The outstanding merit of Mr. Bogdanov's *Course* is that the author adheres consistently to historical materialism. In outlining a definite period of economic development in his "exposition," he usually gives a sketch of the political institutions, the family relations, and the main currents of social thought *in connection* with the basic features of the economic system under discussion.[7]

Bogdanov's book went through numerous editions, ultimately appearing in English translation in 1923, thanks to the Communist Party of Great Britain. As translator J. Fineberg noted at the time:

> It was, as the author says in his Preface, written in the dark days of the Tsarist reaction for the use of secret workers' study circles; and it serves to-day as a textbook in hundreds, if not thousands, of party schools and study circles now functioning in Soviet Russia, training the future administrators of the Workers' Republic.[8]

As it turned out, however, Bogdanov was by no means inclined to restrict his analyses to the realm of economics. He was at the center of a cluster of young revolutionary intellectuals—including Anatoly Lunacharsky, Mikhail Pokrovsky, and Vladimir Bazarov—intent upon utilizing Marxism to develop a comprehensive understanding of society, nature, life, and reality. They were influenced by Ernst Mach, a renowned Austrian physicist also engaged in the study of the history and philosophy of science, and

Swiss-German philosopher Richard Avenarius, whose ideas contributed to philosophical currents known as logical-positivism and empiricism. Among other things, they identified as "monists" who saw reality as a unified whole, denying the existence of a duality between matter and mind, insisting that the mind—rather than reflecting "objective realities" (as Plekhanov argued)—knows only actual or potential sensory experience. It made no sense to separate material reality from what is in people's minds.

Matter could be best understood as inseparable from human sensations, according to Mach. Bogdanov gave this a Marxist spin: "Matter is resistance to activity; thought is the organizing form of activity. Both originally relate to human, collective, laboring activity. . . . In this model, everything is indivisible and inseparable." As he put it, "truth expresses the relationship of the *human collective* to the things of its experience. The power or value of truth derives from the fact that it is crystallized social experience." Bogdanov emphasized that "truth . . . is *produced*—created with the struggle of humanity with the objectives of nature." Reality is "living experience."[9]

The father of Russian Marxism denounced this as un-Marxist philosophical idealism, while the Mach-influenced Marxists insisted that their approach was much closer to the actual orientation of Karl Marx than was Plekhanov's "mechanistic materialism." (In addition, Mach's conceptualizations—as his defenders often note—influenced Albert Einstein's development of the theory of relativity.)[10]

For the so-called Machists, the equivalent of Plekhanov's "objective reality" was a broadening collective comprehension. Bogdanov insisted that socially organized experience had greater validity than individually organized experience. Industrial capitalism "brings together people in large masses for common labor," White tells us (summarizing Bogdanov), and "the mutual understanding which they develop serves to widen and deepen their experience. . . . Whatever machines the machine workers happen to operate, there is much in the general character and content of their labor that is similar, and this similarity keeps increasing in proportion to the degree that the machine approaches perfection to become a completely automatic mechanism."[11]

Paving the way for the socially organized experience required for greater scientifically valid consciousness—"this generality of experience makes for mutual understanding and encourages solidarity among the workers," and "the fragmentation of humanity" though specialization "is gradually overcome." This, in turn, paves the way for a "new type of scholar [who] is widely educated, monist thinking, socially vital. He incarnates the conscious, systematic integration of mankind. For Bogdanov, the best example of this kind of person was Karl Marx, the man who first gave a monist understanding of social life and development."[12]

White's substantial summary of the 1906 essay "Revolution and Philosophy" draws together so many strands of Bogdanov's perspective that it is worth quoting in full:

> Like revolution, philosophy too is a means of overcoming contradictions and establishing harmony. The contradiction here was the lack of correspondence between rational and humane principles which people believed ought to govern their lives and the injustice and inhumanity which characterized actual human relationships. The exploiting classes in society benefited from its irrationality and injustice, whereas, on the side of the exploited classes, the industrial proletariat in its struggle with nature gradually extended the realm of reason and justice in society. The industrial proletariat introduced a new world outlook which was able to eradicate the contradiction between people's social outlook and their social experience. The contradiction was resolved by Marx's social philosophy, which held that it was not people's consciousness that determined their social being, but their social being that determined their consciousness. This realization eliminated everything that was absolute in perception. Marx's philosophy eliminated fetishism from perception and made possible an integrated view of the world corresponding to people's actual experience.[13]

Over time, Bogdanov's philosophical empiriomonism morphed into what he perceived as a science, which he labeled *tectology*, a precursor of what came to be known after the Second World War as "general systems theory." He saw this as a "science of organization" embracing all of reality. Organizing activity, White explains, for Bogdanov permeates both living and nonliving phenomena.[14] "The definition he gave of organization was 'a whole that is greater than the sum of its parts.'" White continues:

> The entire world consisted of an organizing process, an infinitely developing series of complexes of different forms and levels of organization in their mutual relations, in their struggle or their unification. All of these, however remote from each other they were qualitatively and quantitatively, could be subsumed under the same organizational methods, the same organizational forms.[15]

White observes that Bogdanov hoped that tectology would "become the basis for a proletarian science"—but most workers were unable to read it. "To appreciate it fully one would have to have at least some knowledge of physics, chemistry and biology, but an acquaintance with economics, astronomy and linguistics would not go amiss. In other words," White concludes, "readers would have to already possess the kind of knowledge in which *Tectology* was intended to school them."[16]

White presents two other realms of Bogdanov's thought that will be touched on briefly later in this survey: (1) Proletarian Culture ("Proletcult"), and (2) explorations in blood transfusions and what Bogdanov called "the struggle for viability." As White sums it up, "the rewarding task of unearthing the great treasury of his ideas continues until the present day."[17]

Yet Bogdanov was also a revolutionary activist. To do him justice, one must consider the role he played in the Russian Social Democratic Labor Party (RSDLP) and its Bolshevik faction. Even though White's biography does not provide a rounded discussion of this, it does offer useful information that must be integrated into any serious effort to comprehend this aspect of Russian revolutionary history.

Early Bolshevism

It is hardly controversial to say that Bolshevism as we know it would not have existed without the contributions of Vladimir Ilyich Lenin. But as White's biography suggests, it is also questionable that Bolshevism as we know it could have existed without the contributions of Alexander Alexandrovich Bogdanov. In what follows, information on Bogdanov's role provided in White's biography will be dis-attached from the earlier-mentioned "textbook" anti-Leninist innuendo.

When the *Iskra* current of the RSDLP split into Bolshevik/Menshevik factions in 1903, Lenin's opponents mobilized in an effective campaign to overturn decisions of the RSDLP's Second Congress that they opposed, take over the party's influential journal *Iskra*, and build public pressure within the international socialist movement to isolate and denigrate Lenin and his cothinkers who represented in the majority at the Second Congress. Lenin's most influential ally, George Plekhanov, abandoned him, and considerable confusion was generated throughout the revolutionary underground in the Russian empire.

Studying the documents and reports from the Second Congress, Bogdanov and the cluster of bright and energetic comrades around him—all young
and vibrant—concluded that they were in agreement with the besieged faction around Lenin. Bogdanov and Lunarcharsky led a discussion of Lenin's
pamphlet *What Is to Be Done?* at a large meeting of revolutionary activists in
1902–1903. In Bolshevik/Menshevik polemics, considerable factional use
was made of Lenin's assertion that "the history of all countries shows that the
working class, exclusively by its own effort, is able to develop only trade union
consciousness," while "the theory of socialism . . . grew out of the philosophic,
historical, and economic theories elaborated by educated representatives of
the propertied classes, by intellectuals." While this was used by his opponents
(including White) to depict Lenin as an authoritarian elitist, Bogdanov rejected this interpretation. Even after his break from Lenin, he insisted:

> Once Lenin in *What Is to Be Done?* made a slip of the tongue, saying that
> the working class was incapable, independently, without the help of the so-
> cialist intelligentsia, to raise themselves above the ideas of trade unionism
> and come to the socialist ideal. The phrase was uttered quite by chance in
> the heat of a polemic with the "economists," and had no connection with
> the basic views of the author. This did not prevent Menshevik writers in
> the course of three years from concentrating their triumphant polemic
> on the above phrase of Lenin's, by which he had allegedly once and for all
> shown the anti-proletarian character of Bolshevism.[18]

Bogdanov saw the character of Bolshevism quite differently. In 1903 he
produced an essay, mirroring some of Lenin's argument in his description of an
ideal centralized organization involving what he called "the ideologue" (consistent with the conception of "professional revolutionary") and working-class
members in underground conditions:

> A person of the mass both discusses and decides within which limits he
> will follow the ideologue; he "carries out" his organizing orders only in so
> far as they express the aspirations and wishes of the man of the masses.
> He by various ways himself indicates to the ideologue what this latter
> should give to him. He not only subordinates himself to the ideologue,
> but to a certain degree also *subordinates* him to himself. And the more
> synthetic elements there are, the more lively the socializing [*obschenie*]
> of the ideologues with their followers, the more comradely their mutual
> connection becomes, the more progressive the psychology of both sides,
> the more lively will be their cause.[19]

In *Our Misunderstandings*, a 1904 pamphlet coauthored with M. S. Olminsky defending the Bolsheviks against various criticisms (including those of Plekhanov, Karl Kautsky, and Rosa Luxemburg), Bogdanov—as White tells us—"found that the charge of 'Bonapartism' against the 'majority,' the urge to dictate to local organizations and even to dissolve them at will, had no foundation in fact. . . . In Russia local autonomy was the rule." A decisive issue in the split had involved the adoption of Lenin's proposal to reduce the size of the *Iskra* editorial board from six to a more manageable three (Plekhanov, Lenin, Martov), which involved the removal of venerable old-timers Vera Zasulich and Pavel Axelrod. In Bogdanov's opinion, "people in a position of leadership in the party and the members of the editorial board of its central organ . . . ought not to be for life." He agreed with Lenin that "the organization of the RSDLP should be on democratic principles, that there should be majority rule," that there were no "insuperable" divisions between Mensheviks and Bolsheviks, and that "the 'minority' [Mensheviks] have acted reprehensibly in refusing to abide by the decisions of the Second Congress of the party."[20]

Bolshevik Leader

Bogdanov and his comrades threw themselves into the efforts of the Bolshevik faction and were invaluable in the struggle to build the kind of party, a democratic but disciplined revolutionary Marxist collective, that Lenin was reaching for. When "Bogdanov appeared on the horizon," Lenin's companion Nadezhda Krupskaya later remembered, "Vladimir Ilyich was still little acquainted with his philosophical works, and did not know him at all, personally. It was evident, however, that he was a man capable of occupying a leading position in the party." She added that "he had extensive contacts in Russia." Krupskaya and Lenin spent the summer of 1904 with a small cluster of close cothinkers, and "with the Bogdanovs [A. A. Bogdanov and his wife Natalia] we discussed a plan of work."[21]

According to White, an important 1904 appeal, "To the Party," often attributed to Lenin, was in fact coauthored by Lenin and Bogdanov.[22] Decrying the fact that "the Party's capacity for harmonious and united action is fading into a mere dream," they expressed the hope that "the Party's sickness [is] a matter of growing pains" that could be overcome through "the immediate summoning of the Third Party Congress" to "clarify the situation, settle the disputes, and confine the struggle within proper bounds." The Mensheviks should be offered "the widest formal guarantees." They added: "In putting forward this program of struggle for Party unity, we invite the representatives of all other shades and all Party organizations to make a clear statement of their own programs, so as to permit of serious and systematic, conscious and methodical preparation for a congress."[23] White points to the obvious notion, held by Bogdanov and his comrades, regarding "the right of those who disagreed with the decisions of the [RSDLP] congress to express their opinions and have them considered at the following party congress."[24]

In discussing Bogdanov's organizational views, White writes: "He believed that in party organization the slogan of centralism was insufficient; the slogan of democratism ought to be promoted as well." This is, however, a conceptualization also embraced by Lenin and others in both factions of the RSDLP. Views White attributes to Bogdanov were by no means his views alone: "a party which espoused the comradely principle was alien to naked centralization and blind discipline. These were incompatible with the free and conscious character of the comradely connection; this demanded democratic forms of organization." Noting that it is unknown what individual put forward the specific term "democratic centralism" at the unity congress of the RSDLP in 1906, White implies that it may have been Bogdanov himself, and later baldly states that "the very concept of 'democratic centralism' owed its existence to Bogdanov."[25] It would appear that the term was not so new to the workers' movement (perhaps going back at least to the 1870s), was introduced into the RSDLP by the Mensheviks, but was embraced as well by the Bolsheviks. While Bogdanov was eloquent in advancing the concept, it hardly originated with him.[26]

Yet there soon arose a substantive political difference between the Bolshevik and Menshevik factions, somewhat muted in White's account, but certainly seen as of decisive importance to the Bolsheviks. As one of Bogdanov's recruits to Bolshevism Mikhail Pokrovsky later explained: "Lenin set himself the task of *overthrowing* the tsar; the Mensheviks that of compelling the tsar to *give in*. Lenin regarded the overthrow of tsarism as a task of the workers and *peasants*; the Mensheviks believed the best way to extract concessions from the tsar was to act in alliance with the *bourgeoisie*." There had emerged a significant organized liberal current among the more moderate intellectuals—with many connecting with "progressive" industrialists and landowners hoping to work with the tsar to expand civil liberties and craft a representative assembly, and a less conciliatory current forming a party known as Constitutional Democrats. Discussing Bolshevik opposition to a reliance on the liberals, White cites arguments advanced by Bogdanov in late 1904: "one feature common to all liberals was their hostility to socialism. When there was a danger of socialism, the liberals were often prepared to ally with the most reactionary parties and resort to the most extreme measures."[27]

At the same time, differences arose within the Bolshevik faction, particularly with the explosively revolutionary workers' upsurge of 1905, sparked by the brutal repression of a peaceful mass workers' demonstration in January. Masses of radicalized workers streamed to the RSDLP, but many of the practical organizers—often termed "committeemen" (also *praktiki*)—resisted moving too quickly in drawing these raw proletarian militants into the Bolshevik organization. Lenin pushed hard against this organizational conservatism, and in this he was joined by Bogdanov. On the other hand, there was also a holding back among the Bolsheviks from participating in the revolutionary workers' councils (soviets) that were forming in the working-class districts unless they were prepared to accept the program of the RSDLP. From exile, Lenin began urging his comrades to shift—embracing and participating in the soviets. This was a position, White tells us, to which Bogdanov and other comrades were soon won over. A key point of agreement from the start was the necessity of preparing for armed struggle and insurrection. Early in 1905, Bogdanov wrote: "The day of uprising is not far off, but it has still not dawned. The workers and peasants have too few arms, they are still not rallied enough for the struggle."[28]

Yet Bogdanov, Lenin, and Leonid Krasin—functioning as a leading "troika" of Bolshevism—did all that they could to secure arms, to rally masses of the exploited and the oppressed, and to work for what turned out to be the ill-fated December 1905 uprising in Moscow. White's study provides comparatively little of what Bogdanov did in that fateful year, but he does cite comments of veteran Bolshevik V. D. Bonch-Bruevich:

> There were times—such as, for example, in 1905 after 9 January—when in Russia the direct leadership of the party belonged entirely to Bogdanov, and his authority among our most active ranks, among the underground members, was really enormous. When I was an illegal activist for six months during 1905 I had a chance to observe him in action as a leader, and his performance in that role was excellent.[29]

In the aftermath of the defeated insurrection, Lenin and Krupskaya shared a house with the Bogdanovs in nearby Finland. Krupskaya remembers that "Ilyich practically directed all the activities of the Bolsheviks from Kuokkala." The Bolsheviks had decided to make use of legal opportunities provided by the parliamentary body, the Duma, which the tsar had agreed to establish. The shared leadership at the Bolshevik apex meant that while "the Second Duma deputies came to Kuokkala fairly often to have a talk with Ilyich," as Krupskaya notes, "the work of the Bolshevik deputies was directed by Alexander Bogdanov." Yet in the close working relationship that had been established, Bogdanov "consulted Ilyich on everything."[30]

A fundamental political agreement was the key to the close working relationship of Lenin and Bogdanov. This involved a determination to build a democratically centralized working-class party with a revolutionary Marxist program, committed to a worker-peasant alliance that would carry out a democratic revolution to overthrow the tsarist order. It also involved an understanding that the upsurge of 1905 had suffered only a temporary setback—it was not over, but would soon culminate, if the revolutionaries remained firm, in a revolutionary triumph.

A year later, however, Lenin was developing doubts that this common understanding was grounded in the realities of the situation. By 1907 the Bolsheviks were beginning to split apart on the question of how to analyze the current situation and on divergent tactical orientations dictated by the divergent analyses. Philosophical issues also came into play.

Bogdanov/Lenin Split

White's discussion in this volume of the how and why of the Lenin/Bogdanov split is packed with valuable information. Unfortunately, his emphasis on explicating Bogdanov's philosophical contributions tends to overwhelm the political narrative, and combined with his consistently anti-Leninist twist, this obscures much of what happened. Yet he identifies important factors in the situation.

As his son later recalled, "Bogdanov had experienced only two periods of serious depression: after the break with Lenin and after the outbreak of the First World War." The split certainly exacted a great toll on all concerned. "For about three years prior to this we had been working with Bogdanov and the Bogdanovites hand in hand, and not just working, but fighting side by side. Fighting for a common cause draws people together more than anything." This was the comment of Krupskaya, who added: "The conflict within the [Bolshevik] group was a nerve-wracking business." She recalled that upon returning from one of the arguments with these comrades, Lenin "looked awful, and even his tongue seemed to have turned grey."[31]

Comparing White's analysis with Zenovia Sochor's much earlier study *Revolution and Culture: The Bogdanov-Lenin Controversy* is useful. Sochor offers a generalization that White would certainly accept: "cultural change and politics were closely and persistently interwoven in the revolutionary period. The Lenin-Bogdanov dispute led to a split in Bolshevism, one that was never entirely repaired, and challenged any coupling of Leninism with Bolshevism." She adds detail consistent with the findings of White and other scholars:

> The differences between Bogdanov and Lenin began to emerge on both philosophical and political grounds. Bogdanov, although an avowed Marxist, insisted on an open-minded attitude toward new philosophical currents, claiming that some parts of Marxism, such as epistemology, were incomplete. He wrote *Empiriomonizm* (three volumes, 1904–1906), employing the theories of Ernst Mach and Richard Avenarius, as part of an effort to fill in the gaps in Marxism. Lenin at first seemed unaware of the significance of Bogdanov's "revisionism" (despite Plekhanov's warnings) and then decided on a philosophical truce in order to maintain their political alliance.

Her next point, however, on the link between the philosophical dispute with practical politics, goes off the rails in ways that White's study helps to correct: "By 1907," she writes, "Bogdanov's independent streak had begun to show itself in politics as well, and this disdain of 'party discipline,' for Lenin, tipped the scales against his comrade-in-arms."[32]

White succinctly but more accurately identifies the practical issues. He cites Bogdanov, *speaking for the Bolshevik majority* in 1907, arguing that,

> all the factors which had brought about the 1905 revolution continued to operate: the disconnect between the political structure of the country and the demands of its economic development, the ruination of the peasantry, the impoverishment of the proletariat, unemployment, all remained as before. Consequently, the objective historical tasks of the revolution had not been carried out, and, at the same time, the forces of revolution had not fundamentally weakened. Beneath the outward calm, the economic and political organizations of the proletariat were developing, as was

the political consciousness of the peasantry, so that the forces were being gathered for a new and decisive revolutionary struggle.... In this situation the tactical tasks facing the party in the current bourgeois-democratic revolution were explaining to the masses the need for a popular uprising and the convocation of a constituent assembly ... This should be the main focus of party work, and any obstacle to this should be eliminated.[33]

Lenin's disagreement with this was reflected in his insistence on "the priority to be given to participation in the Duma and the use made of other legal openings, such as the trade unions and cooperatives." The too-rambunctious Duma was dissolved by tsarist decree and replaced by a less democratic one. Bogdanov's tactical alternative: "preparation for the coming revolutionary struggle, strengthening the party locally and training up activists to be propagandists of Social-Democracy."[34] It was Lenin, not Bogdanov, who showed "disdain of 'party discipline'" by breaking ranks to vote with the Mensheviks.

"Thus, the man who had sounded the call for armed revolt began to urge us to read the newspaper *Russia* (*Rossia*), which printed stenographic reports on the sessions of the State Duma," Bogdanov's cothinker Pokrovsky later recalled. "What a hail of ridicule this called forth on Lenin—this time not from the bourgeoisie but from our midst! Who did not jeer at him? Who did not bait him? The man had lost his fire, nothing of the revolutionary was left in him. The faction had to be recalled, the Duma faction liquidated; an armed revolt had to be called immediately." This was consistent with what both Lenin and Bogdanov had both been arguing two years earlier.[35]

"A Bolshevik, they declared, should be hard and unyielding," Krupskaya later recalled, explaining:

Lenin considered this view fallacious. It would mean giving up all practical work, standing aside from the masses instead of organizing them on real-life issues. Prior to the Revolution of 1905 the Bolsheviks showed themselves capable of making good use of every legal possibility, of forging ahead and rallying the masses behind them under the most adverse conditions. Step by step, beginning with the campaign for tea service and ventilation, they had led the masses up to the national armed insurrection. The ability to adjust oneself to the most adverse conditions and at the same time to stand out and maintain one's high-principled positions—such were the traditions of Leninism.[36]

Lenin explained the need, in his opinion, to transcend the "outgrown ... narrow framework of the 'circles' of 1902–1905," in which "close-knit, exclusive" committees of "professional revolutionaries" had constituted the RSDLP. "Undoubtedly, the present leaders of the present workers movement in Russia will have to break with many of the circle traditions . . . so as to concentrate on the tasks of Social-Democracy in the present period. Only the broadening of the Party by enlisting proletarian elements can, in conjunction with open mass activity, eradicate all the residue of the circle spirit." He added that "the transition to a democratically organized workers' party, proclaimed by the Bolsheviks in . . . November 1905, . . . was virtually an irrevocable break with the old circle ways that had outlived their day."[37] If such a shift was necessary for the survival and growth of the revolutionary party, Lenin was fully prepared to break factional discipline to achieve it. Ultimately, through tireless efforts involving not a few maneuvers and manipulations, and with the indispensable assistance of a diverse number of experienced and energetic Bolshevik comrades in harmony with the approach he advocated, Lenin was able to declare Bogdanov and his cothinkers outside of the Bolshevik faction.[38]

Bogdanov and his cothinkers called themselves Forwardists, after the Bolshevik journal *Vperyod* (Forward) of 1904–1905, a name they would soon appropriate for their own journal. They believed it was they who were defending "true Bolshevism" (centralized committees of professional revolutionaries, a refusal to compromise with the tsarist autocracy by participating in its "puppet parliament," and an unswerving commitment to armed struggle and a revolutionary uprising) against what they hoped would be the temporary vacillations of Lenin. Bogdanov explained in 1910 that Lenin and others "have come to the conclusion that we must radically change the previous Bolshevik evaluation of the present historical moment and hold a course not toward a new revolutionary wave, but toward a long period of peaceful, constitutional development. This brings them close to the right wing of our party, the Menshevik comrades. . . . Bolshevism continues to exist as before. . . . Comrades, a glorious cause—political, cultural, social—stands before us. It would be shameful for us if leaders who have outlived their times, overcome by adversity, should prevent us from fulfilling it. . . . We will proceed on our way according to the old slogan—with our leaders, if they wish; without them if they do not; against them, if they oppose us."[39]

Lenin by no means considered this to be mere bluster. As late as 1911, he was complaining to Alexei Rykov: "The Vperedists are very strong. They have a school = a conference = agents. We (and the Central Committee) have not. They have money, some 80,000 roubles. Do you think they will give it to you?? Are you really so naïve??" As White points out, "the situation within the Vpered group was not so favorable as Lenin imagined," although it may have been nearer the mark two years earlier as Bogdanov and his cothinkers were being forced out of the Bolshevik faction.[40]

In fact, after being forced out of the Bolshevik faction, despite being graced with an array of talented intellectuals, a significant treasury, and full faction rights in the RSDLP, the Forwardists did not survive for long as a distinctive political force. It was the Leninist-Bolsheviks, not Bogdanov's Forwardist-Bolsheviks, that endured, grew, and triumphed. But why? This is a puzzle that White's biography doesn't resolve.

Philosophy and Revolution

An important aspect of the split, as we have noted, was philosophical. How is one to determine, for example, what is true and what is not? "For Bogdanov, Lenin's main misapprehension was that there was such a thing as absolute and eternal truth, whereas in fact all truths were relative and ephemeral."[41] To what extent is this true? To what extent do the theorizations of Bogdanov (or of Lenin and his philosophical mentor Plekhanov) diverge from the Marxist method of analysis, and to the extent that there is such a divergence, what practical-political difference does it make? White's study of Bogdanov, and especially the translation and circulation of Bogdanov's works, will enable increasing numbers of people to explore, discuss, and debate such matters. But how did the disputants themselves view the matter?

White clearly demonstrates that Bogdanov himself saw intimate links between philosophy and revolutionary activity, which he explains, for example, in his 1906 essay "Revolution and Philosophy." While some historians view Lenin's philosophical polemic as a smokescreen, others have been inclined to agree with Geoffrey Swain that after the emergence of sharp tactical differences between Lenin and Bogdanov, Lenin came to feel that Bogdanov's tactical views "resulted from the un-Marxist philosophy that he propounded. His errors, therefore, could not be confined to this one issue [of boycotting the Duma] but would recur over and over again." This seems to be a reasonable proposition, but the issue is complex. Aside from vague references to "the cycle of ideas of boycottism," Lenin seems to have refrained from drawing a bold, straight line from the tactics of Bogdanov to the philosophy of Bogdanov. At the same time, there did appear to be such a correlation in the minds of the disputants.[42]

In fact, the philosophical orientation of Bogdanov definitely had a profound appeal for many newly radicalized young workers with an intellectual bent and was in harmony with the psychology of a number of militant Bolshevik *praktiki*. It would be an error to think that those commonly considered to be Bolshevik "hards" automatically lined up behind Lenin or simply scoffed at philosophical discussions. One well-known Bolshevik practical functionary, Joseph Stalin, wrote from a Baku jail in 1908 in praise of the "good sides" of Ernst Mach's philosophy and urged that Marxism be developed and revised "in the spirit of J. Dietzgen" (an earlier socialist philosopher, a comrade of Marx and Engels, who was influential among Bogdanov's cothinkers). Stalin also favored what he called "a deviation from strict bolshevism"—the recall of RSDLP deputies from the Duma. Seeing Bogdanov's group as an impressive alternative to "the other part ('orthodox') of our fraction, headed by Ilyich," he praised Bogdanov's latest writings for indicating "individual blunders of Ilyich." Even in late 1909 Stalin was criticizing the earlier removal of Bogdanov from the *Proletary* editorial board and accused Lenin of "schismatic tactics." It was not until 1910, after the consolidation of a Bolshevik majority around Lenin, that Stalin expressed appreciation of his "wisdom."[43]

It is interesting to consider Bogdanov's views on what happened. Believing (as White puts it) "that personal disagreements were inevitable, and indeed, necessary for the health of the party," he insisted—as the polemical disputes were about to become explosive—that "so far the Bolshevik fraction to which he belonged had been able to resolve these differences by wide discussion, democratic voting and party discipline."[44] It is striking that ten years later, he held the same opinion. As White summarizes his position:

> In its early days, in the period 1904–1907, Bolshevism was decidedly democratic, not only in its program, but in the attitudes that permeated the organization. Lenin was the most experienced and influential political figure in the organization, but no one would have thought of waiting to hear Lenin's opinion before forming one's own. Moreover, often on important questions Lenin found himself in a minority and had to put into effect the collective decision which he had voted against.
>
> Things began to change with the victory of reaction after the defeat of the 1905 revolution in Russia. The Bolshevik organization was weakened, and the will of most of its members was broken. Lenin and his entourage at that time underwent a significant turn to the right. They effected a

union with the Mensheviks, despite the opposition of local organizations in Russia. This was a principle for the victory of leadership, causing it to become entrenched. It was precisely from this time that many Bolsheviks began to refer to themselves as "Leninist," a title that had formerly been used by their opponents in polemics against them.

Bogdanov went on to say that although the union with the Mensheviks lasted only a few months, it was followed by a number of instances where Lenin was able to lay down the line in the teeth of opposition from members of his own party fraction.[45]

Leadership and Proletarian Culture: The Capri Party School

This relates to a significant reflection that Bogdanov had earlier developed on leadership, again summarized by White:

> Once a person was designated a leader, and in this way distinguished from the rest of the collective, there was the danger of an authoritarian relationship. The specialized organizer was not wholly a comrade. Even if he had no formal personal "power," even if all the comrades followed his directions voluntarily, and even if they could hold him to account, there was still the serious possibility of a drift towards authoritarianism. The danger was especially great where the level of collective consciousness in the organization was not high, and where the role of the "authority" was filled by an outsider from an environment where authoritarianism was prevalent.[46]

White suggests Bogdanov himself was inclined to apply this analysis to Lenin. But the prevalence of such dynamics can surely be applied to someone like Bogdanov himself. This emerges through an examination of one of his most innovative projects.

Before the split, Bogdanov and other Forwardist-Bolsheviks, assisted by Maxim Gorky and a vibrant, politically experienced young worker-Bolshevik named Nikifor Vilonov, established a school for working-class activists. Working-class activists would be gathered together for a several-month immersive learning situation. In addition to lectures in Marxist theory, economics, history, topics related to struggle (trade unionism, the agrarian question, etc.), literature and other cultural questions, students would be trained in public speaking, the conduct of meetings, and techniques of newspaper printing. Gorky opened his spacious home for this purpose on the Mediterranean isle of Capri.[47]

For years, based on initial experiences with worker education, Bogdanov had been developing conceptualizations that led precisely to this project: the notion that "the intelligentsia played an auxiliary part in the workers' movement, and that the object of educating the workers was to make them completely independent of the intelligentsia," as White puts it. "Indeed, for Bogdanov, the inadequacies of the intelligentsia, their individualism and their consequent metaphysical view of the world, contrasted with the collectivist and monist outlook of the workers." Yet developed proletarian consciousness was hardly a pure and spontaneously developed gift from God. Bogdanov became convinced that "the way to eliminate the authoritarian thinking and the narrow-mindedness among the workers was 'to create newer and newer elements of socialism in the proletariat itself, in its internal relations and its everyday conditions of life: to work out a socialist proletarian culture.' That is, he believed that comradely cooperation was not only a characteristic of a socialist society, but also the means by which that society would be achieved."[48]

This was becoming an urgent practical question by 1908. The defeat of the 1905 revolution had led to a dramatic demoralization especially among many of the young intellectuals who had been part of the RSDLP, with a significant exodus from the ranks of the party. This was "especially felt in all party organizations, because they had acted as party secretaries, treasurers, littérateurs, propagandists and agitators," as White points out. "With their departure these functions had been taken over by the workers themselves, but the workers felt the need to acquire more knowledge and training to carry out these essential party tasks."[49]

Although many of the twenty-seven participants were arrested immediately upon their return to Russia, in many ways the Capri school was a success. One of the students recalled:

A. A. Bogdanov was listened to with enormous interest. He described in a masterful, sometimes even in an artistic, way the epochs of human economic relations. We read together the first chapters of Marx's Das Kapital. He had a good knowledge of the history of philosophy, natural science and mathematics. In a word he was a great scholar in the full sense of the word. It must be added that he was a very good and responsible comrade. He was simple and very attentive. His wife, Natalia Bogdanova, like a good mother, looked after us as we were studying.[50]

Praise was also forthcoming for other lecturers such as Lunacharsky, Pokrovsky, and Gorky. Even the several Leninist-Bolshevik workers in attendance "recognized that knowledge they had received from the lectures at the school as useful and necessary." But extracurricular activities initiated by Forwardist-Bolshevik students and lecturers at the school included the development of a factional platform counterposed to the Leninist wing of the faction. This generated indignation among some of the students (including the worker who had helped initiate the project, Nikifor Vilonov), who vigorously protested and finally resigned from the school. Leninists in Bolshevik publications expressed sharp and open criticism of the entire project. When Bogdanov sought to involve the remaining student body in a polemical response, the school's student council balked, which caused Bogdanov to complain of their "being in awe of the party leadership" (as White puts it) and to threaten his own resignation.[51]

White summarizes a later critique by Nikolai Bukharin, a young Bolshevik who had been attracted to Bogdanov, which gives a sense of the range of Bogdanov's thinking:

> According to Bukharin, Bogdanov's basic idea was that the socialist transformation of society and the socialist revolution should be undertaken according to an organizational plan worked out in advance. First, the working class would create its own science, elaborate its scientific methods in all spheres of knowledge, construct for this purpose workers' universities, write a proletarian encyclopedia, etc. and then make an "organizational plan" to decide the "world organizational tasks." When all this was done, only then would it be possible to achieve socialism. To do otherwise would be "maximalism" and utopia.[52]

By 1910 Gorky himself was becoming disaffected. "As you know, I respect you both as a thinker and as a revolutionary," he wrote to Bogdanov, "but I shall not reply to your letters: they are too severe, written as though you were a sergeant and I a simple private in your squad." He complained more severely of Bogdanov in a letter to another prominent Forwardist, Grigory Alexinsky:

> It seems to me that he does not have the temperament of a revolutionary, but that he is a maker of systems. The inclination towards synthesis is strongly developed in him, and like all people of this kind he is a conservative and a despot. As far as other people are concerned—he despises them all, because he thinks himself incomparably more intelligent and significant than them, hence his arrogant attitude towards them. But he has talent. I am sure he will accomplish much.[53]

And yet the Forwardist-Bolsheviks, which he led, fell apart. The predicted revolutionary resurgence did not materialize. The armed groups that Bogdanov and Krasin had developed, engaged in a sort of urban guerrilla warfare involving "expropriations" that corrupted some of them, became marginal to actual working-class struggles, and tended to descend into simple banditry. There were growing theoretical disagreements, with some close comrades openly critical of Bogdanov's cultural theories. Fierce internal polemics generated by Alexinsky demoralized and drove away key figures in the original Forwardist cluster—including Bogdanov himself, who abandoned organized activist efforts by 1911 in order to devote himself to his studies and literary efforts.

Perhaps predictably, Bogdanov sought to integrate the political experience of 1904–1910 into his philosophical systematizing. In the science of organization, which he designated as *tectology*, he advanced the notion of the "law of the leasts." All phenomena are organized from multiple and diverse elements. The structural stability of all systems—mechanical, physical, psychical, social, etc.—is ultimately determined by its weakest part. To maintain coherence, the more advanced elements must adapt to the least advanced, otherwise the system risks breaking apart at its weakest link.[54]

> Bogdanov saw the danger that the law of the leasts might come to dominate humanity if it was not brought under control. There was, he believed, a problem for tectology to solve: how to master the law in the cultural sphere in order to avoid equalization according to the lowest common denominator, so that humanity's major achievements should not be lost to the survivals of barbarity which threatened to overwhelm them?[55]

Another tectological conceptualization involved the understanding that a system could be considered from the standpoint of its contacts with its environment—branching out in diffusion or limiting such contacts with a more compact structure. Bogdanov "concluded that, as far as the preservation and development of complexes was concerned, under negative selection a compact structure was to be preferred, and under positive selection a diffused structure."[56]

Obviously, the law of the leasts was what Bogdanov's struggles had been designed to overcome, and yet the very same law of the leasts identifies the source of his defeat. Also, the period of reaction in the wake of the revolutionary defeat of 1905 impacted the "relationships between central and local organizations" of the RSDLP by breaking up what was a relatively diffuse structure, so that "the party was turned into a number of scattered groups." However, the triumph of compactness could be seen "where unity was maintained," although "it was only the unity of the program or dogma, which became more stringent." Related to this, "with the merger of political parties," with the Leninist-Bolshevik rightward convergence toward the Mensheviks, "to avoid internal conflict, some programmatic and tactical elements are sacrificed," and "members of the organization who are unhappy with the merger or who can be an obstacle to its implementation are thrown out."[57] Elaborating further:

> Seen from a tectological perspective, Lenin's attempt in 1909 to split the Bolshevik fraction and ally with Plekhanov's supporters among the Mensheviks was doomed to failure. The maneuver involved the Leninists getting rid of the left wing of the Bolsheviks, while Plekhanov detached his group from the "liquidationist" right wing of the Mensheviks. The Leninist Bolsheviks and the "party Mensheviks" would then be required to form a coherent center organization. However the two fractions had become so distant that the desired merger was impossible, and the organization collapsed at its point of least resistance. No center grouping of Lenin's and Plekhanov's forces gelled, and instead of two fractions there were now four.[58]

Yet Lenin's effort to build a coherent version of the RSDLP out of the hoped-for unity conference with "party Mensheviks" in 1912 moved forward without Plekhanov. Lenin was not bound by Bogdanov's schema, worked with what he had, and with like-minded comrades forged a cohesive organization that was able to connect with local organizations throughout Russia while catching wind in its sails from the radicalizing working-class upsurge of 1912–1914. Challenged but then aided by the horrific devastations of the First World War, Lenin's Bolsheviks proved to be a force capable of playing an increasingly vibrant role, ultimately a leadership role, in the revolutionary overturns of 1917.

Revolution, Culture, Blood

Bogdanov had been drafted into the Russian Army as a medical officer during the First World War. The traumas of the war did not disrupt his writing, but he was absent from the urban centers within which tsarism was overthrown in February/March, within which power struggles between the bourgeois-orientated provisional government and working-class soviets unfolded, and within which the Bolsheviks under Lenin and Trotsky swept to power.

Some prominent old Forwardists rejoined the Bolsheviks. Lunacharsky and Pokrovsky, who assumed prominent posts within the new People's Commissariat of Enlightenment, sought to draw Bogdanov back into Bolshevik ranks as well, and it has been said that Bukharin and even Stalin did the same—though Lenin and Bogdanov appear to have sustained a mutual antipathy. Bogdanov maintained a position independent of and at least moderately critical of the Bolsheviks, although he gave critical support to the Bolshevik Revolution and the Soviet regime.

White's narrative suggests a systematic persecution of Bogdanov orchestrated by Lenin, but the matter deserves more careful study. It is true that Lenin openly and persistently criticized the ideas of his old comrade, saw to it that a new edition of *Materialism and Empirio-Criticism* was published with an anti-Bogdanov introductory essay by the Bolshevik activist-scholar Vladimir Nevsky. Lenin also expressed concern about the influence of Bogdanov's ideas in the writings of such comrades as Bukharin. But in the same period, from 1917 through the early 1920s, Bogdanov was able to function with a fair amount of freedom, wrote extensively, was able to publish his writings, and exercised significant influence within the new order. "In the early 1920s it was Bogdanov's works that were the standard works on socialist and Marxist theory," according to White, going through a number of editions, "and they were widely studied in Soviet educational institutions."[59]

Bogdanov was also a founding theorist and organizer in the Proletarian Culture (Proletcult) movement which had begun to develop before the Bolshevik Revolution but by 1920 had a membership of more than 400,000— artists, writers, musicians, scientists, and more, largely from the working class, functioning in a cooperative relationship with the Peoples Commissariat of Enlightenment, headed by Bogdanov's old comrade Anatoly Lunacharsky.[60] While some reference to Bogdanov's views on the necessity of developing proletarian culture and proletarian science has already been offered above, a more thoroughgoing summation of his perspectives is offered in White's study.

Bogdanov "argued for the integrity of the proletarian worldview, unsullied and unaltered by the manipulations of class-alien elements," notes Lynn Mally in her history of Proletcult, though she adds that "he certainly did not question his own ability to articulate the thoughts of the proletariat."[61] The Proletcult movement of this period, however, was hardly following a single set of ideas—it was a complicated social and cultural movement with many conflicting programs, as Mally has shown, with a "heterogeneous social composition and . . . varied cultural practices."[62] It is probable that many would have rejected Bogdanov's relatively conservative notion that, as White sums it up, it was not the "decadent" artistic fashions of "modernism" and "futurism" that should be followed (represented, for example, by the poet Vladimir Mayakovsky), but rather "the simple, clear and pure forms of the great masters such as Pushkin, Lermontov, Gogol, Nekrasov and Tolstoy."[63]

While this corresponded to Lenin's well-known cultural conservatism, however, he had a deep store of distrust for the theoretical orientation of his erstwhile Machist comrade and focused considerable energy on bringing Proletcult under the stricter control of the People's Commissariat of Enlightenment and also to combatting Bogdanov's influence within it, culminating in Bogdanov's resignation in late 1921.[64]

Two years later, Bogdanov was arrested by the Cheka. "Although I had finally given up politics, it had not given up me," Bogdanov wrote, "as my arrest in September-October 1923 has shown." White goes on to quote (uncritically) from Victor Serge's 1942 memoir that Lenin "has Bogdanov, his old friend and comrade, jailed because this outstanding intellectual confronts him with embarrassing objections." Serge is an outstanding witness, to be sure, and the more substantial quotation from which this sentence is wrenched makes a valid point. Serge is telling us that while Lenin describes the dictatorship of the proletariat as "the broadest possible workers' democracy," and that "he believes it and wants it to be so," his regime was contradictory—allowing some freedoms for those considered supporters or potential supporters, yet all too often suppressing those on the Left deemed to pose a counter-revolutionary threat.[65]

But as White should know, in this case Lenin didn't do it. Three decades after the fact, Serge had misremembered. Lenin was felled by his third stroke in March 1923, was severely and increasingly incapacitated, and in less than four months suffered a fourth stroke and died. He was in no position, at that point, to micromanage the persecution and order the arrest of an old opponent. White himself offers the real story. The head of the Cheka, the fiercely uncompromising purist Felix Dzerzhinsky, was convinced that Bogdanov was active in an illegal organization producing the paper *Workers' Truth*, which denounced the Communist Party as having lost its ties with the proletariat and called for "a new Workers' Party to fight for democratic condition under which the workers could defend their interests." One of its articles utilized Bogdanov's terminology and quoted from his writings. Bogdanov was finally able to secure an extensive face-to-face meeting with Dzerzhinsky, whose "attitude changed completely after an hour's conversation," and who had him released shortly thereafter.[66]

Bogdanov's assessment of post-1917 Russia contained interesting elements related to his overall philosophical and theoretical work. One aspect of it involved a sharp difference with a onetime cothinker Vladimir Bazarov who, echoing some of Lenin's writings, believed a transitional form between capitalism and socialism was what Bazarov referred to as state capitalism (state regulation of the economy necessitated by war, which had arisen during the First World War), and which Bogdanov tagged "war communism." Bogdanov argued, White tells us, "that there is an enormous difference between socialism, which was primarily a new form of cooperation, and war communism, which was a special form of consumption, an authoritarian organization of mass parasitism [the "parasites" being military personnel producing no value] and annihilation." The economy "in force in Soviet Russia between 1918 and 1921" consisted of "an attempt to manage scarce resources in a spiral of economic decline." This alleged transition to socialism was, in Bogdanov's words, "a repulsive caricature . . . born of war and the old order."[67]

Combined with this "war communism" was the fact that the new regime's base consisted of a weak working class and a very large number of soldiers, resulting in the tectological "law of the leasts" asserting itself with a vengeance: "A workers' and soldiers' party was objectively simply a soldiers' one. And it was striking to what degree the Bolsheviks had been transformed in this way; they had assimilated the logic of the barracks, all its methods, all of its specific culture and ideals." In fact, there was the ascendancy of "the logic of the barracks, in contrast to the logic of the factory," with every question now regarded "as one of force rather than one of organized experience and labor." It reduced the notion of socialism to "smashing the bourgeoisie and seizing power."[68]

Nonetheless, as Bogdanov explained to Bukharin, "although he disagreed with the Bolshevik party's analysis of the situation, he recognized the objective necessity of its policies." He considered the work of Bukharin and his comrades to be tragic. White summarizes:

> The blood and dirt that had been involved in the revolution was excessive, but it was not individuals that were to blame, but the backwardness of the country. Bogdanov assured Bukharin that the Bolsheviks would be un-

likely to lose their heads or their power. The danger was that what would be lost was the idealism that had inspired Bukharin in the past.[69]

Pushed out of political and cultural efforts, Bogdanov returned to earlier scientific and medical interests. In the mid-1920s he was able to draw together a cluster of like-minded people to study and experiment with blood transfusions. By this time Stalin and Bukharin were at the regime's highest pinnacle, and in 1926 there was official approval for the establishment of an innovative research clinic under Bogdanov's directorship. Scientific historian Nikolai Krementsov describes Bogdanov's 1927 study *The Struggle for Viability* as a text that, reflecting the work Bogdanov was doing, "applied the basic principle of his 'proletarian science' to the studies of blood transfusion and articulated a 'tectological' theory of senescence and rejuvenation as the theoretical foundation of both his vision of 'physiological collectivism' and his research program on blood exchanges."[70]

White seems uncritical, suggesting that Bogdanov was engaged in good science. Krementsov, more critical, disagrees. Bogdanov died in an experimental blood exchange in 1928.

Bogdanov's Legacy

"Whatever Bogdanov studied, be it medicine, natural science, mathematics, political economy, sociology or philosophy, he always studied it thoroughly and in depth," recalled Anatoly Lunacharsky, according to White's summary of the obituary he wrote. "Bogdanov's talent was the ability to deploy his enormous knowledge in constructing and expounding schemes of thought." He added that "the most characteristic feature of Bogdanov's mind was the compulsion to reduce the great multiplicity of being to a number of repeating varieties of a few basic laws," which unfortunately, he concluded, "gave rise to a certain schematism."[71]

"History recruited him for his politics; his personal inclinations made him a philosopher. In both these fields he suffered defeat," commented another old comrade M. N. Pokrovsky. "But as one of the cultural heroes who died at his post, he will remain in the memory of many generations, perhaps he will remain there forever."[72]

Forever is a long time. But what James White and others working on the retrieval of Bogdanov are accomplishing is to make available to new generations around the world the contributions of an extremely important revolutionary thinker. There are old questions still to be wrestled with, not the least of which are challenges posed by Lenin in *Materialism and Empirio-Criticism* and Dominique Lecourt's essay "Bogdanov, Mirror of the Soviet Intelligentsia." Lenin insisted: "Let Bogdanov, accepting in the best sense and with the best intentions all the conclusions of Marx, preach [the empiriomonist notion of] the 'identity' of social being and social consciousness; we shall say: Bogdanov minus 'empiriomonism' (or rather, minus Machism) is a Marxist." What Lecourt has to say in some ways seems more serious: "The Bogdanovist system remained an inexhaustible reservoir for the verbally 'left-wing' themes of Stalinist propaganda," particularly with his conceptualization of "proletarian science."[73]

Whatever conclusions are drawn about such matters, Bogdanov's importance is not contained by them (as is the case of Lenin, for that matter). As K. M. Jensen put it in a pathbreaking study forty years ago, "There is more to Bogdanov's thought than an epistemological position of which Lenin did not approve."[74] With the increasing availability of his ideas, there will be increasing explorations, expositions, applications, and debates.[75] Engaging with what fallen comrades did in the past, one can more fully understand what happened in the past, but also one can sometimes absorb relevant insights and challenging approaches for the present and future, learning from mistakes made and things done right.

Chapter Five

SPIDER AND FLY

The Leninist Philosophy of Georg Lukács

In this new period of global crisis and upsurge, a recurring pattern essential to the dynamic of capitalism, a multiplicity of urgent questions are raised. Just as was the case in the early decades of the twentieth century, these range from elemental issues of ethics (what is right, what is wrong, what is one to do) to more complex questions regarding the interplay between struggle and consciousness, between militant minorities (vanguards) and mass layers of the population, between revolutionary organization and revolutionary tactics.

The story and ideas of philosopher-activist Georg Lukács (1885–1971), particularly from 1917 to 1929, are compelling particularly as we wrestle with the realities and possibilities of our own time. His engagement with Hegel, Marx, Lenin, and the revolutionary experiences of 1917–1921 propelled him to develop a remarkable orientation that found literary expression in writings intimately connected to revolutionary practice—ranging from *History and Class Consciousness* of 1923 to the so-called "Blum Theses" of 1929.

The fact that Lukács partly retreated from this achievement under the immense pressures of Stalinism has obscured much of what that remarkable contribution represented. Our purpose here will be to suggest a reconstruction of this early revolutionary achievement, which can contribute important elements to the perspectives of tomorrow's activists. Through extensive examination of what he wrote in key works of this period, combined with an effort to interweave texts with practical-political contexts (hopefully brought even closer to life with anecdotes), something will emerge—with luck—that we can fruitfully embrace.

In an academic discussion club with which Georg Lukács was involved before he became a Communist, one of his associates challenged: "Isn't there a deep inner bond between the factory owner and the worker?" Lukács replied: "Yes, quite decidedly. The same as that between the spider and the fly in its web."[1] The sticky, multithreaded web of capitalism engages us all, down to the present, in this intimate relationship—yet Lukács as much as any of his contemporaries devoted considerable intellectual labors to defining the nature of the web and (at least in the 1920s) pointing to ways and means of snapping its bonds. These labors were permeated with a materialist understanding that ideas are grounded in our social reality but can be a force for helping us transform reality, especially if our ideas reflect the dialectical (contradictory, interactive, evolving) totality of that reality.

The recent discovery and publication of Georg Lukács's *Tailism and the Dialectic* is an event of importance for more than one reason.[2] Lukács was one of the great European intellectuals of the twentieth century—any newly discovered work by him would naturally merit attention. This particular work necessitates a reevaluation of Lukács in a particularly interesting period of his life. In the early years of the Communist movement following the publication and flurry of polemical assaults on his "forbidden" masterpiece *History and Class Consciousness*, the embattled theoretician composed an explication and defense, previously unknown, which sheds light on the nature of that masterpiece and on Lukács's own political location. And the "new" work itself arguably constitutes a quite valuable contribution to the advance of Marxist philosophy and politics.

A common retelling of the Lukács story runs roughly like this: A radicalized intellectual is horrified by the imperialist slaughter of World War I and inspired by Russia's proletarian revolution of 1917. He joins the newly formed Hungarian Communist Party and is immediately swept up in revolutionary events in his homeland associated with the short-lived Hungarian Soviet Republic. First churning out a flurry of eloquent ultraleftist writings, by 1923 he produces a highly intellectualized volume, saturated with Hegelian interpretations of Marx and a glorification of Lenin's elitist theory of organization which idolizes the Communist Party as the fount of all revolutionary wisdom. But the brilliant book is too unorthodox for the bureaucratic-authoritarian leaders of the world Communist movement, who denounce it. True to his convictions, Lukács himself acknowledges the wisdom of the party and repudiates his work. This is a pattern that will be followed more than once in his life as he becomes enmeshed in the web of Stalinism. The ultraleftist intellectual evolves, in violation of his better self, into a defender and ornament of totalitarianism, only breaking from it (somewhat incompletely) in 1956.[3]

The reality is more interesting, and *Tailism and the Dialectic* is a key for helping us to a truer understanding of the reality. In particular, it helps us to clarify aspects of Lukács's thinking and to retrieve important insights of the revolutionary Marxist orientation represented by Lenin and some of his more thoughtful comrades of the post-1917 period.

Aspirations and Dilemmas

"Ethics relate to the individual," wrote a thirty-four-year-old Georg Lukács in 1919, "and the necessary consequence of this relationship is that the individual's conscience and sense of responsibility are confronted with the postulate that he must act as if on his action or inaction depended the changing of the world's destiny, the approach of which is inevitably helped or hindered by the tactics he is about to adopt." The Hungarian philosopher and culture critic closed off the path of escape for those wishing to evade this challenge: "In the realm of ethics there is no neutrality and no impartiality; even he who is unwilling to act must be able to account to his conscience for his inactivity."[4]

The next comment is a profound challenge for anyone, like Lukács himself, who in this period was drawn to the Marxist banner of socialist revolution: "Everyone who opts for communism is therefore obliged to bear the same *individual* responsibility for each and every human being who dies for him in the struggle, as if he himself had killed them all."

And then this cultured son of the bourgeoisie deepened the argument into an irrevocable break from his class: "But all those who ally themselves to the other side, the defense of capitalism, must bear the same individual responsibility for the destruction entailed in the new imperialist and revanchist wars which are surely immanent, and for the future oppression of the nationalities and classes." Such a starting point in the early Marxist "career" of this middle-aged intellectual promised a remarkably vibrant contribution to the living body of revolutionary theory and practice.

In fact, the quality of his thought might have placed Georg Lukács at the level of such Marxist theorists as Luxemburg, Trotsky, and Gramsci had his revolutionary consistency and intellectual integrity not been so badly compromised by a quarter-century adaptation to Stalinist authoritarianism. Much in his later philosophical and literary analyses, as well as a courageous anti-Stalinism in the 1950s, prevents one from dismissing the "mature" Lukács, but these cannot compare with the contributions made before the onset of his fatal political disorientation stretching from 1930 to 1956 (and in some ways to the end of his life).

This disorientation is particularly striking because Lukács had provided a brilliant and comprehensive interpretation of Marxism—stretching from *Tactics and Ethics* (1919) to the "Blum Theses" (1929)—which stands, philosophically and theoretically, as one of the most profound expressions of Bolshevik politics in the twentieth century.

His earliest efforts to give philosophical expression to the Bolshevik ethos could take odd and even contradictory form. On the one hand, in 1918, he wrote that "Bolshevism rests on the metaphysical notion that good can come from evil, that it is possible . . . to lie ourselves through to the truth," and that "liberty can be attained through oppression," and he concluded that such a position must be rejected.[5]

Yet within days of writing this he decided to join the Hungarian Communist Party and went on to insist: "The human ideal of the realm of freedom must . . . be a conscious principle governing the actions and motivating the lives of all communist parties from the very moment of their inception." Emphasizing that this involves not only organizational forms, consciousness-raising through education, speeches, and literature, but especially "what communists themselves achieve as human beings," he wrote: "The Communist Party must be the primary incarnation of the realm of freedom; above all, the spirit of comradeliness, of true solidarity, and of self-sacrifice must govern everything it does."[6]

It is not clear that he fully rejected his earlier view of the "moral problem" of Bolshevism. Ilona Duczynska (who was on the scene) and others have suggested that the Lukács of the early 1920s sought to "dialectically" reconcile the two notions. It could be said that the failure of reality to conform to this theorization finally dislodged the passionate dialectician from practical political work—that when the ethics of evil surpassed the ethics of freedom and solidarity in the practical organizational life of the Stalinized Communist movement, Lukács chose to abandon any efforts at political leadership in the movement, instead making do with more abstract philosophical and literary pursuits. Yielding to the temptation of reducing Lukács's revolutionary career to the dramatic playing out of stark formulations from 1918, 1919, and 1920, however, prevents one from considering a far more interesting reality.

In fact, the more mature practical-political approach Lukács developed in the 1920s had implications for the development of an ethical resolution to which we shall return at the conclusion of this essay.

Achievement's Context

For a politically mature expression, one must turn to his *History and Class Consciousness*, which sought to "integrate Lenin's theory of revolution organically into the overall framework of Marxism," as Lukács himself put it.

It is worth pausing for a moment to consider how to place this work in its context. John Rees, prefacing an extremely positive reading, has asserted that this book was "born in the greatest period of advance the world has ever seen," constituting "a reflection on three revolutions—the Hungarian, the Russian, and the German—shot through with a new understanding of Marxism based on Lukács's studies in exile." On the other hand, in a more critical reading, István Mészáros has stressed that it was written "against the background of the military defeat of the Hungarian Council Republic and the restoration of capital's international dominance and stability, after the short revolutionary interlude initiated by the Russian Revolution."[7]

Both points are well taken, yet Lukács himself emphasized a different aspect of the context in his fragmentary autobiographical notes—"crucial for the whole enterprise: the method and contents of the Hungarian factional struggles." And more: "Relationship to Landler. The theoretical importance of "minor" causes of the party split. My attention shifted from the "great" questions (their existence perhaps only postulated) to the actual problems of the movement—here: the effect revolutionizes."[8]

As these notes suggest, *History and Class Consciousness* paralleled— and would have been impossible without—Lukács's commitment to the faction inside the Hungarian Communist Party led by Eugen (or Jenö) Landler. A veteran of the left wing of the socialist movement and leader of the railway workers' union, Landler—remembered years later as "the truest of the true" even by such a disillusioned ex-Communist as Franz Borkenau—represented a practical working-class opposition to the ultraleftist and bureaucratic-sectarian party leadership of Bela Kun. Four decades later, Lukács described Landler as being "notable not only for his great and above all practical intelligence but also for his understanding of theoretical problems so long as they were linked, however indirectly, with the praxis of revolution. He was a man whose most deeply rooted attitudes were determined by his intimate involvement in the life of the masses." Lukács saw a sharp contrast between Kun's demagogy, dishonesty, glory-seeking and the qualities of Landler: "Landler was different from Kun—and this is what made me become his loyal supporter—in that he had no program which he could have used to appear before the world as a leader of the Communists. He simply concerned himself with the practical possibilities of reviving the Hungarian movement. That made a great impression on me, and from then on I supported him enthusiastically."[9]

After the bloody defeat of the short-lived Hungarian Soviet Republic of 1919, Kun sought to establish a supercentralized Hungarian Communist Party built up among exiles living outside of Hungary—seeking "to create a movement from above, directly from Moscow," as Lukács put it, that would then be transplanted onto native soil. "Landler took a very skeptical view of such a proposal, arguing that the real movement would have to originate in Hungary and that the émigrés could not do anything but assist it from abroad by virtue of their more advanced ideological development. In the eyes of the Landler camp the émigrés were always subordinate to the indigenous movement."[10]

While the entire Communist movement of this period was afflicted by what Lukács has termed a "messianic sectarianism," in his view Kun represented one of the most destructive variants of the trend.

> I attribute the fact of this trend . . . not having become the sole dominating one, to the underground Hungarian movement, to Jenö Landler's and Janos Hirosik's influence in the first place. The opposition headed by Landler and Hirosik took a determined stand against Bela Kun's bureaucratic utopias . . . and—in the true spirit of Lenin—strove to deduce the political and organizational tasks of the communist movement in Hungary from the actual problems of the real situation in that country.[11]

Lukács himself was centrally involved in the underground Communist Party in Hungary. Some saw him as "the philosopher lost in the jungle of conspiratorial party work." But he had no hesitation in risking arrest in order to travel from Vienna to Budapest for weekly clandestine meetings with leading Communist workers in Budapest to discuss "the tactics and methods of working within the trade unions," to lead study groups, and oversee the party's semilegal press. (His underground party-name was "Blum," and workers described him as "a frail man who smokes cigars during party meetings.")[12] While left-wing intellectuals and sectarian grouplets have all too often lost sight of the fact, the Lukács of the 1920s was absolutely clear that there can be no revolutionary Marxism that is detached from the actual lives, consciousness, and struggles of the working class.

A working-class militant in Vienna, Sandor Vajda, later recounted how Lukács encouraged him to take seriously the realities around him, and to write down his observations of the workers' living and working conditions, what they read, what they talked about on the job, their thoughts on the current regime and on communism. "I showed him my notes about the workers' lives: the squabbles of women, the factory meetings, the quality of textiles we produced, the prices and wages in the textile industry," he later remembered. "I wrote about what was said during lunch breaks, including some interesting comments of workers." He recalled Lukács's comments: "It is often the insignificant and seemingly meaningless human acts that become important."[13]

Lukács later recalled that "the correct policy of the Landler faction began to bear fruit. The party, working in conditions of strict illegality, steadily increased its influence on the left-wing of the Social Democrats so that in 1924–1925 it came to a split and the founding of a Workers' Party that would be radical and yet legal." Covertly led by Communists associated with Landler, this Hungarian Socialist Workers Party, according to historian Miklos Molnar, was able to develop some national and even international influence as it "attempted to establish a common plan of action with the Social Democratic party and . . . published periodicals, participated in the organization of social struggles, and conducted an energetic agitation in the poorest regions, particularly in the countryside."[14]

One additional element in this crystallization of the Lukács achievement was international. Lukács himself later emphasized:

> We were all messianic sectarians. We believed that the world revolution was imminent. The Hungarian work was determined by Landler's realism on actual Hungarian questions. This produced a dualism. Internationally we were messianic sectarians, in Hungarian affairs we were practitioners of *Realpolitik*. This dualism finally resolved itself in favor of realism with the Blum Theses.[15]

By "messianic sectarian," however, he was not referring to the perspective represented by Lenin, who (Lukács stressed in his brief Lenin book of 1924) was no less committed to "the actuality of revolution." Rather, he was referring to an "ultraleft" political current targeted by Lenin's polemic *Left-Wing Communism: An Infantile Disorder* (1920) and even more sharply criticized at the Third Congress of the Communist International in 1921. Central to the 1921 controversy was the notorious March Action of 1921, which involved a disastrous effort by the Communist Party in Germany (supported both by Bela Kun and Lukács, among others) to seize power in a minority putsch—going against the sentiments of the great majority of the German workers influenced by the Social Democratic Party. Lenin had sternly lectured them that a Communist Party could not "replace the proletariat as the spontaneous historical agency," elaborating:

> He who fails to understand that in Europe—where nearly all the proletarians are organized—we must win over the majority of the working class is lost to the Communist movement. If such a person has not yet learned this in the course of the three years of a great revolution, he will never learn anything. . . . We achieved victory in Russia, not only because we had the undoubted majority of the working class on our side (during the elections in 1917 the overwhelming majority of the workers voted for us and against the Mensheviks), but also because half the army—immediately after we seized power—and nine-tenths of the peasantry—within the course of a few weeks—came over to our side.[16]

Lukács later noted: "At that time Trotsky himself had not been a Trotskyist but supported Lenin."[17] In summing up the Third Congress, Trotsky had commented on the "revolutionary subjectivism" of the ultraleftists which "mistakes the second or fifth month of pregnancy for the ninth." He observed that the failure of the mass revolutionary upsurges that shook Europe in 1919–1920 had made the working class more cautious—not because workers "have become less revolutionary, but because they are less naive and more exacting." He elaborated:

> They have understood and sensed that the prerequisite for success is a firm leadership, that one must know how to calculate and plan, that revolutionary strategy is indispensable. . . . Only that party will be able to lead them in decisive battles which reveals in practice, under all conditions and circumstances, not merely its readiness to fight, i.e., its courage, but also its ability to lead the masses in struggle, its capacity to maneuver in attack or retreat,

its skill in leading them out of the line of fire when a situation is unfavorable, its ability to combine all forces and means for a blow, and, in this way, systematically to enhance its influence and its authority over the masses.[18]

The Congress advanced a perspective of careful party-building and serious efforts to advance class consciousness through organic connection with the actual struggles of the working class—engaging in trade union work, reform struggles, and united fronts. In other words, the perspectives of the Comintern's Third Congress represented on an international plane the orientation advanced by the Landler faction inside Hungary. Lukács's embrace of the perspectives of the Comintern's Third Congress is an essential component of what he became in this phase of his political evolution.

Premature "Popular Frontist"?

The culmination of this phase of Lukács's life came after the 1928 death of Landler. Lukács assumed leadership of the faction at a moment when it was becoming obvious that the increasingly Stalinist-dominated Communist International—under an ever more bureaucratic-authoritarian interpretation of its "Bolshevization" policies—would not tolerate any resistance to its political dictates. Lukács committed political suicide by advancing the "Blum Theses," essentially challenging the application in Hungary of an "ultraleft" zigzag advanced by the Stalin leadership at the Comintern's Sixth World Congress. The faction quickly disintegrated as many of its members transferred their allegiance to Bela Kun.

The "Blum Theses" were—as Lukács later commented—"a precise expression" and "a theoretical resumé" of the political orientation of the Landler faction. At the same time, he asserted, they were fully confirmed by "the Seventh Comintern Congress and the policies arising from it." Or as his one-time student István Mészáros put it, "they anticipate the strategy of the 'Popular Front.'"[19] While this undoubtedly represents the way that the politically compromised Lukács later chose to see himself, it seriously distorts the reality of both the Landler faction and the "Blum Theses."

The Seventh Congress of the Communist International of 1935 marked, as E. H. Carr commented, "the twilight of the Comintern."[20] The organization lingered on until 1943, but it never had another congress after this one. The original purpose of the Comintern had been to organize and mobilize men and women throughout the world for the purpose of bringing about revolutions of workers and the oppressed masses in various countries, culminating in socialism on an international scale. By 1935, however, the Comintern had been fundamentally compromised by the corrupted personalities and bureaucratic apparatus dominating the "socialist homeland," the Union of Soviet Socialist Republics, and increasingly its revolutionary purpose was subordinated to the foreign policy priorities of the Stalin leadership.

From 1928 through 1934, the line of the Comintern had been characterized by the sort of ultraleft and "bureaucratic-sectarian" approach that was utterly inconsistent with the orientation both of the Landler faction and of the Comintern's own Third Congress of 1921. This had contributed to the disastrous inability of the large German Communist Party to form a united front with the German Social Democratic Party to prevent the coming to power of Adolf Hitler's Nazi dictatorship. The victory of German fascism created a new situation in world politics, one which posed an increased threat to the security of the USSR. The Stalin leadership (while never ruling out—albeit covertly—the possibility of seeking a nonaggression pact with Hitler[21]) urgently and actively called for the development of a global alliance of "democratic" forces—including "progressive" layers of the capitalist class and their political representatives—to block the expansionism of Germany and its Italian and Japanese allies (the so-called "anti-Comintern Axis"). The line shaped at the Comintern's Seventh Congress, known as the Popular Front strategy, conformed to this orientation.

Comintern chairman Georgi Dimitrov clearly identified the defining principle underlying the new strategy: shifting from the struggle for "proletarian dictatorship" against "bourgeois democracy" to that of defending bourgeois democracy against fascism.[22] Instead of utilizing the united front tactic to draw together all workers for victories in the class struggle as part of a strategy leading to socialist revolution, the Comintern advanced a Popular Front strategy to save bourgeois democracy: united efforts of communist and socialist workers, joined with farmers, small business people, and others—including those liberal (and even conservative) sectors of the capitalist class feeling threatened by the rise of fascism—in order to form broad electoral alliances that would establish "Popular Front" governments. These governments would preserve both democratic political forms and capitalist property relations, implementing some social reforms beneficial to workers and others in the "lower classes" while also following a foreign policy that maintained friendly relations with the USSR and resisted the expansionism of the Axis powers.

The "Blum Theses" were fundamentally different. One of the key slogans it calls for stands in direct contradiction to the defining principle of the Popular Front: "Fight against the slogan of 'democracy or fascism,' which misleads the workers." Another slogan: "No pact with the bourgeoisie. Class against class—long live the alliance of workers and peasants." Drawing various elements from the democratic perspectives that Lenin articulated in 1905, in the World War I period, and at the Third Comintern Congress, they advanced a perspective, under the banner of replacing Hungary's dictatorship with a republic, of fighting for democratic rights and advancing the struggle for economic justice of the workers and peasants, culminating in "a democratic dictatorship of the proletariat and the peasantry" that would grow over into a full-blown workers' government and transition to socialism.[23]

A starting point of the "Blum Theses" involves an understanding of the centrality of imperialism to capitalism, and of the desire of increasing numbers of capitalists to secure the American model of "democracy"—one "in which every possibility for the free development, accumulation and expansion of capital is given, while at the same time the external forms of democracy are preserved—but in such a way that the working masses cannot exert any influence whatever on the actual political leadership." In addition, the development of the global economy generates a need to prevent the organizations of the working class, especially trade unions, from maintaining their independence. Instead, there is a need for bureaucratic structures, government controls, legislatively required arbitration, etc., to enforce harmony between employers and workers. Such an approach has been given the label of *corporatism* by some analysts.[24]

This corporatist approach to maintaining the health of capitalism was most dramatically advanced by ex-socialist Benito Mussolini with the establishment of his fascist dictatorship in Italy. In fact, Lukács speaks of two variants of "fascism" one democratic (the American model), and one authoritarian (the Italian model). Lukács notes that the reformists of the Social-Democracy, themselves entrenched in the old trade union bureaucracies, prefer the American model and "nowadays pose the question as: democracy or fascism?" He argues:

> By posing this question it hides from the workers the real class goals of the
> kind of democracy which is possible under present-day imperialism, and
> it lends its support to the suppression of class struggles, the institutional
> prevention of wage struggles, the fascisization [actually corporatization,

or subordination to the state] of the trade unions, and the integration of social democracy and the trade-union bureaucracy into the fascist [i.e., corporatist] state apparatus.[25]

This forms the analytical framework within which Lukács articulates a revolutionary strategic orientation for Hungarian Communists:

> During this struggle, the high-point of which is necessarily the fight to achieve democratic dictatorship, the party must retain its earlier slogan of the "republic." As long as the tranquil and unruffled power of large-scale landed property and large-scale capital expresses itself in advocating the coronation of the legitimate king, the struggle for the republic will also continue to represent, in the eyes of the masses, the struggle for all basic liberties, for the right to combine, assemble, and even to strike.... Naturally, the party must not, either now or in the future, employ the republican slogan in isolation. The republican slogan can only be used in the sense of a struggle for total democracy, for the republic headed by a government of workers and peasants, a struggle against the democratic liquidation of democracy, a fulfillment of the slogan, "Class against class," a mobilization for the struggle which had to be conducted to secure democratic dictatorship.... There must be no concessions to the view that this is "a long way to socialism" or that maintaining production and providing for the working class are interests which call for very different policies, etc. All party members must understand that what is at issue is a question which is fundamental to the transition from bourgeois revolution to the revolution of the proletariat; they must understand that the power of large-scale landed property and large-scale capital cannot be destroyed except by this kind of revolution, and that the remnants of feudalism cannot be wiped out except through the elimination of capitalism.[26]

There is nothing here of the People's Front orientation advanced by Dimitrov, Stalin, and other Comintern leaders in 1935. E. H. Carr has commented on "the silent relegation of the proletarian revolution to as inconspicuous a place as possible in the proceedings and resolutions of the seventh congress." While Lenin's *united front* was a means to move forward to working-class revolution, Dimitrov's *popular front* was designed to set aside working-class revolution in in order "to deal with the pressing emergency of Fascism."[27] It is obvious that the "Blum Theses" remain consistent with the revolutionary perspective of Lenin that Lukács had embraced by 1922.

The newly discovered *Tailism and the Dialectic* (1926) comes third in the major works reflecting Lukács's 1920s theoretical achievement, the others being *History and Class Consciousness* (1923), *Lenin—A Study in the Unity of His Thought* (1924), and the "Blum Theses" (1929). The achievement involves what is in many ways an unsurpassed expression of Marxist and Leninist theory, an expression intimately connected in Hungary with the practical working-class radicalism of the Landler current.

Revolutionary Marxism and "Orthodox" Critics

Steeped in European "high culture" and revolutionary working-class politics, Lukács offers in these four works a remarkable blend—subtle yet tough-minded—of Hegelian dialectics, Marxist social and economic analysis, and Leninist politics. Most frequently commented on is the fact that in *History and Class Consciousness* Lukács produced a remarkable Hegelian reading of Marx's *Capital* which independently reproduced the then unknown conceptualization of "alienation" contained in Marx's yet-to-be discovered *Economic and Philosophical Manuscripts of 1844*. But there is much more to Lukács's 1923 masterpiece: in particular, there are insightful elaborations on the nature and development of class consciousness, a discussion which has remained vibrant until our own time. In addition, one finds a sophisticated fusion of classical Marxism with the revolutionary strategic, tactical, and organizational orientation of Russian Bolshevism. Marx and Lenin are presented as if *Capital* leads logically and necessarily to *What Is to Be Done*).[28]

It is significant, but hardly surprising, that the book became a polemical target. Bela Kun and others in his faction among Hungarian Communists would obviously need to find fault with it and denounce it as "un-Marxist." But there were also reasons within the Communist International for then-president Gregory Zinoviev to attack the volume and its author. Of course, there was the prevalence of émigré Hungarians—in particular, Kun and others in his faction—among Comintern functionaries, and their political alignment with the Comintern leaders (whether this was Zinoviev or, later, Bukharin, and finally Stalin), but more significant was a deepening crisis developing within 1920s Bolshevism.

An aspect of this crisis involved a dispute inside the Russian Communist Party initiated, covertly, by Lenin in alliance with Trotsky, and then resumed by Trotsky after Lenin's death, challenging policies associated with an increasingly dominant triumvirate of Zinoviev, Lev Kamenev, and Stalin.

A lack of sufficient democracy and principled functioning, and also a politically disorienting approach to revolutionary possibilities in Germany were among the points of contention. Trotsky issued a polemic calling for a "New Course" in the Soviet Republic, and in another—"Lessons of October"—he condemned the bungling, through excessive caution, of revolutionary opportunities in Germany, pointing the finger at Zinoviev who (he emphasized) had displayed similar hesitations on the eve of the 1917 October Revolution.[29]

Zinoviev and those around him defended their authority by orchestrating a generalized campaign against "Trotskyism" (alleged to be anti-Leninist and a deviation from Marxism) in the Communist movement, and also by tightening organizational norms and the borders of "political correctness" in the Comintern. This included intimidating potential "leftist" opposition through attacks on intellectuals such as Lukács and Karl Korsch who formed—Zinoviev alleged—"an extreme left tendency growing into theoretical revisionism."[30]

An additional concern among the leaders of the increasingly bureaucratized and authoritarian Communist movement, István Mészáros has suggested, is the emphasis Lukács's book places on the vibrant workers' democracy represented by the soviets (councils). Mészáros points out that in 1923, "where workers' councils still existed, they had effectively lost all their power." Connecting threads with Trotsky's critique could be imagined in the passages of Lukács's book glorifying the soviets, which "had become a tragic reminder of the contradiction between the original aspirations of the revolution and the sociohistorical constraints which by then actually prevailed also in postrevolutionary Russia."[31]

It could be argued that all of this was related to limitations in the Marxist education of many leading Bolsheviks. It is certainly the case that a profoundly influential interpretation of Marxism—in which many Russian, German, and other Marxists were trained in the years before World War I—involved a relatively one-sided and mechanical economic and historical determinism that Lukács attacked as being insufficiently dialectical. This could all too easily degenerate into a fatalism, which restrained its adherents from attempting to influence events in a revolutionary direction. A consequence might involve an underestimation of the revolutionary potential of the working class and might cause such "vulgar Marxists" to tail-end behind so-called "objective conditions." In addition to Kun and Zinoviev, full-scale attacks were launched by a Marxist philosopher in the Soviet Union named Abram Deborin, and by

Lazslo Rudas, who had become Kun's ideological hatchet-man in the Hungarian party. They accused Lukács of "subjectivism" and of a philosophical "idealism" that contradicted the dialectical materialism associated with Marx.

Tailism and the Dialectic is a powerful polemic which effectively defends *History and Class Consciousness* from its critics but also explains essential aspects of Leninist politics in a manner that continues to resonate after six decades. Even touching on a limited portion of that work here will give a sense of this.

Reality, Consciousness, Action

In his polemic, Lukács reproduces the assertions of Rudas, expressing a particular interpretation of Marxist "materialism" that has been influential among rather diverse currents in the socialist movement—whether "progress-is-inevitable" reformists or adherents of revolution's inevitability or spontaneists and dogmatists of various persuasions. "Today's society is subjected to certain laws, which prescribe the future direction of society just as necessarily as the direction of a stone that has been thrown is prescribed by the laws of gravity," Rudas explained. "The stone does not know that its fall is prescribed necessarily by natural forces, and it might just as well be the case that at this moment the proletariat knows nothing of its role either." But, said Rudas, "since the proletariat consists not of stones but of people, who possess consciousness, so they will become aware of their historic mission in time." With the philosophical flourish that "I know as a materialist that consciousness depends on social being," Rudas elaborated: "Since this being is constituted such that the proletariat through its suffering, etc., is absolutely of necessity forced into action, so too is it absolutely necessary that in time its consciousness will awaken."[32]

This approach, according to Lukács, is neither Marxist nor Leninist nor correct—rather, it represents an historical fatalism that results in causing would-be Marxists to "tail-end" after events rather than helping to shape the future. This touches on the relationship between *"objective" conditions* (existing social and economic realities) and *"subjective" factors* (the consciousness and activity of the working class and of revolutionary groups). Lukács shows that both Marx and Lenin correctly saw a fundamentally different relationship between objective conditions and subjective factors than is expressed in Rudas's explanation.

First of all, while it is possible for the working class—due to its location in capitalist society and the "objective" conditions (living conditions, working conditions, experiences and relationships related to these) bearing down on it—to develop an accurate understanding of its situation that could lead to revolutionary class consciousness, it is not the case that workers always develop such consciousness. There is often a significant gap between the "ripeness" of objective conditions (the blatant oppressiveness and destructiveness of capitalism, intensified suffering among the masses of people who are part of the working class) on the one hand, and on the other hand a level of consciousness among a majority of workers that fails to grasp clearly the sources of their misery and what to do to end it. Many workers have an insufficient level of knowledge and revolutionary determination even under the most oppressive conditions. A failure to understand this possibility could cause one to incorrectly conclude that the absence or failure of a revolution proves its impossibility because the "objective" conditions were presumably lacking.[33]

Bad conditions are not inevitably reflected in an increasingly revolutionary consciousness of workers. Among the first layers of the working class to turn to socialism and labor action, assuming a vanguard position within the class as a whole, have not been the most oppressed unskilled workers, but rather the less downtrodden skilled workers. At the same time, this same relatively "privileged" layer of the working class can be, and historically often has been, an "aristocracy of labor" that follows an utterly "opportunistic" policy, that—as Lenin put it—sacrifices the basic interests of the mass of workers in favor of the temporary interests of a small number of workers. An example would be skilled workers adopting a narrow "pure and simple" trade unionism that cares for the needs of a small number of organized workers (themselves) while excluding women, immigrants, racial and ethnic minorities, and unskilled and unemployed workers and in general rejects broader social concerns. There is nothing that inevitably pushes this layer in the direction either of opportunist labor aristocracy or principled revolutionary vanguard. What is decisive is the ability of revolutionaries within this layer, as within the entire working class, to organize for the purpose of winning their workmates, and their sisters and brothers in the working class as a whole, over to a revolutionary understanding of what's what and what's needed.[34]

In arguing against a fatalistic approach, Lukács poses the question of what the boundaries are between objective conditions and subjective factors. Rudas "conceives the opposition of subject and object undialectically, inflexibly," whereas the correct (and Marxist) approach is as complex and interactive as the relationship between being and consciousness. Lukács pursues this philosophical difference on the plane of practical politics, focusing attention on the perspective advanced by Lenin during World War I: "Because it is not the case that out of every revolutionary situation a revolution transpires, but only out of such a situation where, in addition to the objective conditions outlined previously, a subjective factor comes along, namely the capability of the revolutionary class to carry out revolutionary mass actions that are of sufficient strength to break the old government (or shake it), which never, even in a period of crisis, 'collapses' unless one 'rattles' it." Lukács goes further in drawing our attention to Lenin's most practical appeal at the Second Congress of the Comintern (1920) that "we must now 'prove' through the praxis of revolutionary parties that they are sufficiently self-conscious to forge organizations, contacts with the exploited masses, that they possess determination and knowledge to exploit this crisis for the benefit of a successful, a victorious revolution."[35]

Obviously, the subjective factor here has sufficient relative autonomy that it can (and must) decisively impact on the objective situation—just as "objective reality" itself is insufficient, simply on its own, to generate revolutionary consciousness within the working class. Successes or failures on the part of the workers' movement shape the subsequent objective realities within which the working class later finds itself, which means that "objective causes were . . . previously subjective ones," and that "people actually—and not only in their imagination—make their own history." More than this, the development of class consciousness and class struggle do not occur "as a continuous intensification, in which development is favorable to the proletariat, and the day after tomorrow the situation must be even *more* favorable than it is tomorrow, and so on." To the contrary, it involves a profoundly dialectical process in which "objective" and "subjective" factors interact in ways that preclude the revolutionary-fatalist "inevitabilities" of Rudas. "It means rather that at a particular point, the situation demands that a decision be taken and the day after tomorrow might be too late to make that decision."[36]

At certain points, everything depends on class consciousness, which plays a decisive role in the dialectical interaction with objective factors in the historical process. This is the key to Leninism. "How is it possible even to imagine Lenin's basic idea of the preparation and organization of revolution without such an active and conscious role of the subjective moment?" Lukács stresses:

"Moments that are consciously *made*, that is to say brought into being by the subjective side," involving "purely subjective" qualities such as "decisiveness, moral superiority," at certain points in the political process "have decisive predominance," although they cannot play their role independently of social and economic development. Over time the dynamic and interactive blend of objective and subjective factors can result in the emergence of a Communist Party which could have the potential to concentrate and advance the subjective factor to such an extent that—at the decisive moment—it would provide effective leadership for a socialist revolution. "The subjective moment reaches in this 'moment' its comprehensive significance precisely because and inasmuch as it has already acted consciously and actively during earlier developments."[37]

Lukács quotes Lenin: "It depends on us." He is referring to the more conscious and organized activists and revolutionaries in the working-class movement. This doesn't mean the party substituting itself for the working class, but instead helping the working class to become an effective revolutionary force. He challenges those who explain Communist failures by viewing the working class as "immature" or "wavering." If the working class "is subjectively too immature for revolution, then evidently that has objective, social causes, on whose ranks, however, an extraordinarily large role is played by subjective moments that have become objective moments." The development of the working class as revolutionary force is a process which must be understood "not as an evolutionary one or an organic one, but as contradictory, jerkily unfolding in advances and retreats in every—apparently—calm moment. 'There is no moment,' say the organizational theses of the Third Congress [of the Comintern], 'when a Communist Party cannot be active.' Why? Because there can be no moment where this character of the process, the germ, the possibility of an *active* influencing of the subjective moments is completely lacking."[38]

Class Consciousness and Organization

In responding to critics of *History and Class Consciousness*, Lukács offers striking formulations regarding class consciousness that—as in his discussion of the subjective/objective dialectic—underscore the logic of Leninist organizational perspectives. We already saw an important aspect of this in the comparison of possible "revolutionary" as opposed to "opportunistic" orientations among skilled workers that could make them either part of a revolutionary vanguard of the working class or part of a self-interested "aristocracy of labor." Lukács makes a distinction between revolutionary working-class consciousness and the actual consciousness of workers. The revolutionary party plays an essential role in establishing and spreading true class consciousness.

But what is it that makes one form of consciousness more "true" or "correct" than another?

Lukács addresses the question quite directly. "The answer is simple: because one consciousness corresponds to the economic and social position of the class as a totality, while the other sticks at the immediacy of a particular and temporary interest." The outlook which involves a more thorough, factually complete understanding of reality and one's place within reality, and in addition, the outlook which provides the most adequate guidelines for action, is the superior outlook. He notes that such a level of consciousness does not arise spontaneously but must involve a certain amount of deliberation. It is possible for many workers (sometimes a majority) not to have deliberated sufficiently to come to such a level of consciousness. Lukács repeats from his own *History and Class Consciousness* that class consciousness represents "the thoughts and feelings that men would have in a particular situation if they were *able* to assess both it and the interests arising in it in their impact on immediate action and on the whole structure of society. That is to say, it would be possible to infer the thoughts and feelings appropriate to their objective situation."[39]

Obviously, this begs the question: with what justification does Lukács identify this "correct" consciousness as class consciousness? This was precisely the question posed in the polemic leveled against him by Laszlo Rudas. Lukács answers that "any agitator or propagandist" could respond by:

> asking Comrade Rudas whether he may not speak of class-conscious workers *in contrast* to those who are not class-conscious (who are just as much workers whose thought is just as much determined by their proletarian being). He would ask Comrade Rudas whether he had the right to dispute the proletarian class consciousness of a strike-breaker, indeed, even a wavering worker. And, in appealing to the class consciousness of workers through an analysis of the objective situation and the slogans that follow from it, does he have the right to awaken or heighten this class consciousness?[40]

Lukács links Marx and Lenin. Marx says that class consciousness is not "a matter of what this or that proletarian or even the whole proletariat *imag-*

ines for itself as a goal at any point," and Lenin says that "the communists are only a drop in the ocean of people. They will only be in a position to lead the people, to take them down the right path, *if they correctly define the path*." There is need for "an organization of class-conscious elements of the proletariat" for helping to answer the questions of:

> *how*, on the one hand correct recognition of the class position of the proletariat ("level of consciousness" in Lenin, "sense of the historical role of the class" in me) can be raised to an ever higher level, that is to say, become ever more correct in terms of content, ever more to the actual situation.... [and] how, on the other hand, this consciousness can be *made* conscious in as large a section of the class as possible.[41]

The organization that communists create for the purpose of accomplishing such a task is the revolutionary party. This is the target of many anti-Communist critics. "The party is the visible embodiment of class-consciousness, the sole guarantor of the correct political orientation of the proletariat and the sole exponent of its 'real' will," is how Leszek Kolakowski sums up Lukács's views, and thus "we arrive at the desired conclusion: the party is always right." Perhaps something akin to this crystallized for Lukács in the 1930s when he declared that "only Lenin and Stalin, and the Bolshevik Party they founded and led, were and are able to sweep away the so-called theories of revisionism in all domains of Marxism," etc., etc.[42] But this despairing (and, given his residency in Moscow, also fearful) adaptation to Stalinism constituted a break from the perspective articulated in the 1920s. For his conception of the revolutionary party was thoughtful, critical-minded, with revolutionary optimism seasoned by a practical-minded seriousness. In fact, *Tailism and the Dialectic* focuses our attention on moments when the party is wrong.

Noting that the "raising of the level of class consciousness is . . . not an endless (or finite) progress, not a permanent advance towards a goal fixed for all time, but itself a dialectical process," Lukács even suggests that "an unsuccessful action of the proletariat, caused by vacillation or the low level of consciousness of the vanguard, can change the objective situation in such a way that further development—in a certain sense—sets in at a lower level." In such a situation, he argues, it is essential that the revolutionary party avoid placing the blame for such a development on "objective" causes (which "looks, at best, like fatalism"). He highlights the need for "Bolshevik self-criticism with its unprecedented significance for the development of parties, and mediated to the whole proletariat through those parties." The ability for revolutionary activists to self-critically examine their activities means that, when a party is organized and functioning according to Leninist principles, "the development of the level of class consciousness can be more strongly encouraged through mistakes that are correctly recognized and, correspondingly, thoroughly corrected." There are similar formulations in Lukács's *Lenin*: "The party called upon to lead the proletarian revolution is not born ready-made into its leading role: it, too, *is* not but *is becoming*. And the process of fruitful interaction between party and class repeats itself—albeit differently—in the relationship between the party and its members."[43]

In Defense of Vanguard Organization

The "organizational forms recognized and applied by Lenin" are designed to help committed revolutionary activists to "work out rather practical measures from a correct knowledge of the historical process as a whole, from the totality of its economic, political, ideological, etc., moments" Lukács explains. "These practical measures are those with whose help, on the one hand *one part* of the proletariat is raised to the level of consciousness that correctly corresponds to its objective position in the totality, while on the other hand, the broad masses of workers and other exploited people can be led correctly in their struggles."[44]

The "one part" of the working class that can develop the high level of class consciousness that Lukács talks about represents a revolutionary vanguard layer. It is the nucleus around which increasing numbers of workers may rally. It constitutes the energetic, insightful, experienced elements that provide leadership in social struggles. By definition, and in historical reality, this may be (and in a revolutionary situation needs to be) a growing percentage of the working class as a whole but does not and cannot constitute the entire working class or even the majority of the workers. "But even in this portion of the working class," Lukács asserts, "consciousness does not only not arise 'by itself,' but not even as an immanent result of its immediate economic position and the inevitable class struggles that develop from it at the base." He goes on to affirm Lenin's notorious point in *What Is to Be Done* that socialist consciousness (what Lukács calls "correct class consciousness") must be brought to workers from outside of the working class.[45]

If one believes that Marxism provides the best orientation for workers to understand and change the world, of course, then there is a case to be made for this apparently elitist assertion. After all, Marx and Engels were not proletarians. Lukács himself, however, says that in spite of this there is "a dialectical interrelationship between this 'from without' and the working class." He explains that:

> while Marx and Engels stem from the bourgeois class, the development of their doctrine is, nevertheless, a product of the development of the working class—of course not in any immediate way. And not only the doctrine itself; even elements of its foundation (Ricardo, Hegel, French historians and socialists) more or less consciously summarize in thought that social being out of which and as a part of which the proletariat arose.[46]

This coincides with a point made ten years later by the revolutionary Marxist Franz Jacobowski, a Polish Trotskyist influenced by Lukács's *History and Class Consciousness*:

> Of course it cannot be denied that [nonworking-class] intellectuals founded and developed Marxist theory. But Marx and Engels and their descendants could only do so from the standpoint of the proletariat and in close contact with the proletarian movement. Marx and Engels were the founders of the First International and "introduced" their theories into the workers' movement, but they could only work out these theories because there was already an existing proletarian movement for them to observe. Among the English chartists and French blanquists and other similar groups they found not only a movement but also, from the beginning, the content of a consciousness to which their theory gave form and expression. Theory and the working-class movement, therefore, do not develop along parallel lines that only meet in an external sense; they form a unity of living interaction.[47]

Nonetheless, Lukács affirms that Lenin is "profound and correct" in denying that "the whole working class can 'spontaneously' reach the level of consciousness that corresponds to its objective economic position." Only an understanding of this—the "outsideness" of such knowledge and insight to the majority of workers—makes it possible to increasingly win workers, and finally a working-class majority, to this level of class consciousness. Lukács accepts Lenin's insistence that revolutionary class consciousness necessarily includes but also goes beyond the simple confrontation of workers and bosses at the workplace. This means that "the spontaneous struggle of the proletariat will not become its genuine 'class struggle' until the struggle of the proletariat is led by a strong organization of revolutionaries." He by no means assigns leadership to bourgeois intellectuals such as himself, nor does he view intellectuals and workers as distinct categories. Within the revolutionary party "all distinctions as between workers and intellectuals, not to speak of distinctions of trade and profession, in both categories, must be effaced."[40]

What is essential is that increasing numbers of workers develop revolutionary class consciousness. According to Lukács, "forms of organization are there in order to bring this process into being, to accelerate it, in order to make such contents conscious in the working class (in a part of the working class), which once made conscious turn the workers into class-conscious workers, precisely those contents that correspond as adequately as possible to their objective class situation." This involves far more than simply socialist educational work:

> Every Bolshevik knows exactly that 'the struggle over consciousness' embraces the whole activity of the party, that its struggle against the class enemy is inseparable from the struggle for the class consciousness of the proletariat and for making conscious the alliance with the semi-proletarian layers (as much in these layers as in the proletariat). For the consciousness of the masses at any one time does not develop independently of the party's politics, and the class consciousness embodied in it.[49]

Confronting Limitations

Yet there are gaps—ultimately fatal gaps—in Lukács's discussion of the "forms of organization" required to advance the working class as an effective revolutionary force. In *Tailism and the Dialectic* there is no discussion of the internal structure and functioning of this vitally important organization. In other works from this period, Lukács offers only very general and sometimes ambiguous formulations. There is reference to party leaders and party members, the need for centralization and discipline, and also the necessity of self-criticism. We have noted that Lukács, in his book on Lenin, indicates the need for members to engage in "a process of fruitful interaction."

In *History and Class Consciousness*, he had gone somewhat further. "If every member of the party commits his whole personality and his whole existence to the party," according to Lukács, "then the same centralizing and disciplinary principle will preside over the living interaction between the will of the members and that of the party leadership, and will ensure that the will and the wishes, the proposals and the criticisms of the members are given due weight by the party leaders." He argued against "blind trust" of the membership in the leadership, and against restricting criticisms by members to rare and special occasions that would prevent them from exerting "any influence on future actions." He stressed the need for "true democracy" in a context of an active membership sharing a revolutionary programmatic commitment, "closely integrated and collaborating in a spirit of solidarity."[50]

But there is no elaboration of institutional forms within the revolutionary party that would guarantee freedom of written as well as oral debate, especially in regular preconvention discussion periods, the right of organized oppositional currents, the supremacy of the elective principle and majority rule (subordination of leadership to membership), and the encouragement of relative autonomy for local party units. All of these things were aspects of the internal life of the pre-1917 Bolshevik party, but they were—by the late 1920s—increasingly eliminated within the mainstream of the Communist movement.[51]

Nor is there any discussion of the relationship of member parties of the Communist International to each other, and in particular to the Russian Communist Party. The way that Lukács discusses the abstract conception of *revolutionary party*, or Communist Party, one would assume that it is akin to the historical Bolshevik party in being a relatively autonomous organization, in no way subordinated to the dictates of a powerful governing party in another country. But by the late 1920s, this was the case with no member party of the Comintern—rather, as E. H. Carr has noted, there was a "deep-seated trend, long apparent to the discerning critic, to identify the aims of the Comintern with the policies of the USSR." What was true of the internal life of the Communist Party of the Soviet Union also became true of its "sister parties" in the Comintern:

> During the nineteen-twenties controversies on major topics had been conducted in congresses and committees, the proceedings of which were published in the daily press and in a multitude of journals. It was not difficult to discover the reasons for any important decision, who had supported it, who had opposed it, and on what grounds. By the end of 1929 this freedom had been slowly eroded. Orthodoxy was the road to promotion, heresy was punishable. The press was rigidly controlled. Congresses and committees met no longer to debate decisions, but to register and popularise them.[52]

Such realities—associated with the triumph of Stalinism in the USSR and Comintern—decisively cut across the elaborate and insightful perspectives outlined in Lukács's work. To be true to the perspectives in *Tailism and the Dialectic*, it would have been necessary to confront this reality. This would, of course, have resulted in the expulsion of Lukács from the Communist mainstream. He chose another path: adapting to Stalinism while at the same time seeking to keep alive elements of his revolutionary and Marxist commitments through more abstract, philosophical, and cultural studies that were substantially removed from practical politics.

The fact that Lukács had to turn away from his philosophical achievement in order to remain in the Communist movement stands as an obvious and quite substantial defense of Leninism—as an historical reality in its own right, and as reflected in the 1920s writings of Lukács—from the charge that it finds its realization in Stalinist totalitarianism. To be true to itself, it would have to push beyond the deadly limitations of Stalinism, and also beyond Lukács's post-1929 compromises.

Revolutionary Ethics

Breaking free from the Stalinist web through his association with the Hungarian workers and students uprising of 1956, Lukács devoted his remaining years to a reconstruction of Marxism that, among other things, would establish a revolutionary ethics true to the method of Marx and Lenin. After decades of political compromise and distance from practical revolutionary work, Lukács was hardly able to retrieve the ground that he had occupied in 1923–1929.

In his final writings Lukács insisted, of course, that the myth that Stalin was "the only genuine and worthy successor of Lenin" must "be torn to pieces" by those seeking to "reestablish genuine Marxism," adding that "Leninism, in which the spirit of Marx lived, was converted into its diametrical opposite" by the method and practice of Stalin, and that within the Stalinist system ideology "loses that immense free play, the contradictory multiplicity and asymmetricity that it has in Marx." Lukács added that "the long duration of the Stalinist system had ruinous effects on the creativity of the masses. They lost faith in themselves, in the belief of the possibilities of their own personal-social praxis." The explosive, spontaneous insurgency of the 1917 Revolution had resulted, through the soviets, in a situation in which "the masses accustomed themselves to participatory behavior in the conduct of public affairs." In the Stalin era that crystallized in the late 1920s, however, "not active but passive behavior became the rule, because this was appropriate under such authoritarian circumstances."[53]

Such abstract formulations, however, failed even to consider the possibility of challenging exclusive political rule by the Communist Party, which Lukács imagined might be peacefully transformed from within into an instrument of socialist democracy. Yet his philosophical and theoretical reach of the 1960s clearly went in the direction of his 1920s trajectory—"one must speak of a reciprocal process between the subjective and the objective," as he emphasized in his 1968 draft *The Process of Democratization*, which—as he elaborated in his fragmentary *Ontology of Social Being* in the same period, in formulations reminiscent of *Tailism and the Dialectic*—should be seen as "something in process, changing itself in process, renewing itself, taking part in the process, and yet preserving itself in essence."[54] What Lukács is focusing on here is democracy—rule by the people—which he sees as "a process and not a condition," an interplay of objective and subjective factors, and *within the latter* an interplay of spontaneity and organization in the form of socialist democracy:

> Socialist democracy—taking man to be an active creature, which is the true nature of his human species being since he is forced to be active in his everyday praxis—transforms the objectified and objective products of human labor into objects that are consciously created by man himself and that fulfill human purposes. Socialist democracy is the political framework that allows objectivity, without violating the inherent law of objectivity, to become a tool in the teleological designs of conscious active men. It is the conquest of consciousness and self-determination over blind objectivity.[55]

The revolutionary ethics that shine through here involve the necessity of being true, in the very *process of struggle* (whose goal is rule by the people over political, social, and economic structures) to the democratic humanism that is essential to both ends and means. This is the case, Lukács tells us, in Lenin no less than in Marx: "Lenin had a deep insight into the relationship between the subjective and objective forces, and he was an advocate of human self-determination. He wished to place a knowledge of the power and creativity of the subjective and objective in the service of the coming Kingdom of Freedom."[56]

This was the outlook that animated Lukács's writings from *History and Class Consciousness* to the "Blum Theses." On the other hand, it goes in the opposite direction from his less mature 1918 notion, cited earlier in this essay, that "Bolshevism rests on the metaphysical notion that good can come from evil, that it is possible . . . to lie ourselves through to the truth," and that "liberty can be attained through oppression." That notion was truly consistent with what became Stalinism—and perhaps his dark premonition of 1918 somehow made it easier for him to adapt, as he acquiesced to the mutilation and rejection of his own 1920s revolutionary standpoint.

The tragedy of Lukács is mitigated at least somewhat by this second triumph. Mutilated by the spider from which he had more than once barely escaped, his latter-day reach for revolutionary ethics contains unmistakable traces of vibrant theorizations reflecting his 1920s activism.

As his life was drawing to a close, he perceived that "although it is still not existent, the present world economy provides increasing signs of a coming crisis, and a Marxist interpretation of the crisis—unfortunately still inadequate—suggests a revival of the democratization process." The youthful upsurges of the 1960s, of course, did not possess "electrifying spontaneity of the earlier, volcanic upheaval" of 1917–1923. In the so-called "socialist" countries, protests gave way to "the continuance of routine manipulatory agreements." At the same time, capitalist regimes were "experimenting with the tactics of co-option, since they are eager to incorporate the still chaotic spontaneous protest movements into the establishment and thereby pacify it." And yet, insisted the seasoned Marxist, "a sociopolitical crisis of worldwide proportions is visible."[57] In fact, its playing out would take even longer, perhaps, than Lukács had imagined, and it would certainly take a number of turns that would have astonished, disappointed, and excited the old survivor. It may be that the tactics and ethics that had been part of his life and writings would have relevance for what was to come.

Chapter Six

ANTONIO GRAMSCI AND THE MODERN PRINCE

Antonio Gramsci (1891–1937) offers an incredibly rich way of articulating and applying Leninist perspectives. As a Marxist, Gramsci saw future possibilities as being conditioned by past and present "objective" economic and social realities. But his thought was also alive to multiple possibilities— grounded in the understanding that not only are "objective" factors too complex and fluid to be *fully* grasped in analysis, but that the consciousness and actions of human beings (especially when informed by revolutionary theory and focused through effective organization) can alter the "objective" factors. Consistent with Lenin's conceptualization of Marxism, this approach dovetails as well with that articulated by Georg Lukács in 1923–1928.[1]

In the 1920s, Gramsci and Lukács were key leaders, respectively, in the Italian and Hungarian Communist parties. Each sought, at a moment when Stalinist influences were about to swamp the Communist movement with authoritarian and sectarian policies, to remain true to principled revolutionary perspectives of the first four congresses of the Communist International. As Perry Anderson has noted, while in prison Gramsci "categorically opposed [Stalin's] 'third period' line from 1930 onwards, maintaining positions not unlike those of Lukács in 1928, which stressed the importance of intermediate democratic demands under fascism, and the vital need to win the alliance of the peasantry to overthrow it."[2]

Gramsci and Lukács have been associated with a trend that has been given the misleading label of "Western Marxism," associated with a diverse assortment of theorists including Karl Korsch, thinkers affiliated with the

Frankfurt School (including Max Horkheimer, Theodor Adorno, Herbert Marcuse), Henri Lefebvre, Jean-Paul Sartre, Louis Althusser, and others. The so-called Western Marxists shared in common fairly sophisticated philosophical orientations, rejecting the intellectual narrowness of Stalinism as well as the somewhat rigid interpretation of Marxism associated with many of the so-called orthodox Marxists of the Second International (or Socialist International) of 1889–1914. They refused to view "subjective" factors of culture and consciousness as being merely reflections of "objective" economic factors. Questions of capitalism and socialism, and how to get from one to the other, could be adequately grasped—they insisted—only through engagement with both "subjective" and "objective" factors, whose interplay was far more complex than "vulgar Marxists" were inclined to acknowledge.[3]

Gramsci was profoundly influenced by the dialectical philosophical orientation of G. W. F. Hegel, popularized in Italy by such academics as Benedetto Croce and Antonio Labriola, and was vibrantly alive to a multiplicity of cultural questions. This approach emphasizes the complex dynamism and fluidity of reality, which can be understood as an evolving totality of contradictory and interactive elements. Economics and class conflict are central to him, but these are understood in rich interplay with history and culture. Far from being simply a philosophical culture critic, however, Gramsci was a political leader concerned with the practicalities of revolutionary strategy, tactics, and organization within the revolutionary wing of the workers' movement. Yet in the late twentieth and early twenty-first centuries, with his political commitments all too often set aside, he has been a primary reference point in much "postmodernist" discourse dealing with innumerable (and often quite interesting) cultural issues. Abstracting his ideas from the person that he actually was, however, can distort the meaning of what he actually said.[4] An examination of one of his best-known works, "The Modern Prince," highlights Gramsci as a theorist focused on practical revolutionary politics.

Who Gramsci Was

To gain a better sense of this remarkable person in the short moment of this essay, we can first refer—all too fleetingly—to knowledgeable people who have written about Gramsci. If we consider our common humanity with this world-famous thinker, we might find meaningful entry-points for considering his ideas.

We are our bodies. "Antonio never grew to be more than four and three-quarters feet tall. He had two humps, one in front and the other in back, giving him a deformed appearance," Gramsci scholar Dante Germino tells us. "His normal-sized head appeared huge and awkward on his short frame. He also walked lamely." According to biographer Giuseppe Fiori, "from earliest childhood he was kept going by extraordinary will-power and a determination to make up in every possible way for his deformity."[5]

We are shaped through experiences from childhood to youth. "As a boy he felt unloved, alienated, humiliated," according to another scholar, John Cammett. Yet this seems too sweeping as we consider the tenderness and caring reflected in stories of and letters to family members (he was the fourth of seven children). There were certainly happy times as he grew up in the village of Ghilarza, on the island of Sardinia. Yet his father was a downwardly mobile white-collar worker, a civil servant convicted of stealing, which resulted in a four-year imprisonment. Fiori also tells us "Antonio was deeply disturbed by the terrible poverty in the family after his father's arrest, by the psychological repercussions of this calamity as well as by his own physical ailment." For two years a teenage Gramsci was forced to labor for ten hours a day, six days a week plus Sunday mornings, in a physically demanding job at a local registry office. His interrupted education was finally resumed, largely through the family's sacrificial efforts and his own hard work.[6]

We are what we feel. Writing in the 1970s, an editor of his prison letters, Lynne Lawner, commented that "local people still speak of a certain closed quality of his personality" during Gramsci's adolescence but that "he is mostly remembered for his cheerfulness, taste for jest and horseplay, and expansive character." In letters to intimates, written in 1923–1926, Gramsci refers on the one hand to memories of "colorful" childhood days "that bring back pleasure," but also to "the other side of the coin," musing: "My life has always been a spent flame, a desert." There were awful memories in which "the sewer of my past brought things back up that for some time left me poisoned." He wrote: "For many, many years I have been truly used to thinking of the absolute impossibility, almost a decree of fate, that I might be loved by somebody." From the age of ten, "I was convinced I was a burden that intruded into my family." He wrote of "a way of life that I have had since I was a boy . . . hiding my states of mind behind a hard mask or behind an ironic smile."[7]

As a multiply disadvantaged outsider striving to prove himself, his perceptions and his mind were naturally sharpened. As one observer at the time reported, he "dominated his own unhappiness with an iron will for study, making efforts way beyond the strength of his organism." A brilliant student with a passion for reading ("I'm getting on like a house on fire," he commented at the time), Gramsci won a scholarship that enabled him to enter the University of Turin in 1911. He had been reading Marxist pamphlets and the Socialist Party's paper *Avanti* since his early teens. An older brother had become a militant in the Italian Socialist Party, but the younger sibling would make his own way politically. Dante Germino has emphasized, "the fact that Gramsci eventually became a revolutionary has everything to do with his early experience of injustices in Sardinian soil."[8] Germino's elaboration merits attention:

> Gramsci particularly seethed over descriptions of Sardinians as biologically inferior to Italians on the mainland. He learned early to recognize the intellectually and morally disgraceful tendency of some who belong to social groups temporarily enjoying power, wealth, and prestige to attribute inequalities brought about by their own selfish policies to the genetic "inferiority" of the people who have been oppressed. As Togliatti expressed it, Gramsci "sought for the explanation for the poverty and backwardness of the island in the actual relationships that prevailed between the different social groups." For Antonio Gramsci, Sardinia was the laboratory in which the injustice of the larger world could be measured. As an entity, Sardinia was oppressed by the mainland; as a reflection of the social order prevalent on the Italian peninsula, the island's own social order reflected the pattern, prevalent in Italy, of oppression by the powerful over the weak.[9]

We are what we do. Within two years, Gramsci became an activist within the Italian Socialist Party. As was the case with a majority of his Socialist Party comrades, he opposed the First World War (1914), although took up his own position in the revolutionary wing of that party. In 1919 he helped to found a new weekly, *L'Ordine Nuovo* (New Order), which sought to apply the lessons of the 1917 Russian Revolution to Italy. This paper became the voice of militant factory workers who engaged in a general strike and factory occupations that in 1920 seemed to threaten the overturn of Italian capitalism and a workers' revolution. Socialist Party moderates who led the trade union movement quickly effected a compromise, however, which ended the strike, resulting in modest concessions for the workers and the continued (if temporary) survival of a liberal capitalist regime.[10]

Frightened by the workers' militancy, however, the landed aristocracy and industrialists concluded that a right-wing counterforce was needed, and they poured substantial resources into the rising fascist movement led by ex-socialist Benito Mussolini. Disgusted by the moderate Socialist sell-out, Gramsci and many others on the left end of the political spectrum concluded that a genuinely revolutionary workers' party was needed. The result was the foundation of the Italian Communist Party (PCI) in 1921.

Revolutionary Leader

More than a key figure of the PCI in the early 1920s, Gramsci worked for the Communist International (or Third International) in Moscow and Vienna in this period. Victor Serge, who worked with him in the early Comintern in Vienna, remembering him as "an industrious and Bohemian exile, late to bed and late to rise," tells us:

> His head was heavy, his brow high and broad, his lips thin; the whole was carried on a puny, square-shouldered, weak-chested, humpbacked body. There was grace in the movement of his fine, lanky hands. Gramsci fitted awkwardly into the humdrum of day-to-day existence . . . indifferent to the comfort of his lodgings and the quality of his meals—but intellectually he was absolutely alive. Trained intuitively in the dialectic, quick to uncover falsehood and transfix it with the sting of irony, he viewed the world with an exceptional clarity.[11]

The rise and succession of victories of the fascist movement was a major concern to Gramsci and his comrades, but there was not agreement on appropriate perspectives for the PCI. Gramsci developed a perspective that was independent of the moderate line advanced by Angelo Tasca and also an alternative to what he saw as a sectarian and ultraleft line represented by Amadeo Bordiga. His perspective became predominant in the PCI, and he was considered to be its central leader. His columns in the Communist daily L'Unitá profoundly influenced and helped to educate his party's working-class base. Gramsci was elected to parliament in 1924, where he was the leader of the Communist representatives. At a PCI national congress in January 1926, a party majority was won to Gramsci's positions, advanced with the support of Palmiro Togliatti. Later in the year, however, he was arrested as the fascists consolidated their dictatorship.

Mussolini had once referred to him as "this Sardinian hunchback and professor of economics and philosophy" who had "an unquestionably powerful brain." The prosecutor at Gramsci's trial—where he was convicted on six different charges of treason—warned the court of the dangers this posed in calling for a sentence of two decades: "We must stop this brain from functioning for twenty years."[12] Gramsci doubly cheated the authorities—dying in eleven years and doing intensive brain work during his incarceration that has kept his thoughts "functioning" down to our own time.

During his ten years in prison, where his health was finally broken, Gramsci was able to fill thirty-four thick notebooks with a remarkable range of political, social, historical, and cultural writings. The presence of fascist censors forced him to use code words and obscure formulations. The rising influence of Stalinism within the international Communist movement—and his resistance to aspects of Stalinist ideology combined with a desire not to be isolated from that movement—also contributed to obscure and contradictory formulations. This is especially so due to a number of indications that his theoretical and political orientation was fundamentally incompatible with that which Stalin imposed. There seems to be a consensus among those who knew him and later scholars that, had he openly espoused some of the positions he held shortly before imprisonment and while in prison, he would have been expelled from the Communist movement—his Communist brother Gennaro and his comrade Togliatti shielded him, refusing to transmit certain communications to higher authorities.[13] Carl Marzani, the first person to introduce Gramsci's thought to an English-speaking readership, has given a vivid sense of the drama of Gramsci's final years:

> Consider this man, for ten years in Mussolini's jails. Even in the most humane prisons, the physical and psychological pressures in imprisonment are a terrible ordeal; what must it have been like to be in a fascist jail? Add the burden of pain and fatigue as tuberculosis ravages the organism; insomnia. Hemorrhages, faintings, deliriums. In August 1931, the most serious symptoms appear and by March 1933, the first complete physical breakdown. He recovers somewhat and continues writings until 1935, when he can no longer work as the disease burns the last remaining reserves of the body.
>
> Watch him at work, day after day, fighting with the penal administration and with the government up to Mussolini himself for the right to get a few books, a few magazines. Denied any Marxist writings, he has to quote from memory, paraphrase, use in his study of Croce [a liberal political philosopher and critic of Marx] only what Croce gives of Marx, in other words make his argument on Croce's own grounds. He has to think of the censorship, avoid the well-known words and names, so he develops

a code: Marxism is called the philosophy of praxis (from the Greek, to do; practice); Marx becomes the founder of the philosophy of praxis and Engels the second founder; Lenin is the greatest modern theorist of praxis; *Capital* becomes the critique of political economy, and so on.

Yet he continues writing; an assiduous, incredible labor. How the greatness of humanity is reaffirmed by the tenacity of his will, particularly in the last few years as he writes with wasted body, death a hovering companion. The enormous effort is reflected in the physical act of writing. The first notebooks were neat, in a clear and regular calligraphy. At the end, the handwriting wavers, wanders, is erratic and weak. But the thinking remains lucid, vigorous, trenchant, while the style continues poised and professional, spiced with humor, irony, and a genial twist of phrase.[14]

Gramsci's intellectual achievement would have powerful impact years after his death. Among the most important works embedded in the prison notebooks is the extensive essay "The Modern Prince," composed between 1929 and 1934.

It is impossible to understand this text unless one is clear that Gramsci's primary goal is to help develop a Leninist-type organization that will be capable of mobilizing the working class and its allies in an effective struggle for political power. Such an understanding has been contested by certain influential Gramsci scholars, such as Carl Boggs and Anne Showstack Sassoon, each of whom has offered valuable discussions of Gramsci's thought. Sassoon asserts that "Gramsci's analysis of a mediated relationship between masses and state, between people and intellectuals is . . . very different from Lenin's," since the Russian leader envisioned "the substitution of one set of elite intellectuals for another."[15] Boggs elaborates:

> The concrete meaning of politics in Gramsci's Marxism . . . was its role in enlisting mass energies in the struggle for ideological hegemony and in establishing a new socialist "national-popular" community out of the cleavages and crises of the old society. . . . Lenin's type of Jacobinism . . . was *elitist* and authoritarian to the extent that it envisaged the revolutionary transition as a project defined and led by a tightly-organized nucleus of professional cadres. What Gramsci outlined was neither an anarchistic spontaneous mass movement nor an *elite* party that would be the exclusive repository of consciousness, but a synthesis of the two—an organic linkage between elite and mass, the organized and spontaneous, the planned element and the vital impulse. . . . Gramsci's Jacobinism, thus contained a "popular" or consensual component that was not normally associated with the primacy of politics.[16]

As Alastair Davidson has demonstrated, however, this difference between Gramsci and Lenin is definitely *not* something that Gramsci himself believed he was articulating. Considered by many of his closest comrades as "an expert on Lenin," Gramsci believed that the Bolshevik party "acquired its definite character" in 1907–1909, that "the fundamental emphasis of Leninism was on the links with the working class," that (in Gramsci's view) Lenin in fact "regarded the links between the party and the mass was what were at stake in discussing the 'leading role' of the party."[17]

Peter Thomas has gone further to demonstrate that what Gramsci believed was neither an illusion nor a "politically correct" fiction. Polemicizing against the "mechanical and caricatured interpretation" of Russian revolutionary experience, Lenin insisted (in debates within the Communist International) that "in Europe, where almost all the proletarians are organized, we must win the majority of the working class and anyone who fails to understand this is lost to the Communist movement." Thomas concludes: "Lenin's advice on the need to win over the majority of the working class (understood in the broadest sense) as the *sine qua non* of revolutionary politics, whether in East or West, before *or* after a successful assault on bourgeois state power, became Gramsci's fundamental orientation."[18]

A considerable amount of recent scholarship corroborates the understanding of Lenin's thought referred to in the analyses by Davidson and Thomas. More than this, a comparative analysis of the extensive document on party organization which Lenin helped to produce for the 1921 Third World Congress of the Communist International with Gramsci's own elaboration in "The Modern Prince" reveals innumerable common themes and formulations.[19] Gramsci's seminal work is nothing if not Leninist.

Machiavelli and Gramsci

Steeped in Italian history and cultural traditions, Gramsci turned to the classic text *The Prince* by Niccolò Machiavelli (1469–1527)—foremost political theorist of the Italian Renaissance—for the purpose of theorizing the question of political power in modern times. Like Machiavelli, Gramsci sought to examine the question in a manner that superficially seems chillingly amoral. It is a science that can serve heroes and villains, democrats and reactionaries, those bent on self-defense and those bent on murder—the emancipatory goals of Marx and Lenin, but also the despotic designs of Mussolini and Stalin.[20]

Like Machiavelli, Gramsci sees the key to politics as the question of leadership: "The first element is that there really do exist rulers and ruled, leaders and led. The entire science and art of politics are based on this primordial and (given certain general conditions) irreducible fact." A difference between Machiavelli and Gramsci lies in the phrase "given certain conditions." These are the conditions of modern class society, which have not always existed (first crystallizing roughly 5,000 years ago) and which—as a Marxist—Gramsci believes can and must be overcome. As he puts it: "In the formation of leaders, one premise is fundamental: is it the intention that there should always be rulers and ruled, or is it the objective to create the conditions in which this division is no longer necessary?"[21]

Another difference between Machiavelli and Gramsci is that the theorist of the Middle Ages believed that leadership would be provided by individual heroes and villains—princes—whereas Gramsci believed that the *modern prince* must be collective and can only be a political party, which is the focus of his text. As he notes, "the formation of the party system" involves "an historical phase linked to the standardization of broad masses of the population (communications, newspapers, big cities, etc.)."[22]

Fertile Ambiguities

In Gramsci's discussion, there are a variety of ambiguities, deriving from several problems. One is his desire to elude the watchful eyes of various censors—certainly those of his fascist jailers, but also potentially some of his own comrades who are coming under the powerful influence of Stalinism. Intertwined with this is the fact that he is dealing, more or less, with all political parties of modern times, and sometimes it seems unclear whether he is talking about a fascist party, a more or less democratic-republican bourgeois or petty-bourgeois party, a reformist social-democratic party, or a communist party (and of the latter, one that is healthy or one that is infected with bureaucratic or sectarian tendencies).

Other ambiguities are perhaps more profound. In particular, at one point Gramsci states that "every party is the expression of a social group, and one social group only." But only a few pages later he tells us that "the great industrialists utilize all the existing parties turn by turn, but they do not have their own party," observing that in England the industrialists shifted from the Liberal to the Conservative Party, even reaching a significant accommodation with the Labor Party. He adds that some parties (it is tempting here to think of our own Democratic and Republican parties in the United States) represent "a nexus of classes, great and small, rather than a single, great class." But he then enunciates "the theoretical truth that every class has a single party."[23] Without trying to unravel here what seems like a contradictory knot, it can be suggested that such a critical "working-out" process might provide a fruitful way of developing rich insights into complex political realities.

An additional ambiguity can be found in Gramsci's assertion that "the counting of 'votes' is the final ceremony of a long process, in which it is precisely those who devote their best energies to the State and the nation (when such they are) who carry the greatest weight"—but then he tells us that "the historical rationality of numerical consensus is systematically falsified by the influence of wealth."[24]

Revolutionary Goals Shape Revolutionary Organization

Actually, from this point, Gramsci moves immediately to a veiled discussion of an expansive, revolutionary democracy—based on governance by democratic working-class councils (or soviets) in which, as he puts it, political life moves beyond "the canons of formal democracy," and "the people's consent does not end at the moment of voting," but rather also involves active participation in implementing the decisions, giving new life and deeper meaning (or proletarian content) to the idea of *self-government*.

This relates to Gramsci's remarks regarding "that determinate party which has the aim of founding a new type of State (and which was rationally and historically created for that end)." From his 1921 mini-essay "Real Dialectics," we can understand that Gramsci unambiguously views the Italian Communist Party in this light, emerging from lessons learned from momentous events, "the real dialectics of history," by growing numbers of individuals who are part of "the worker and peasant masses."[25]

While he refers in "The Modern Prince" to this party's "inevitable progress to State power," however, he was convinced that victory would also be dependent on the revolutionary party developing in a manner that linked it organically to the laboring masses. Elsewhere in "The Modern Prince" Gramsci is critical of so-called parties made up of what he dismissively refers to as "'volunteers,' and in a certain sense *declassés*," that "have never or almost never represented homogeneous social blocs," but are instead "the political equivalent of gypsy bands or nomads."[26]

This seems a slap at the kinds of left-wing (often ultraleft) sects which have proliferated over the years. Their sectarianism prioritizes their own small-group needs and "purity" at the expense of possibilities for real struggles that could benefit and help politicize masses of people. This contrasts with Gramsci's vision of what is needed in moving forward to drawing together massive "social blocs" actually capable of bringing revolutionary change.

Gramsci, after all, had not been a product of "far-left," small-group politics, which became prevalent in many countries on the Left in the late twentieth century. The Italian Socialist Party had a membership that rose from 81,000 to 216,000 in 1920, with a vote in parliamentary elections that rose from 347,000 in 1913 to 1,756,000 in 1919—its seats in parliament rose from 47 to 156, making it the strongest single party in parliament. It controlled half of the local governments in the country, involving 2,162 villages, towns of various sizes, and such cities as Milan, Bologna, and Turin. Trade unions linked to the party rose in membership from 320,000 in 1914 to 1,159,000 in 1919 and 2,320,000 in 1920. The cooperative movement intimately connected to the party had nearly three million members in 1921. This was the moment when working-class socialist forces split and the Italian Communist Party crystallized, with a membership of about 40,000 and a militant youth movement of 28,000. The Communists had support of about one-third of trade unionists in Italy's major labor federation. After the split, they were able to elect thirteen representatives to parliament (in contrast to 128 from the Socialist Party). This was seen as only the beginning, and Gramsci envisioned it becoming a force not only of the radicalized industrial workers in urban Italy but also winning "the support and consent of other layers, of the poor peasants and the intellectual proletariat." Suggesting that the old Socialist Party had "drawn a crowd" with "the methods of fairground demagogy," he concluded: "The more the Italian population has plunged into chaos and disorientation, and the more the forces dissolving the past alignment of revolutionary forces have operated and continue to operate, the more evidently necessary it appears to bring about a new alignment of loyal and trusty soldiers of the world revolution and of communism."[27]

To achieve this, Gramsci advanced a particular way of developing and utilizing Marxism. In his discussion of Gramsci's open Marxism, Carl Marzani commented: "The deeper one's Marxism, the less one's dogmatism." Frank

Rosengarten—exploring Gramsci's prison writings—makes a similar point. "As in the past, he insisted on the discipline, the rigor and the united will of the Party," yet from his prison cell a deepened way of explaining this comes to the fore, a notion in stark contrast with the Marxist "orthodoxy" permeating the Communist International in the late 1920s and early 1930s: "it was necessary to adapt theory to events and not events to theory." Or as Gramsci himself put it: "Reality is teeming with the most bizarre coincidences, and it is the theoretician's task to find in this bizarreness new evidence for his theory, to 'translate' the elements of historical life into theoretical language, but not vice versa, making reality conform to an abstract scheme."[28]

Flowing from this, Gramsci followed his theoretical mentors in seeking to translate Marxist theory into the distinctive cultural specifics and language of his own homeland. "For [Antonio] Labriola, as for Lenin at around the same time and later for Gramsci," Gramsci scholar Valentino Gerratana tells us, "Marxism becomes a truly living force in the consciousness of a country and can produce in each country all of its effects only when the general principles of the doctrine assume a particular national form, tied to a tradition and open to an independent development."[29]

Qualities of the Revolutionary Party

To understand the nature of a genuinely revolutionary party, Gramsci speculates on how the history of such an organization might be written. "A simple narrative of the internal life of a political organization"—focusing on the first groups that bring it into being, "the ideological controversies through which its program and conception of the world" are formed—will provide only an account of "certain intellectual groups," or even "the political biography of a single personality," but it will not provide an adequate understanding of the political party. To develop such an understanding, much more is required:

> The history will have to be written of a particular mass of men who have followed the founders of the party, sustained them with their trust, loyalty and discipline, or criticized them "realistically" by dispersing or remaining passive before certain initiatives. But will this mass be made up solely of members of the party? Will it be sufficient to follow the congresses, the votes, etc., that is to say the whole nexus of activities and modes of existence through which the mass following of the party manifests its will? Clearly it will be necessary to take some account of the social group

of which the party in question is the expression and the most advanced element. The history of a party, in other words, can only be the history of a particular social group. But this group is not isolated; it has friends, kindred groups, opponents, enemies. The history of any given party can only emerge from the complex portrayal of the totality of society and State (often with international ramifications too). Hence it may be said that to write the history of a party means nothing less than to write the general history of a country from a monographic viewpoint, in order to highlight a particular aspect of it. A party will have had greater or less significance and weight precisely to the extent to which its particular activity has been more or less decisive in determining a country's history.[30]

The richness of Gramsci's discussion is deepened as he takes up a variety of questions. This includes an examination of different layers within the party: the "mass element" of "ordinary, average" members, who are essential to the organization's existence but who by themselves cannot ensure the party's existence; the experienced, knowledgeable, and "innovative" layer constituting the party's leadership, whose qualities make it the essential ingredient to the party's existence; and "an intermediate element" of party militants who provide the crucial physical, intellectual and moral interconnections between the other two layers. The cohesion (or "centralism") of the party is dependent on a so-called "policing" function that can either be educational, progressive, and democratic or repressive, reactionary, and bureaucratic. "The problem of assimilating the entire grouping to its most advanced fraction" is an educational problem that is threatened by the "danger of becoming bureaucratized."[31]

Related to this is Gramsci's discussion of spontaneity. Gramsci insists that "pure" spontaneity does not exist in history, "that every 'spontaneous' movement contains rudimentary elements of conscious leadership, of discipline." At the same time, it is not possible for "modern theory [Marxism] to be in opposition to the 'spontaneous' feelings of the masses." Nonetheless, he sees "spontaneity" as an ideologically contested terrain, with the possibility of either "progressive" or "regressive" outcomes, and often involving "bizarre combinations." The revolutionary theoretician (and revolutionary party) must "unravel these in order to discover fresh proof of [revolutionary] theory, to 'translate' into theoretical language the elements of historical life." But he warned that "it is not reality which should be expected to conform to the abstract schema," and that it is a mistake to see "as real and worthwhile only such movements of revolt as are one hundred per cent conscious, i.e., movements that are governed by plans worked out in advance to the last detail or in line with abstract theory."[32]

The appropriate interplay of spontaneous upsurges with conscious revolutionary organization, in Gramsci's opinion, "can only be found in democratic centralism, which is, so to speak, a 'centralism' in movement—i.e. a continual adaptation of the organization of the real movement, a matching of thrusts from below with orders from above, a continuous insertion of elements thrown up from the depths of the rank and file into the solid framework of the leadership apparatus which ensures continuity and the regular accumulation of experience."[33]

Pessimism of the Intellect, Optimism of the Will

A phrase commonly associated with Gramsci appeared on *L'Ordine Nuovo* under his editorship: "Pessimism of the Intellect, Optimism of the Will." It was a maxim taken from Romain Rolland (1866–1944), the French musicologist, pacifist, and Nobel Prize–winning novelist who was a favorite of Gramsci's.[34]

Rolland's watchword, Gramsci argued in a 1920 polemic with the anarchists, characterized two essential aspects of "the socialist conception of the revolutionary process." Observing that some anarchists wanted to repudiate Marx's pessimistic notion that revolution "comes about as a result of an excess of poverty and oppression," he affirmed that "socialist pessimism has found terrible confirmation in recent events: the proletariat has been plunged into the deepest abyss of poverty and oppression that the mind of man could ever conceive." In the face of this reality, anarchist spokesmen "have nothing to counterpose but vacuous and irrelevant pseudo-revolutionary demagogy, interwoven with the most tired themes of street-level, simple-minded optimism." It was, instead, the revolutionary pessimist who truly expressed an optimism of the will:

> The socialists . . . counterpose an energetic organizing campaign using the best and most conscious elements of the working class. In every way open to them, the socialists are striving via these vanguard elements to prepare the broadest sectors of the masses to win freedom and the power that can guarantee this freedom.

He went on to insist on the necessity for what he would later label *the modern prince*—working "systematically to organize a great army of disciplined and conscious elements, ready for any sacrifice, trained to carry out slogans as one person, ready to assume effective responsibility for the revolution and become its agents," thereby making possible the mobilization of "the creative capacity" of "the masses who are reduced to such conditions of bodily and spiritual slavery."[35] Some years later (December 1929), from a fascist prison, he assured his youngest brother Carlo,

> you must realize that I am far from being discouraged or feeling beaten.... It seems to me that . . . a man ought to be so deeply convinced that the source of his own moral forces is in himself—his own energy and will, the iron coherence of ends and means—that he never despairs and never falls into those vulgar, banal moods, pessimism and optimism. My own state of mind synthesizes these two feelings and transcends them: my mind is pessimistic, but my will is optimistic. Whatever the situation, I imagine the worst that could happen in order to summon up all my reserves and willpower to overcome each and every obstacle.[36]

It is interesting to see the way in which Gramsci's example inspired the European cultural icon whose early work had inspired him. In 1934 Romain Rolland sought to summarize for an international readership the meaning of Gramsci's life, ideas, and impending death:

> An iron spirit in a weak body. Ill from childhood—a fever of study and reflection. No bitterness. The joy of learning and sharing his knowledge. A passion for culture which he wished so ardently to communicate, which he later made an absolute duty for the proletariat....
>
> This philosophical mind, fed on Hegelianism, and specializing at the University in linguistic studies, was powerful above all in dialectic.... He founded in May 1919, the *Ordine Nuovo*, with the collaboration of the executive of the Italian Communist Party....
>
> He turned himself into the schoolmaster of the proletarian revolution; but his lessons were inscribed in action, in bold characters. It was around him that there sprang up in Turin in 1919–1920 the movement of *factory councils*, which he intended to turn into unit of the revolutionary army during the struggle and the units of the Workers' State after victory. This victory he was not to see. . . . But a new example has been set which will be taken up, an example which links up with the great and victories experiment of Bolshevik Russia at the other end of Europe.... Nor did Gramsci, who made no separation between philosophy and politics, escape the animosity and bitterness of the Duce [Mussolini]; but he was at any rate struck down fighting. . . . They did him the honor of sentencing him, as the leader, to twenty years of imprisonment.

That means death for a man suffering from Pott's disease, tuberculous lesions, arteriosclerosis, with arterial hypertension . . . in his prison-tomb of Turi do Bari, where all possibility of serious attention is lacking. . . . So, he will die. And Italian Communism, too, will have its great martyr, whose shadow and whose heroic flame will guide it in its future struggles.[37]

In his mind and notebooks, Gramsci systematically labored to develop conceptualizations of the modern prince, the disciplined and conscious collective, the revolutionary party, that he saw as essential to unleashing and mobilizing the immense creative energy of the oppressed. Those who continue the struggle for human liberation may find nourishment and strength from this gift.

Chapter Seven

ROSA LUXEMBURG AND THE ACTUALITY OF REVOLUTION

In this chapter, I want to do three things. First, I want to suggest an approach to Rosa Luxemburg that makes sense to me, while mentioning other approaches that do not. Then I want to suggest an answer to a question that has been raised about how Luxemburg was inclined to view and characterize—in the final years of her life—the Social Democracy in Germany and in general. From there, I want to consider advice on political strategy that she seems to offer socialist activists of today, to be found in volumes two and five of her *Collected Works*, which I have helped edit, at the same time suggesting connections of this with a broader revolutionary tradition.

Let's engage with Luxemburg in the manner she deserves. This has several aspects. One involves opening our minds and hearts to her—and for many of us this is incredibly easy, given her vibrant sensibilities, her energy, her personal and intellectual animation and depth, and the very way she talks to us in her writings. Another aspect involves trying to understand what she actually said and meant and did (as opposed to settling for a Rosa simply of our own making). I have heard people describe Rosa Luxemburg essentially as a utopian radical-feminist or as a rigidly "Marxist" antifeminist. I have heard people talk about her—and quite positively—as if her thinking was compatible with Emma Goldman's anarchism or Eduard Bernstein's social-democratic reformism or Deng Xiaoping's bureaucratic state-capitalism. She is also very frequently cast in the role of Lenin's Most Magnificent Enemy in some cosmic morality play.

One can get negative too. Simply because Luxemburg is a Marxist, believing in the class struggle and opposing capitalism, she is for some on the

119

Right a precursor of Joseph Stalin and a herald of horrific tyranny. Among some on the Left, on the other hand, she is criticized as a woolly-minded "spontaneist" who does not understand the need for organization in the revolutionary struggle.

Luxemburg was qualitatively different from, and more interesting than, any of this, and she deserves better from us.

Related to this, she deserves from us an effort to make use of what she is actually offering us. She was brilliant, insightful, with considerable knowledge and practical experience. She said and wrote things that are worth comprehending, actively considering, and testing out as we try to understand and change the world around us.

Through our engagement with her, we must treat her as a person, not as a "revolutionary goddess." Just because she thinks or says or writes something does not necessarily make it true. It is possible that she could be wrong. Given her humanity, it is *inevitable* that she would get some things wrong. It has been argued intelligently that she got certain things terribly, even disastrously wrong—and such arguments deserve serious consideration.[1] I should add that, from my own experience, even when I conclude she was wrong about something, it is not the case that she is wrong about every aspect of that thing—her mind and insights are so good that one can learn from her even when she is partly or largely wrong.

She deserves being taken seriously. We owe that to her and to ourselves, as well.

Now I want to quote from one of Luxemburg's comrades with whom she sometimes crossed swords—Vladimir Ilyich Lenin. Here is something Lenin wrote about her, in 1922, which has been quoted over, and over, and over again:

> Not only will Communists all over the world cherish her memory, but her biography and her *complete* works ... will serve as useful manuals for training many generations of Communists all over the world. "Since August 4, 1914, Social-Democracy has been a stinking corpse"—this statement will make Rosa Luxemburg's name famous in the history of the international working-class movement.[2]

The 1914 reference is to the eruption of World War I, and to the betrayal by the leaders of Luxemburg's party—the Social Democratic Party of Germany (the SPD)—in supporting this imperialist war. Indeed, there are revolutionary-minded people today who wag a finger at those who join Democratic Socialists of America while repeating this Luxemburg quote: "Social-Democracy is a stinking corpse."

Some of us who are involved in editing the complete works that Lenin had called for went looking for this formulation and could not find it in any of Luxemburg's already-translated published writings. We concluded that this must be Lenin's formulation—perhaps his own summary of her sharp critique of the German Social Democracy in, for example, the Junius Pamphlet. As Helen Scott and I pored through her writings from the years 1910 to 1919, we were not able to find those exact words: "Since August 4, 1914, Social-Democracy has been a stinking corpse."

Just as we were concluding that Rosa Luxemburg never said what Lenin claimed—we discovered that, in fact, she *did* say something very much like it.

In a set of lengthy and fascinating rough notes that Luxemburg wrote in 1918, to appear in volume 5 of *The Complete Works of Rosa Luxemburg* under the title of "Historical Fragments on History," she essentially characterizes the Social Democracy (particularly the Second International but including the SPD) as a "corpse" that has been in a process of "decay" since 1912, and especially since 1914. In these notes, she recalls that projected May Day actions of 1912 had been decisively and cold-bloodedly watered down in order to prevent an escalation of mass actions that might decisively challenge the status quo.[3]

The significance of such backtracking, for a perceptive and unyielding militant such as Luxemburg, posed the sharpest question about the revolutionary fiber of Social Democracy. Looking back on it from 1918, her conclusions were severe. With this, she reflected, "the International was already inherently a corpse, the ostentatious Basel Congress [of the Second International in 1912] was already, unconsciously, a wake." Later in these notes is a section entitled: "Decay Process in Social Democracy & the International since August 4, 1914."

Not a stinking corpse, then—just a decaying corpse.

One could argue these notes were not published in time for Lenin's comment, but in both formulation and conceptualization, they seem too similar to be coincidental. It seems likely that in the same period of time that these notes were composed, Luxemburg was saying and perhaps even writing such things beyond these rough notes, and within venues to which Lenin had access. The further publication in English of Luxemburg's complete works should make it easier to resolve this matter.

The fact remains, however, that the basic outlines of Luxemburg's political orientation have been clear for roughly a century, even to those limited to the English language. She was always very critical of the increasingly nonrevolutionary orientation in the SPD leadership, and starting in 1914 doubly and triply so. And at the end of her life, she helped to form the German Communist Party. But for most of her life—with varying degrees of patience and impatience—she labored to win working-class comrades of the Social Democracy to a revolutionary Marxist orientation. She warned left-wing activists of what she called twin evils. One would be cutting themselves off from the mass of workers and their struggles, maintaining their purity as a little revolutionary-minded sect. The other would be adapting to opportunities offered by shrewd capitalist politicians, potentially resulting in what she termed "a movement of bourgeois social reform."[4]

In her battle against reformism, she by no means opposed the struggle for reforms—changes for the better within the framework of capitalism. The problem with reform*ism*, she insisted, is that it seeks simply to pile up one reform after another with the intention of gradually, painlessly transitioning to a more just and humane society. Luxemburg saw winning reforms as essential to building a strong and self-confident working-class movement capable of overturning capitalism and replacing it with socialism. Describing her approach, she explained: "the struggle for reforms is its means; the social revolution, its aim."[5]

Luxemburg's analysis of the economic dynamics of the capital accumulation process, to be found in volume 2 of her collected works, indicates that the success of reformist gradualism is impossible. She described capitalism's global expansion as "capital's relentless war on the social and economic interrelations" of the world's peoples, and "the violent looting of their means of production and their labor power." She emphasized the destructive impact of all this—what she called "the ravenous greed, the voracious appetite for accumulation, the very essence of which is to take advantage" of human and natural realities "with no thought for tomorrow."[6] Imperialism, militarism, and war are essential to the capitalist system that Luxemburg describes and analyzes. We must now add to this environmental degradation. This leads, as she put it time and again, to a choice: "the destruction of all culture or a transition to the socialist mode of production."[7]

The fifth volume of her works highlights the pathway she felt could lead to this final, transitional victory of Social Democracy. It was *transitional* not simply in the sense of leading from the capitalist to the socialist form of economy but also in the way working-class consciousness and workers' struggles should develop, with struggles for reforms that can actually flow into the social revolution. Mass struggles to protect people's dignity and quality of life generate what she called "a lovely madness" among the workers, the vision that "a huge effort full of sacrifices" can result in "a socialist ordering of society." Luxemburg called upon the socialist party and trade unions of Germany to help prepare the intellectual spirit and idealism among masses of workers that (in her words) "all struggles that we conduct, all mass strikes that lie in front of us, are nothing other than a necessary historical stage towards the ultimate liberation from capitalism, on the way to a socialist order."[8]

I would like to conclude by suggesting perspectives that Luxemburg shared with other revolutionary Marxists of the early twentieth century. In combing through her contributions that constitute the fifth volume of her complete works, I was struck by how thoroughly a well-known phrase from the 1924 writings of Georg Lukács applies to her—"the actuality of revolution" is at the core of her thought. "The theory of historical materialism therefore presupposes the universal actuality of the proletarian revolution," Lukács explained. "In this sense, as both the objective basis of the whole epoch and the key to an understanding of it, the proletarian revolution constitutes the living core of Marxism."[9]

In her ongoing defense and continual elaboration of the mass strike concept in this fifth volume, Luxemburg advances the notion of how this must unfold in the actual class struggle of her time. "Above all else, a political mass strike demands determined leaders who are ready for action," she insisted in 1913. Lamenting the SPD leadership's lack "of such determination and readiness for action," she argued:

> We need to reexamine and forge new methods of struggle for this occasion. The masses are pushing for action, they wish for a fight. Recognize that the fire that has taken hold of the masses amounts to something more than a flash in the pan. Do not allow the working class's desire to fight to fall asleep, as we would find it difficult to shake the masses back to life.[10]

Six years later, as the Spartacus League was preparing to help create the German Communist Party, she denounced "the rotten and bankrupt traditions of the old Social Democracy and its parliamentary shadow life," emphasizing that "the Spartacists paved the way for the new revolutionary tactics: for extra-parliamentary mass action, they tirelessly . . . called for mass strikes until the first successes strengthened and raised their self-confidence and the workers' fighting courage."[11] One is struck by the fact that Luxemburg's conception involves an essential interplay of organizational leadership with semispontaneous mass action.

This approach reminds one of Antonio Gramsci, who in "The Modern Prince" considers the revolutionary party "the decisive element in every situation" involving revolution but warns that there is a danger of "neglecting, or worse still despising, so-called 'spontaneous' moments" of mass action among the workers and the oppressed. In fact, he argues, "unity between 'spontaneity' and 'conscious leadership' or 'discipline' is precisely the real political action of the subaltern classes, in so far as this is mass politics and not merely an adventure by groups claiming to represent the masses." The essential organic quality necessary for such revolutionary politics, Gramsci insisted, involves (in his words) "a continual adaptation of the organization to the real movement, a matching of thrusts from below with orders from above, a continuous insertion of elements thrown up from the depths of the rank and file into the solid framework of the leadership apparatus which ensures continuity and the regular accumulation of experience."[12]

If we take these ideas of Luxemburg, Lukács, and Gramsci seriously, we must realize that all of them were referring to a context that no longer exists in the early twenty-first century. A hundred years ago there existed a substantial global labor movement, profoundly influenced by the theory of historical materialism, and with a dynamic and influential left wing infused with the sense of the actuality of revolution. That was obliterated between the First World War and the twilight of the twentieth century. Something like it remains to be rebuilt.

Yet early in the second decade of our own century, a renewed sense of revolution's "actuality" has been emerging amid deepening crises that afflict our planet. Insurgent currents of youthful activists are moving away from an anarchism that seemed to lead nowhere, in some cases connecting with the remnants Social Democracy, in some situations connecting to one or another remnant of the old Communist movement. Some of those in the swirl of activism are wrestling with how to gather useful insights from revolutionaries of the past.

Rosa Luxemburg told us, as she explained her revolutionary orientation of mass action: "We can only grow through struggle, and it's in the middle of struggle where we learn how to fight."[13] Her words are worth taking to heart as we labor to rebuild our socialist movement and, with a lovely madness, reach for a future of the free and the equal—learning how to fight, through engaging in the actual struggles of today and tomorrow.

Postscript on Luxemburg and the Communist Tradition (2021)

Luxemburg's revolutionary Marxist approach developed independently of, and in critical symbiosis with, the Leninist tradition. Yet the reflections of Karl Kautsky are worth pondering. Once a leader, with her, of the revolutionary Marxist Left within the socialist movement, Kautsky broke decisively from Luxemburg in order to remain in the good graces of the increasingly reformist leadership of the German Social Democratic Party. A few years following her murder in the aftermath of the abortive uprising of 1919, Kautsky commented that "Rosa Luxemburg came ever closer to the Communist ideological world in the course of the [First World] War," and he concluded (explicitly agreeing with his Communist foe Karl Radek), "with Rosa Luxemburg, the greatest, most profound theoretical mind of Communism has died." There is a logic to this assertion, since she was one of the central founders of the German Communist Party two weeks before her death.[14]

Luxemburg was reaching for a more adequate way of organizing for the working-class revolution and socialist democracy to which she had devoted her life. Her critique of what the German Social Democracy had become is certainly reflected in the 1921 *Theses on the Organizational Structure of the Communist Parties and the Methods and Content of their Work*, adopted by the young Communist International:

> In the organizations of the old, non-revolutionary workers' movement, a pervasive dualism developed, similar to that of the bourgeois state, between bureaucracy and "people." Under the paralyzing influence of the bourgeois environment, functionaries became estranged from members, a vibrant collaboration was replaced by the mere forms of democracy, and the organizations became split between active functionaries and passive masses.[15]

The early Communist movement, in the spirit of Luxemburg, sought to create organizations that would maintain "living ties and interrelationships both within the party, between its leading bodies and the rest of the membership, and also between the party and the masses of proletarian masses outside its ranks." The eminent historian F. L. Carsten, in his youth an idealistic Luxemburg partisan in the early Communist movement, notes that as the

German Communist Party was being created, Luxemburg sought to infuse the new organization with the understanding of the appropriate relationship between the revolutionary "vanguard," the working-class majority, and the socialist revolution: "It is no desperate attempt of a minority to fashion the world according to its own ideals, but the action of the many millions of the people, which is called upon to fulfill its historical mission and to transform historical necessity into reality." She saw an organic bond between the qualities of the revolutionary organization, the struggle for socialism, and the nature of the new socialist society: "The essence of a socialist society consists in this, that the great working mass ceases to be a regimented mass, but lives and directs the whole political and economic life in conscious and free self-determination. . . . Highest idealism in the interest of the community, strictest self-discipline, a true civic spirit of the masses, these constitute the moral basis of a socialist society."[16]

All too soon, the Communist movement crystallized and evolved in ways inconsistent with what Luxemburg was saying here. Writing in the Cold War years of the early 1960s, Carsten would bitterly comment: "For Rosa Luxemburg, socialism and freedom were inseparable: those who have abolished freedom have no use for her ideas."[17] One might add that this was as true for the partisans of corporate capitalism dominating the planet as for partisans of the ill-fated Stalinist dictatorships that claimed to represent an alternative.

It can be argued that, had Luxemburg and some of her closest comrades survived and been successful, things could have turned out differently. It is indisputable that those who reach for socialism and freedom in the twenty-first century will find that Rosa Luxemburg offers them essential gifts.

Chapter Eight

THE "ANTI-PHILOSOPHY" OF KARL KORSCH

The Marxist tradition involves an incredibly rich pool of ideas and approaches, fed by multiple streams and feeding into a diversity of tributaries. It nourishes countless intellectual labors and explorations, and in our time of crisis and turmoil, it promises to inform an increasing number of struggles to change the world—which is precisely the purpose of the methodology and doctrines developed by Karl Marx and his cothinkers.

The unique interpretation of Marxism developed by Karl Korsch (1886–1961) is perhaps not the best place to start for someone just coming to terms with Marx's approach. But there is no denying the impact of challenging perspectives associated with his incredibly stark and lean analyses. Korsch's two most salient works are available in English: *Marxism and Philosophy* (1923—a mere sixty-eight pages in its 1970 English-language edition, published in a slim volume with a few other writings) and *Karl Marx* (1938—in its 2016 edition less than 173 pages). The second of these has recently come out in a new edition, part of Brill's Historical Materialism series. Both books—along with the complex life of their author—bristle with contradictions, in some ways mirroring the contradictory qualities of the time in which he lived, but also reflecting the author's idiosyncrasies.

Korsch is often identified, with Georg Lukács and Antonio Gramsci, as part of the foundational trio of what has been called "Western Marxism."[1] As was the case with Lukács and Gramsci, Korsch (1) blended G. W. F. Hegel's dialectical philosophy with the revolutionary approach of Marx and Lenin, and (2) was a prominent figure in the early Communist movement, with a sophisticated orientation incompatible with the dogmatic rigidities of Stalinism. Korsch's works do not compare well, however, with the richer and more substantial output of the other two. In the movement's early heroic years, all three were leading figures in their respective Communist parties (Hungary, Italy, and—in Korsch's case—Germany), yet Korsch was far less of a political leader, less consistent, in some ways less durable than either Gramsci or Lukács. "Whatever Korsch's merits as a Marxist," David Renton has noted, "Lukács was more successful in bringing his theory and practice together." The same is certainly true of Gramsci.[2]

Who He Was

The lived experience from which Korsch's writing flowed, however, suggests that he can have important insights to offer.[3] A relatively privileged family background enabled him to follow academic pursuits in philosophy and law, but the well-educated young man was troubled by the social inequalities and oppression of the working class in his industrial German homeland, and he was initially drawn to the ideas of Britain's moderate "Fabian" socialists. The brutalizing shock of the First World War profoundly radicalized him—drafted into the military, he was an actively antiwar soldier. The revolutionary ferment of 1918–1920 propelled him into the upper circles of the rapidly growing German Communist Party. Korsch became editor of its theoretical journal in 1924.

As befitted someone in his position, the uncompromisingly militant tenor of Korsch's Marxism was matched by his uncompromisingly militant Leninism, a good introduction to which could be found—he informed his readers—in a newly translated pamphlet by Joseph Stalin, *Foundations of Leninism*. He also explained to his comrades the virtue of the new workers' state, the Soviet Republic, enforcing "scientific organization and ideological dictatorship."[4]

And yet Korsch was destined to run afoul of authoritarian currents taking hold within the movement to which he had committed himself. For example, he identified the perspectives of his *Marxism and Philosophy* with the brilliant essays contained in *History and Class Consciousness* by Georg Lukács—who was engaged in a factional battle with Bela Kun, a favorite of Communist International chieftain Gregory Zinoviev. And Korsch, as one friend later commented, was inclined to "lay too much stress on his own integrity" (for example, allowing the expression of different points of view in the theoretical journal), an approach which did him damage within the emerging power struggles in the Communist movement. In 1924, Zinoviev publicly lashed out at both Lukács and Korsch as bourgeois-tainted "Professors" who didn't understand Marxism.[5]

Things got even worse after Zinoviev was shunted aside by Stalin. Korsch was marginalized and, leading a small leftist faction, he was finally ejected from the party altogether in 1926, definitively giving up on it by 1928. In 1930—now associating with leftist "council communists," whom Lenin had targeted in the 1920 polemic *Left-Wing Communism: An Infantile Disorder*[6]— Korsch was offering an open critique of Lenin as not truly representing Marx's revolutionary perspectives, a view corresponding to that of his new-found comrades, although his consistency on this matter sometimes flagged.

On a dozen different pages in his 1938 work, Korsch cites Lenin as a reliable authority who gives accurate voice to the meaning of Marx's approach. Not only does he make inclusive reference to "Marx and other dialectical materialists as Engels, Antonio Labriola, Georgi Plekhanov, and Vladimir Ilyich Lenin," but he seems to take Lenin's side in the famous conflict with his own "left-wing communist" friends:

> Just as, after the final defeat of the 1848 revolution, Marx and Engels had confronted the subjective and emotional hopes of the leftists of 1850 with the cruel materialist analysis of the objective economic position and the sober perspective resulting from this, so Lenin came to grips with the activist-revolutionary tendencies of the left communists of 1920 who, in an objectively changed situation, adhered to the slogans of the direct revolutionary situation unleashed by World War I.[7]

Korsch, at various times, articulated themes common among "Western Marxists"—seeing Marx's materialist dialectics *not* as a universal methodology applicable to nature, but as relevant only to social realities. Also typical was his inclination to see the Marxism of the Second International and even of Engels as different from and inferior to Marx's perspectives (although, as already indicated, for Korsch this hardly amounted to thoroughgoing rejection).

There is little doubt that the author of *Karl Marx* was a thoughtful and knowledgeable theorist with more than two decades of experience in the workers' movement. A veteran educator in the substantial revolutionary circles of pre-Hitler Germany, he was seen by one of the twentieth century's greatest playwrights, Bertolt Brecht, and also by the influential U.S. philosopher Sidney Hook, as a highly valued teacher of Marxism. While both

Brecht and Hook acknowledged learning much of value from Korsch, both could also be devastatingly critical of him precisely in the period when he wrote the work under consideration. "He is very much in favor of the struggle, but he himself does not actually struggle," Brecht once commented. And Hook recalled that "an impressive air of revolutionary integrity about Karl Korsch" coexisted with "a baffling obscurity about his specific beliefs." Korsch "believes in the proletariat," noted Brecht, implying that that there was something almost mystical about this belief, since it led to a fatalistic optimism: "Sometimes it seems to me that he would feel it his duty to do more if he believed in it less." Hook described the theorist, in his 1930s exile, as having "an idealized version of the worker as the center of his political allegiance but no firsthand contacts with actual workers."[8]

All of this may have something to do with some of the problematically sweeping assertions in his *Karl Marx* volume. Perhaps this simply involves a leap over a logical step or two. It can be argued that Marxism is a perspective influenced by the struggles of the working class (the proletariat), and that it exists for the purpose of advancing the interests of the working class. Historically it has sometimes been, and in the present and future it can be, influential within the working class. It has been and can be embraced and utilized by working-class activists committed to advancing the class struggle against the capitalists, winning improvements for workers, and eventually replacing capitalism with the economic democracy of socialism. What Korsch does with this is to employ telescoped formulations which will strike some readers as highly problematical.

For example, Korsch tells us that (1) Marx was "an outspoken revolutionary and even a proletarian socialist" (although no knowledgeable person, Korsch included, would claim that Marx was actually a wage-worker), that (2) "Marx instilled in the minds of the workers the materialist lesson that . . . they themselves must bring . . . a social revolution penetrating the economic basis of existing bourgeois society" (although there are many, many, many workers—of Marx's time and since—who have not been "instilled" in this way), and that (3) "the principles of the Marxian critique of existing society" are "proletarian" and that "Marxian theory . . . represents the new views and claims of the oppressed class in bourgeois society" (although this would be news to a majority of those who labor as part of the world's working class).[9]

"My teacher is a disappointed man," Brecht once wrote of Korsch. "The things he took part in did not turn out according to his ideas." Fifteen years after the publication of *Karl Marx*, a demoralized Korsch was teaching at an American university in relative isolation and obscurity. US capitalism's widespread affluence in the late 1950s had a seeming stability, matched by the seeming lack of working-class struggles—quite different from realities that had propelled him in a revolutionary direction decades before. Within his small circle of political friends, Korsch began raising critical questions about the Marxism in which he had believed for so many years—some later claiming that he had abandoned Marxism at the end of his life, others interpreting this (as his wife insisted) as an attempt to clear the decks and further develop his revolutionary perspectives.[10]

When one utters the name "Karl Korsch," however, what is generally being referred to are the views articulated in his two remarkably brief works of 1923 and 1938. In the remainder of this review, I will touch first on idiosyncrasies and limitations before working to the strengths of Korsch's *Karl Marx*.

Ironies and Idiosyncrasies

Marxism and Philosophy, the work for which Korsch is best known, is a readable essay offering a well-informed exploration of the philosophical background and context that contributed to the development of Marx's outlook. The very title suggests that this may be the first stop for anyone wishing to engage with the philosophical aspects of Marxism.

Yet there is an irony here, grounded in Korsch's understanding of the eleventh of Marx's "Theses on Feuerbach" (1845): "The philosophers have only interpreted the world in various ways, the point is to change it." Korsch suggests Marxism is best seen as *"anti-philosophy."* This poses a challenge. Alex Callinicos also comments that Marx and Engels saw this as asserting "their final and irrevocable departure from speculation's realm of shades for the firmer ground of empirical science, whose premises are not the abstractions of philosophy, but 'the real individuals, their activity and the material conditions of their life'"—although he adds, "it is one of the many paradoxes of Marxism's history that this parting of the ways between philosophy and historical materialism seems never to have been finally accomplished." This raises the obvious question of whether Marx and Engels actually, seriously meant what Callinicos and Korsch say they meant. Helena Sheehan argues, to the contrary, "that the pronouncements of Marx and Engels on the 'end of philosophy' ran counter to the basic truth of their thinking on the status of philosophy."[11] Different Marxists have certainly done different things with all of this. As Marxist philosopher Roy Edgley once summed it up:

> Either there is a distinctive Marxist philosophy that opposes bourgeois philosophy, perhaps as Marxist social science opposes the bourgeois social sciences. Or there is a philosophy in Marxism that is not distinctively Marxist, a philosophy Marxism shares with bourgeois social thought, the opposition being between Marxist and bourgeois theory being at a scientific level. Or there is no such thing as a philosophy of any kind in Marxism because Marxism opposes bourgeois philosophy by opposing philosophy as such.[12]

Korsch's *Marxism and Philosophy* appears to articulate the third of these positions. Marx and Engels, Korsch tells us, were not attempting to create some new socialist or communist philosophy. "They rather saw the task of their 'scientific socialism' as that of definitively overcoming and superseding the form and content, not only of all previous bourgeois idealist philosophy, but thereby of philosophy altogether." This approach is maintained in *Karl Marx*:

> Marx's materialist science, being a strictly empirical investigation into definite historical forms of society, does not need a philosophical support. . . . The only reason why, from a certain point in their development, the materialist philosophers Marx and Engels turned their backs on every philosophy, even materialist philosophy . . . , is the fact that they wanted to go one step further and outbid the materialism of philosophy by a directly materialist science and practice.[13]

A similar irony is related to the fact that Korsch's 1938 work was part of a prestigious series entitled "Modern Sociologists" (also including volumes on Auguste Comte, Edward B. Tylor, Vilfredo Pareto, and Thorstein Veblen)—and yet Korsch took the same stance toward this discipline as he did toward philosophy, distinguished only by being even more dismissive:

> If we think of the Sociology begun by Comte and in fact first named by him, we shall not find any affinity or link between it and Marxism. Marx and Engels, with all their keen desire to extend and enhance the knowledge of society, paid no attention to either the name or contents of that ostensibly new approach to the social studies. . . . The science of socialism as formulated by Marx, owed nothing to this "sociology" of the 19th and 20th centuries which originated with Comte and was propagated by Mill and Spencer. . . . Bourgeois sociologists refer to the revolutionary socialist

science of the proletariat as an "unscientific mixture of theory and politics." Socialists, on the other hand, dismiss the whole bourgeois sociology as mere "ideology.". . . [S]ociology as a special branch of learning . . . represents nothing more than an escape from the practical, and therefore also theoretical, tasks of the present historical epoch. Marx's new socialist and proletarian science which, in a changed historical situation, further developed the revolutionary theory of the classical founders of the doctrine of society, is the genuine social science of our time.[14]

In exploring more deeply the meaning of these critical remarks, it may be helpful to define terms. "Philosophy" is commonly defined as the study of general and fundamental problems concerning existence, knowledge, values, reason, etc., so it would seem that Marxism itself is inseparable from—not some kind of "advance beyond"—such stuff. "Sociology" is, likewise, commonly defined as precisely the sort of thing that Marxism does: the study of society, including its origins, development, organization, as well as the existence, the interaction, and clashes between social groups, also involving attention to matters having to do with social stability and social change.

But Korsch insisted that both philosophy and sociology as we know them (as well as all the other social sciences, in fact what he sweepingly terms "the positive sciences") represent "bourgeois ideology." Not only have they developed within bourgeois society, but they are saturated with positive assumptions regarding the capitalist status quo, which is seen as representing "the natural order of things," in fact reflecting biases that favor its perpetuation.

We will want to return to this understanding of "bourgeois ideology" shortly, but the point is that Korsch's terminology can sometimes pose challenges and misunderstandings. "Korsch declared that the revolutionary process was a total attack on bourgeois society that brought the abolition not only of its philosophy but of all of its sciences," as Helena Sheehan sums it up, adding the perturbed complaint: "Just how the new revolutionary man, endowed with mystical proletarian class consciousness, was to come to terms with the natural world without the positive sciences and without philosophical interpretations of the results of positive sciences was something that was never quite explained." The shrewd ex-Marxist philosopher Leszek Kolakowski comments that, for Korsch, Marxism "is neither a science nor a philosophy, but a theoretical and practical critique of existing society" which is "'subordinated' to revolutionary aims"—the overthrow of capitalism by the organized working class, and its replacement with socialism. Or as Korsch himself emphasizes, Marxism "is not only a theory of bourgeois society but, at the same time, a theory of the proletarian revolution."[15]

This hardly whisks away the critical questions posed by Sheehan, whose objections might best be met by the terminological shift articulated in comments by radical sociologist C. Wright Mills, dropping the idiosyncratic usage that Korsch employs. Marx, he insisted, "is both a philosopher and an empirical sociologist. . . . Marxism is at once an intellectual and moral criticism. In its documents, in its very conceptions, the two *are* often difficult to separate, but it *is* political philosophy and at the same time it *is* definitely social science."[16]

In justice to Korsch, however, he himself offers formulations that seem consistent with the understanding of Mills. "Marx's materialist research, while not for a moment abandoning its character of a strictly theoretical science," Korsch writes in *Karl Marx*, "yet consciously assumes its particular function within the whole of a movement striving to transform existing society, and thus constitutes itself as a necessary part of the revolutionary action of the modern proletariat." Similarly, in *Marxism and Philosophy* (in a manner seemingly inconsistent with other formulations) he refers to "the independent essence of Marxist philosophy," and to "the revolutionary materialistic dialectic, which is the philosophy of the working class."[17]

Theoretically close to Korsch in this period, Sidney Hook expressed the central thrust of Korsch's (and his own) Marxism this way:

> If a man's life has any connection with his thought, then Marx's revolutionary activity should provide the clue to the central purpose of his thinking. Whatever Marxism might mean to his disciples, there can be no question but that for Marx it meant the theory and practice of the proletarian revolution. Every one of his doctrines was a generalization of an historic experience in the class struggle or a proposed solution of some problem in that struggle. . . . If Marxism is the theory and practice of social revolution in capitalist society, then its first consideration must be a persistent and critical survey of all the social and political factors which affect the possibilities of successful political action.[18]

It might be argued, however, that the insight in this assertion needs to be balanced with another, one that will help revolutionaries avoid a potential debilitating rigidity. It might go against the grain of Korsch's schema to posit an objective reality whose complex and fluid dimensions can be perceived by various approaches—not simply the "revolutionary proletarian" stand-point associated with Korsch's understanding of Marx. But cutting one's self, or one's Marxism, off from these other approaches in a self-contained grandeur—convinced of the inherent incorrectness of those not sharing one's distinctive revolutionary outlook—could pave the way for a failure to understand important aspects of reality's complex totality.

To restrict one's self to the narrow confines of what will advance the revolution may, in fact, undermine one's ability to advance one's understanding of the world, as well as one's ability to advance the revolutionary liberation struggle.

Strengths

The chapters of Korsch's *Karl Marx* are grouped into three parts—Society, Political Economy, and History. Particularly fruitful in the book's first part is his emphasis on what he terms *the principle of historical specification*, which he combines with what he sees as two other elements of Marxism—the *principle of change* and *the principle of criticism*.

Comprehending "all things social in terms of a definite historical epoch," Marx "criticizes all the categories of the bourgeois theorists of society in which that specific character has been effaced." Korsch stresses: "Every truth, according to the Marxists, applies only to a definite set of conditions; it is therefore not absolute but relative, not independent and complete in itself, but contingent upon external facts." This is in contrast to economists and other "bourgeois" social scientists who "ingenuously regard society's basic relationships as having the immutable character of a genuine natural law, and are for just this reason unable to become aware of any other than this actually given form of society. . . . When they speak of 'society' in general, we can still, with only slight variations, recognize in that so-called general society the well-known features of present-day bourgeois society."[19]

Korsch also notes that "bourgeois society may contain the conditions of earlier societies in a further developed form," although sometimes "in degenerate, stunted, and travestied forms." Present-day society also "contains within itself the germs of its future developments, though by no means their complete determination." He comments that the notion of "evolution as applied by bourgeois social theorists, is *closed* on both sides, and in all past and future forms of society rediscovers only itself," while the Marxist approach to development "is, on the contrary, *open* on both sides." He adds that in "the principle of evolution as used by the bourgeois social investigators, there is no room for the conscious human-social act, which shall radically transform and overthrow the present order of society." Noting the "unhistorical" quality permeating bourgeois social science when dealing with contemporary realities, he quotes Marx's taunting critique: "Thus there was history, but there is no more." Free from such a status quo bias, Marxist social analysts would be capable of a "critical investigation of the existing conditions," enhanced by an understanding of the possibility of "a *transition from the present historical phase to a higher form of society.*"[20]

Yet another strength in this volume is Korsch's approach to history, with its emphasis on the creative energies of human beings—particularly of the masses of oppressed laborers—in making history. He cites the compelling comment of Marx and Engels from *The Holy Family*:

> History does *nothing*, it possesses *no* immense wealth, it fights *no* battles! It is rather *man*, real, living man—who does everything, who possesses and fights; it is not history which uses men, as a means to carry out its end, as if it were a separate person, but it is *nothing* besides man in the pursuit of his ends.[21]

Korsch adds (seeing the "motor force" of history as an interactive blend of technological development and class struggle) that "Marx and Lenin did not think for a moment of supplanting the real revolutionary action of the working class by a passive belief in a mere economic process of development which would after a considerable amount of waiting finally achieve the revolutionary change with the inevitability of a natural process." Rather, the workers "must with their own hands break the fetters that obstruct the development of the productive forces and establish the higher production-relations of a new progressive epoch of society."[22]

A number of notable points can be found in Korsch's discussion of political economy. "*Capital* is only nominally the subject of Marx's new economic theory," he writes. "Its real theme is *labor* both in its present-day economic form of subjugation by capital and in its development, through the revolutionary struggle of the proletariat, to a new directly social and socialist condition." He argues that "the great illusion of our epoch that capitalistic society is a society consisting of free and self-determining individuals can only be maintained by keeping the people unconscious of the real contents of those basic relations of the existing social order." Bourgeois economists mask reality "by representing the real social relations between the classes of the capitalists and the wage laborers as an inevitable result of the free and unhampered 'sale' of the commodity 'labor power' to the owner of the capital," without acknowledging the unequal power, coercion, and exploitation inherent in this "free" exchange.[23]

The way that Korsch presents Marx's economics may strike some readers as having a contemporary resonance. Consider his discussion of the *labor theory of value* and *theory of surplus value*. Marx, following the classical political economists Adam Smith and David Ricardo, saw labor as the creator of "value." This means the amount of labor contained in each *commodity* (products that are made for the purpose of being sold) determines the amount of value contained in that commodity. The worker's ability to work (his or her "labor-power") is itself a commodity to be sold, for wages, in this voraciously buying-and-selling economy, an economy of "generalized commodity production." But the value of the products needed to sustain the worker (reflected in the worker's wages, the payment for the utilization of his or her labor-power) is less than the amount of value that the worker creates for the capitalist employer (the amount of labor actually squeezed out of the worker by the employer). The consequent surplus-value is the key to the capital accumulation process, through which the capitalists spectacularly increase their profits, at the expense of the exploited workers.

Stressing that "it was never the intention of Marx" to utilize this analysis of provide a "direct determination of the price of commodities" (which had become a center of debate between some critics and partisans of Marx[24]), Korsch notes Marx's own belief "that the 'production prices' of commodities produced by capitals of various organic constitution can no longer be identical with their 'values' as determined by the 'law of value.'" He goes on to explain:

> It would be nearer the truth to say that the working of this law appears in the general *development* of the prices of commodities, in which the continuous depreciation in value of the commodities, effected by the ever-increasing productivity of social labor consequent upon the further accumulation of capital, constitutes the decisive factor. The ultimate meaning of this law as shown in its operation by Marx in all three volumes of *Capital* does not consist, however, in supplying a theoretical basis for the practical calculation of the businessman seeking his private advantage, or for the economico-political measures taken by the bourgeois statesman concerned with

the general maintenance and furtherance of the capitalist surplus-making machinery. The final scientific purpose of the Marxian theory is rather to reveal "*the economic law of motion of modern society*" and that means at the same time *the law of its historical development.* Even more clearly was this expressed by the Marxist Lenin when he said that "the direct purpose of a Marxist investigation consists in the disclosure of all forms of the antagonism and exploitation existing in present-day capitalist society in order to aid the proletariat to do away with them."[25]

The dynamics of the capital accumulation process—an insatiable quest for more profits, to be invested to realize more and more profits, which must be invested to secure more and more and more—have the dual impacts of spectacular creation and spectacular destruction, with yesterday's creations needing to be demolished to make way for tomorrow's profit-making creations, and

this increasing *destruction* of its own foundations is forced upon present-day capitalism by an objective development of its inherent tendencies. It is produced by the ever-increasing accumulation and concentration of capital; by the growing monopolist tendencies of the big industrial and financial combines; by the increasing appeal to the State to rescue 'the community at large' from the dangers brought about by the impending collapses of hitherto proud and tax-evading private enterprises.

Korsch focused on related developments which would soon help generate the global holocaust of World War II:

hyper-ultra-super-dreadnought demands for subsidy raised by the various direct and indirect producers of armaments encroaching ever more on the field formerly occupied by the activities of the less directly war-producing industries. In trying to escape from the periodical crises which threaten more and more the existence of bourgeois society, and in a desperate attempt to overcome the existing acute crisis of the whole capitalist system, the bourgeoisie is compelled, by continually fresh and deeper "interferences" with the inner laws of its own mode of production, and continually greater changes in its own social and political organization, to prepare more violent and more universal crises and at the same time, to diminish the means of overcoming future crises. In organizing peace it prepares for war.[26]

Commenting that "the mass-employment offered by a new war" was already being "partially anticipated by a hitherto unheard-of extension of the direct and indirect armament industries both in the fascist countries and in democratic Britain and pacifistic U.S.A.," he observed that war "has the incomparable advantage that it will never cause an undesirable glut of the market because it destroys the commodities it produces simultaneously with their production and, incidentally, destroys a considerable portion of the 'excessive' workers themselves."[27]

And so it came to pass: the horrific Second World War, followed by the decades' long Cold War—which gave capitalism a glorious new lease on life, pulling it out of the Great Depression that had seemed to promise the very different, revolutionary outcome anticipated in Korsch's 1938 study. That the destruction of his hopes was the result of forces he himself had identified in that work is not without interest. No less significant is the fact that much of what Korsch wrote about almost eight decades ago seems consistent with what is happening all around us in the twenty-first century.

Chapter Nine

THE ODYSSEY OF JAMES BURNHAM

There have been many journeys made from the left to the right end of the political spectrum over the past two centuries by intellectuals who originally believed in giving "power to the people," but who—for one or another reason—became disappointed with the effort to achieve such a goal. Some of the most influential political and social theories have been developed out of such disappointment. The radical-democratic conception of socialism developed by Karl Marx and others of his persuasion, especially because of the intellectual power of its "historical materialist" underpinnings, has first attracted and subsequently repelled many an alert and critical mind.

The "collapse of Communism" has given even greater impetus to post-Marxist theorizing. Much of this "new thinking," however, simply goes over ground covered many decades before by such people as James Burnham (1905–1987). His own trajectory led to conclusions that would certainly be unpalatable to the democratic inclinations of many "post-Marxists" in the 1990s, and he would hardly have had patience for intricate theorizations of those turning from Marx to Foucault and from Lenin to Derrida. A greater kinship can be found with those "new Leftists" migrating to the "neoconservative" banner.[1] Yet from all of those disappointed with Marxism and Leninism, regardless of their present location on the political spectrum, we can hear echoes of the critique Burnham articulated in 1941.

The full-scale biography that Burnham deserves has yet to be attempted although we have fine sketches by such intellectual historians as John Diggins, Alan Wald, George Nash, and Gary Dorrien, who focus on one or another as-

140

pect of his career.[2] Missing from all of these, however, is the kind of in-depth exploration of Burnham's evolution from left to right that highlights his power as a thinker and (most important, given the importance for Burnham of the interpenetration of theory and practice) what he actually did about the things he thought: his impact as a history-maker. Even restricting ourselves to published materials (Burnham's papers have been deposited with the Hoover Institute), we can trace continuities and discontinuities between his Marxist and conservative phases that illuminate aspects of Marxist (and post-Marxist) theory, of democratic (and antidemocratic) thought, of US politics and foreign policy, and of anti-Communist and conservative ideology.

Commitment to Change the World

Burnham's writings were meant to be far more than intellectual reflections. They were produced by a man who was committed to action, first from the far-Left, later from the far-Right, and who was intent upon having an impact on world events. Articulated with a great boldness and clarity, his political analyses were both sweeping and closely reasoned. In his lifetime they profoundly affected the thinking of US and European intellectuals, of influential shapers of public opinion, and of powerful decision-makers. The access to such power seems reasonable, given his personal background. Burnham was born into a wealthy Chicago family in 1905. His father had emigrated from Britain as a child and became vice-president of the Burlington Railroad. There was no difficulty, therefore, in sending his son to Princeton University, where Burnham graduated first in his class in 1927. He then went abroad to round out his education at Oxford, where he studied literature and received a master's degree at Balliol College in 1929.

Although he had left the Catholic Church midway through Princeton, at Oxford he studied philosophy under Father Martin C. D'Arcy, concentrating on medieval and Thomist philosophy. While there are no indications that Burnham had ever been plagued by "ill feelings toward the business world of his father," (who died in 1928), he was soon affected by the revolutionary currents of his time. "At the onset of the Great Depression, he was torn by incongruous sentiments," writes Alan Wald. "Propelled leftward by the economic crisis, he started reading Marx while living in the south of France during the summer of 1930; yet that same autumn he and Philip Wheelwright initiated a magazine, *The Symposium*, modeled after T. S. Eliot's *Criterion*." Assuming a position in the philosophy department of New York University, he produced with Wheelwright *Introduction to Philosophical Analysis*, "a highly imaginative textbook," according to John P. Diggins, which at the time Susanne K. Langer praised as a "pedagogical masterpiece." Yet Burnham, through the medium of *The Symposium* and increasingly in his practical activity, began to utilize his philosophical and literary talents to deal with questions of contemporary politics.[3]

Sidney Hook (Burnham's colleague at New York University's philosophy department and at the time a prominent young Marxist) later recalled that *The Symposium* "was required to deal with social and political issues; and . . . the worsening of the Depression, which destroyed much of the world in which Jim had grown up," helped to move the young editor further leftward. Among those writing for the magazine were a number of left-wing intellectuals such as F. W. Dupee, Paul Goodman, Dwight Macdonald, William Phillips, Harold Rosenberg, Morris U. Schappes, and Lionel Trilling. Hook's essay "Toward the Understanding of Karl Marx" (later expanded into an influential book) was also published in *The Symposium*, offering a sophisticated interpretation of Marxist theory. Burnham himself wrote a lengthy review of Trotsky's *History of the Russian Revolution* for the magazine, commenting: "Reading this remarkable book was an exciting experience; and it left me with the impression of understanding very clearly those events of which it claims to be an accurate record and a valid explanation."[4]

Reviewing Ralph Fox's biography of Lenin for the Communist Party's *New Masses*, he declared the Bolshevik leader to be "the chief political leader of all time." In this period he began to work with the Young Communist League at New York University and became the group's educational advisor. US Communist leader Earl Browder met with him to explain the Communist program in an almost-successful effort to recruit him. Hook recalls that Burnham was critical of the dogmatic and rigid qualities of the Stalinists but believed that "the overriding significance of the Communist Party was its effective centralized structure, without which all social criticism was just talk."[5]

Some commentators on Burnham's intellectual trajectory (Lasch, Diggins, Dorrien) assume that there is a link between such Leninism, which they see as inherently manipulative and totalitarian, and the conservative elitism to which Burnham later gravitated. This distorts the Leninism to which Burnham committed himself, however, and consequently underestimates the ideological distance that Burnham had to travel from the 1930s to

the 1950s. In the early 1930s Burnham was deeply influenced by the revolutionary-democratic interpretation of Marx and Lenin, which Sidney Hook
had advanced in his classic *Towards the Understanding of Karl Marx*. "Burnham . . . became what the Communist Party used to call a Hookworm, at
least for a short period of time," Hook later recalled.[6]

Like Hook, Burnham soon broke with the Communist Party—believing that it was not in harmony with the valid revolutionary perspectives of
Marx and Lenin—and went on to participate (with Hook, the former minis-
ter A. J. Muste, the prominent trade union official J. B. S. Hardman, the talented labor organizer Louis F. Budenz, and others) in forming the American
Workers Party (AWP) in 1934. The new organization attempted to combine
a nondogmatic revolutionary Marxism with a rootedness in distinctively
American radical traditions plus practical labor organizing. During its short
existence, it played a significant role in the unemployed movement and in a
number of militant labor struggles, particularly the Toledo Auto-Lite Strike.[7]

Soon Muste, Burnham, and a majority of the AWP decided to join with
the Communist League of America, a Trotskyist organization led by James
P. Cannon and Max Shachtman, to form the Workers Party of the United
States. According to Sidney Hook, essential to this merger was the Trotskyists' "willingness to accept the AWP conception of a workers' democracy."
This had been articulated by Hook himself, who argued that Marxists, far
from being opposed to democracy, "hold that a true democracy is possible
only in a socialist society." Citing Marx and Lenin, he explained: "Since in
a capitalist society, only a small minority holds ownership, and the actual
reins of control, over the means of production, what we really have under the
guise of formal democracy is the dictatorship of a minority owning class."
He asserted that "against the dictatorship of the bourgeoisie, Marxists have
always opposed the ideal of workers' or proletarian democracy," and that
the method by which such a workers' state would achieve a classless society
was "the progressive expansion of democratic processes to a point where the
whole population is drawn into the ranks of the producers and the repressive
functions of the state apparatus becomes unnecessary." Hook noted that
Marx and Lenin had "employed interchangeably" this notion of workers'
democracy with the concept of "dictatorship of the proletariat," the political rule by the working class which would constitute the ever-increasing
democratic transition from capitalism to communism. Even though Hook
remained no more than a "fellow-traveler" of the enlarged Trotskyist group,

Burnham and others—embracing this revolutionary-democratic understanding of Marxism—helped to make the fusion a living reality.[8]

In 1936 the Trotskyists briefly merged into the left-wing of the Socialist Party, emerging with a doubled membership of about 1,500 a year later to establish the Socialist Workers Party (SWP) in early 1938. Throughout this period and up to 1940, Burnham was one of the foremost leaders of American Trotskyism. The Trotskyists—a dissident faction in the Communist movement influenced by the ideas and example of Leon Trotsky—opposed what they considered to be the corruption of Marxist and Leninist perspectives by the bureaucratic dictatorship of Joseph Stalin in the USSR. They insisted that socialism was inseparable from such principles (which they believed Stalinism had betrayed) as "workers' democracy" and "revolutionary internationalism." They insisted that the progressive achievements initiated by the Bolshevik Revolution in Russia must be defended not only from the imperialism of the capitalist world but also from the bureaucratic cancer of Stalinism. Only a relative handful of idealistic workers and intellectuals rallied to the Trotskyist banner in the United States and various other countries in the 1930s, although they had influence well beyond their numbers.[9]

Max Shachtman later recalled that Burnham "was very much welcomed in the Trotskyist movement, although he was regarded as something of a curio, a personal curio, not a political curio. He was very much respected by everybody—the leadership and the ranks, not just by the intellectuals but by the proletarians, including the pseudo-proletarians in the party. It was known that he came from the bourgeois aristocracy." He was very scholarly, not "in demeanor but in knowledge. Very urbane." Burnham "immediately acquired a reputation for impersonality, impartiality, fairness, and logical thought."[10] Sidney Hook, who continued to identify himself as being on the Left (but not as a Trotskyist, and in later years as a pro-Reagan "socialist") describes him in this way:

> What were the sources of Burnham's intellectual appeal during his radical years? They were more manifest in his writings than in his speeches. First was his fresh, forceful, direct style, completely free of "radicalese." Second was the organization of his arguments, so that his conclusions seemed to flow naturally from his points as he clicked them off. Third, although he was not a professional economist, he was quite familiar with economic history and contemporary currents of economic thought. Finally, although

he wrote simply, there was a certain elegance in his diction, an occasional cultural reference that suggested depths of meaning to be explored.[11]

With Max Shachtman he served as coeditor of the Trotskyists' impressive theoretical magazine *New International*, writing a number of lucid articles on theory, current politics, and culture. In 1937 Burnham penned a penetrating critique of the Stalinists' new reformist orientation, *The People's Front: The New Betrayal*. In 1938 he wrote a popular party pamphlet, *Let the People Vote on War!* He maintained an extensive correspondence with Trotsky and enjoyed considerable influence throughout the Trotskyist movement and beyond. "Yet all of us," Shachtman recalled, "and this went for Cannon and myself in particular, felt that although he was with us and with us thoroughly, he was not, so to say, of us." In a letter to Trotsky, Cannon expressed concern over Burnham's tendency "to deprecate his party co-workers and to resist the idea of being influenced or taught anything, even by our international comrades."[12] Alan Wald provides this portrait:

> Tall, thin, bespectacled, conservatively dressed, and a good speaker, Burnham, however, displayed little warmth in personal relations. He was liked by the young party members and admired by Shachtman, but he kept aloof from the party rank and file. An excellent teacher, he was asked one summer to give classes on socialism to Trotskyists in Minneapolis [a stronghold of the movement where his comrades had led a militant and successful general strike] but refused to give up his vacation in Connecticut. He lived at Sutton Place in New York City and would occasionally attend political committee meetings in a tuxedo because he had just come or was en route to cocktails at the Rockefellers or at the home of some other wealthy family with whom he was friends.[13]

Burnham was known to have philosophical differences with Marxism, operating—in the words of one philosophically inclined comrade from that period, George Novack—from "positivist rather than materialist premises" and opposing "the historical necessity of socialism on the general ground that no categorical determinism existed either in nature or society; any and every proposition about reality was no more than probable." But Burnham's imperfect connection with his revolutionary Marxist comrades was rooted in life more than philosophy. Both Cannon and Shachtman recognized that Burnham was personally torn, in crisis over the contradiction between his upper-class lifestyle and his left-wing commitments. Respecting his talents and sincerity, they gently sought to help him make the transition to being a full-time revolutionary. "There were clearly times," according to Shachtman, "when he was on the very verge of throwing it all up—namely, his job at the University—and perhaps other personal involvements—and coming to work for the party, and that he felt this urge very strongly and very sincerely." Yet he could never bring himself to take that step, in large measure because he was wracked by doubts, which he freely expressed to Shachtman: "questions that had arisen in his mind about Marxism—not just about dialectical materialism, toward which he was always skeptical, but about Marxism in general, socialism in general, about the social capacities of the working class in general." These doubts were nourished by the triumph of Stalinism in the USSR and throughout the world Communist movement, the triumph of Nazism and fascism throughout much of Europe, the failure of revolutionary socialists to mobilize the working class around an alternative course anywhere—including in the United States, where the New Deal enjoyed mass support for its welfare-state reforms of capitalism and its substantial military build-up.[14]

Nonetheless, in this period Burnham distinguished himself by publishing in *New International* a combination of seemingly razor-sharp political analyses and sophisticated defenses of revolutionary Marxism. Most interesting of these was a remarkable essay coauthored with Shachtman, "Intellectuals in Retreat," in which a substantial layer of left-wing intellectuals of the 1930s was subjected to a penetrating and extensive critique, accused of constituting a "League of Abandoned Hopes" that was "moving from a revolutionary Marxian position, or one close to it, *towards* reformism, or a little beyond it to bourgeois liberalism (or in some instances, scarcely concealed passivity)," all under the banner of opposing "totalitarianism."[15]

Burnham did more in the revolutionary movement than simply write impressive articles. As a member of the SWP Political Committee, he played an influential role in shaping party policy. In 1938, as a minority of one he urged support of the Ludlow Amendment to the US Constitution, which would have mandated a national referendum before the nation could go to war. In the same year, he also advanced a minority position favoring SWP support for forming a mass labor party, in the face of growing sentiment among radicalizing workers in unions affiliated to the recently formed Congress of Industrial Organizations (CIO) for independent politics. Both positions appeared to fly in the face of long-held Trotskyist "orthodoxy." Yet Burnham advanced them with a boldness and lucidity that finally helped persuade a majority of his comrades (including Trotsky). The demand to "let the people vote on war," and the call for a labor party based on the trade unions subsequently became standard ordnance in the arsenal of American Trotskyism.[16]

In January 1939 Burnham won a plurality in the Political Committee for a more problematical position regarding a factional war that had erupted in the United Automobile Workers of America (UAW), one of the most combative and effective affiliates of the CIO. UAW President Homer Martin, supported and advised by the dissident-Communist splinter group of Jay Lovestone, was in battle with the Unity Caucus, which included Socialists around the dynamic Reuther brothers (Roy, Walter, and Victor) and activists associated with the Communist Party. Rival UAW conventions were organized in Detroit (by Martin) and Cleveland (by the Unity Caucus). The Trotskyists, with a significant grouping in the UAW, were confronted with a choice of which side they were on. Maintaining that "everything healthy in the labor movement withers under the touch of Stalinism," Burnham characterized the Cleveland convention as "a 100% Stalinist stooge assembly" in advance, predicting that "every move, every motion, every resolution will be dictated by Earl Browder," the General Secretary of the US Communist Party. This outlook, which Burnham developed into an editorial for the SWP's weekly newspaper, *Socialist Appeal,* was consistent not only with the perspective of the Lovestoneites (with whom Burnham had collaborated on the short-lived *Marxist Quarterly* in 1937), but also with the analysis of prominent labor journalist Ben Stolberg, who had been active in the American Committee for the Defense of Leon Trotsky (and the Dewey Commission which discredited Stalin's purge trials) and who had just authored *The Story of the CIO,* which critically focused on "Stalinist influences" in the CIO. Burnham's orientation was not consistent, however, with the perspectives of a majority of SWPers in the UAW, not to mention SWP leader James P. Cannon (who was out of the country). Aware of these differences, Burnham nonetheless chose to push forward for an implementation of his policy—only to find that the party's UAW fraction voted to junk the issue of *Socialist Appeal* which contained his editorial.[17]

"The formal logic here is perfect," said prominent SWP activist George Clarke of Burnham's analysis. "But just one little thing is omitted from the syllogism, just as it is omitted from all formal logic: an understanding of events in the process of motion and change, an understanding of the interaction of human beings and events. Or in other words, an understanding of the dynamics of the workers' movement." Burnham's perspective was consciously and consistently ignored by Trotskyists in the auto union, and he sought to bring them to heel for their indiscipline. But this proved impossible, and the orientation he had pushed through was quickly dropped by the Political Committee.[18]

The Cleveland UAW convention turned out to be, in fact, broadly representative, enthusiastically militant, profoundly democratic. The sessions of Homer Martin's rival convention, on the other hand, "were devoted to flag-waving patriotism and rabid red-baiting," as Martin prepared to lead his shrinking following out of the CIO and back to the more conservative American Federation of Labor. "This convention marked the public suicide of the Lovestoneites in auto," Clarke commented, "just as it would have marked our own had we participated in it." Burnham's behavior, he added, "revealed strong tendencies towards bureaucratism in administration, an arrogant approach to the rank and file, a hateful attitude towards the workers who correct his line, sterile and formalist in analysis."[19]

While some of his comrades were to look back on this as a "moment of truth" revealing Burnham's inevitable trajectory, it is conceivable that more time and additional experience in the Trotskyist movement might have helped him mature into a more capable left-wing leader. But 1939–1940 brought events that would fundamentally alter Burnham's commitments: the signing of the Nazi-Soviet pact in 1939, the German-Soviet overrunning of Poland, the onset of World War II, and the Soviet war against Finland. All this sent many left-wing intellectuals reeling and precipitated a fierce factional conflict in the Socialist Workers Party. Burnham now insisted, with growing support from Shachtman and others, that the USSR was not a bureaucratically degenerated workers' state (Trotsky's position) but represented a new form of class society, which they labeled *bureaucratic collectivism*, that was in no sense progressive and was fully as exploitative and reactionary as fascism and capitalist imperialism. They argued that in the face of the two oppressive and expansionist camps of capitalism and Stalinism, revolutionary socialists must establish a "third camp" to which all the workers, oppressed people, and progressive-minded people should be rallied. The SWP split, and with a sizeable minority Shachtman and Burnham created a new organization, the Workers Party.

Yet Burnham's evolution did not end there. According to one of his comrades, reminiscing eight years later, Burnham "announced his resignation from the Workers Party one lonely morning in 1940 [not long after its founding] by leaving a note at the office with a secretary who was trying to fix a radiator, tipping his hat politely and leaving." This "note," actually a long letter, asserted: "Of the most important beliefs which have been associated with the Marxist movements . . . there is virtually none of which I accept in its traditional form. I regard those beliefs as either false or obsolete or meaningless; or in a few cases, as at best true only in a form so restricted and modified as no longer properly to be called Marxist."[20] In the following year, he published The *Managerial Revolution*, in which he elaborated his critique of (and alternative to) Marxism, summing up:

> The grander scientific pretensions of Marxism have been exploded by this century's increases in historical and anthropological knowledge and by the clearer contemporary understanding of the scientific method. The Marxian philosophy of dialectical materialism takes its place with the other outmoded speculative metaphysics of the nineteenth century. The Marxian theory of universal history makes way for more painstaking, if less soul-satisfying, procedures in anthropological research. The laws of Marxian economics prove unable to deal concretely with contemporary economic phenomena. It would be wrong, of course, to deny all scientific value to Marx's own writings; on the contrary, we must continue to regard him as one of the most important figures in the historical development of the historical sciences—which sciences, even today however, are only in their infancy. But to suppose, as Marxists do, that Marx succeeded in stating general laws of the world, of man and his history and ways, is today just ludicrous.[21]

Some years later Burnham himself succinctly summarized the practical orientation of his alternative to Marxism:

> Throughout the world . . . informed and thoughtful men have come to a double realization: first, that the capitalist era, in anything like the traditional meaning that we derive from the eighteenth and nineteenth centuries, is drawing to a close, or may even be regarded as finished; but second, that it is not to be replaced by socialism, if "socialism" is taken to mean the free, classless, international society of the abstract Marxian ideal. If these two negative facts are accepted, there then remains a double positive task: from a theoretical standpoint, to analyze the precise nature of this present historical transition and of the form of social, economic and political organization into which it is developing; from a human and practical standpoint, to act in such a way as to promote those variants of the evolving

new order that permit at least that minimum of liberty and justice without which human society is degraded to merely animal existence.[22]

In what follows, we will (1) touch on Burnham's reasons for dismissing the possibility of socialism, (2) summarize his analysis of the nature of the new social form which he called managerial society, and (3) explore the manner in which he sought to act to ensure a "minimum of liberty and justice" within the new form of society.

The Impossibility of Socialism

Burnham's 1941 study *The Managerial Revolution* stands as one of the most salient critiques of Marxian socialism. After making the case that the notion of socialism's *inevitability* is an indefensible dogma, Burnham argued that "there is ample evidence from actual events that socialism is not coming." He presented what he called "sets of facts" to demonstrate this:

> (1) Since the 1917 socialist revolution in Russia, socialism (defined as a free, classless, international society) is further away than ever. The upper 11 or 12 percent of the Soviet population in 1940 received approximately 50 percent of the national income (as opposed to the top 10 percent receiving 35 percent of national income in the United States). The freedom and democracy—"never very extensive," and yet existing to "a considerable measure"—maintained under the early Bolsheviks had disappeared under Stalin, and "the tyranny of the Russian regime is the most extreme that has ever existed in human history, not excepting Hitler." The early internationalism of the Bolsheviks had given way to "an ever growing nationalism which has in recent times come to exceed anything ever present under the Czars themselves. The pseudo-internationalism, still occasionally manifested and allegedly represented by the existence of the Communist International and its parties, is simply the extension of Russian nationalism on the world arena and internationalist only in the sense that Hitler's fifth columns or the British or United States intelligence services are internationalist."
>
> (2) Socialist revolutions did not succeed anywhere else. "All the important conditions supposed to be necessary for the transition to socialism were present in the immediate post-war era. The working class, presumed carrier of socialist revolution, proved unable to take power, much less to inaugurate socialism. Yet most of the capitalist world was in shambles; the workers, as the principal part of the mass armies, had arms in their hands, and the example of Russia was before them."

(3) The abolition of capitalist private property rights in Russia "not merely did not guarantee socialism, but did not even keep power in the hands of the workers—who, today, have no power at all."

(4) "*If* socialism is to come, the working class . . . has always, and rightly, been held to be the primary social group which will have a hand in its coming." According to Marxist theory the overwhelming bulk of the population would eventually be "proletarianized" under capitalism, leaving a massive working class facing a tiny capitalist minority. This has not happened: "Small independent properties remain in many lines of endeavor; and the last seventy-five years have seen the growth of the so-called 'new middle class,' the salaried executives and engineers and managers and accountants and bureaucrats and the rest, who do not fit without distortion into either the 'capitalist' or 'worker' category." In fact, "the social position of the working class has gravely deteriorated." The rate of increase of industrial workers has slowed and in many countries changed to a decrease, the bulk of the unemployed come from the working class, and the development of technology and economic organization has resulted in a situation in which "the workers, the proletarians, could not, by themselves, run the productive machine of contemporary society." Also, militarily it has become impossible for workers to make a revolution: "Just as the new techniques of industry weaken the general position of the workers in the productive process as a whole, so do new techniques of warfare weaken the potential position of the workers in a revolutionary crisis. Street barricades and pikestaffs, even plus muskets, are not enough against tanks and bombers."

(5) Marxism, as a political movement and as an ideology committed to socialism, has collapsed. "During the past two decades Marxist parties have collapsed on a world scale. Their fate can be pretty well summed up as follows: they have all either failed socialism or abandoned it, in most cases both." Throughout Europe, the left-wing workers' movement with tens of millions of adherents, has "simply disappeared from existence in nation after nation. Wherever fascism has arisen . . . the Marxist parties have gone under, usually without even a fight for survival." Although a Marxist party took power in Russia, "within a short time it abandoned socialism, if not in words then at any rate in the effect of its actions." In countries where Social Democratic governments have been established through elections, "the reformist Marxist parties have administered the governments, and have uniformly failed to introduce socialism or make any genuine step toward socialism; in fact, have acted in a manner scarcely distinguishable from ordinary liberal capitalist parties administering

the government." The fate of those continuing to embrace the socialist goals and commitments of traditional Marxism clinches the argument: "The Trotskyist and other dissident opposition wings of Marxism have remained minute and ineffectual sects without any influence upon general political developments."[23]

All of this, Burnham added, has been paralleled by the collapse of Marxist ideology:

> The power of an ideology has several dimensions: it is shown both by the number of men that it sways and also by the extent to which it sways them— that is, whether they are moved only to verbal protestations of loyalty, or to a will to sacrifice and die under its slogans. This power is tested particularly when an ideology, in reasonably equal combat, comes up against a rival. From all these points of view the power of Marxist ideology, or rather of the strictly *socialist* aspects of Marxist ideology, has gravely declined. . . . The only branch of the Marxist ideology which still retains considerable attractive power is the Stalinist variant of Leninism, but Stalinism is no longer genuinely socialist. Just as in the case of the Stalinist party, the Marxist ideology has kept power only by ceasing to be socialist.[24]

The coherence of Burnham's critique of his own former orientation is demonstrated by the fact that its echoes reverberate through the next several decades among intellectuals of various persuasions—in sociological explorations of working-class deradicalization and the exhaustion of revolutionary ideology, in historical analyses of the Russian Revolution's decline, and in exegeses on the multiple deficiencies of Marxist thought.[25]

Managerialism

If Burnham had simply stopped here, his destructive critique would still be considered a classic of post-Marxist thought. What followed, however, is what made *The Managerial Revolution* (in the words of John Kenneth Galbraith) "an important book which changed people's minds on the nature of the modern corporation," for Burnham's argument "legitimized what in the interests of reality the schools of business were already beginning to teach." As Alfred Kazin put it, "Burnham was now reaching American business executives, scientists, and the technocratic elite with the news that they were the leaders of the future. Burnham's analysis was still functionally Marxist. History was nothing but the domination of one class over another. In

this eternal power game, it was the managers' turn to walk off with the pot."
Left-wing sociologist C. Wright Mills scoffed that Burnham was "a Marx for
Managers." Indeed, Burnham argued that there was a global transition underway from bourgeois society to managerial society. Key decision-makers
and policymakers in the increasingly complex economy (in the United States
this would include growing corporate conglomerates interpenetrating with
the growing state apparatus) "will, in fact, have achieved social dominance,
will be the ruling class in society." Yet this transition to managerial society
takes different forms in different parts of the world and assumes different
ideological expressions:

> The ideologies expressing the social role and interests and aspirations of
> the managers (like the great ideologies of the past an indispensable part
> of the struggle for power) have not yet been fully worked out, any more
> than were the bourgeois ideologies in the period of transition to capital-
> ism. They are already approximated, however, from several different but
> similar directions, by, for example: Leninism-Stalinism; fascism-nazism;
> and, at a more primitive level, by New Dealism and such less influential
> American ideologies as "technocracy."[26]

In fact, while not quite saying so, Burnham himself was engaged in a
process of helping to shape an ideological orientation that would rise above
the "primitive level" of New Dealism, one characterized by "sufficient clarity
about what is happening in the world," helping to advance the transition in
a manner consistent with "law and order," as he put it, and "in a comparatively democratic fashion." We will see that the term "democratic" was soon
jettisoned from Burnham's program—without weakening its thrust in the
slightest. To repeat how he put it in 1959, it involved acting "in such a way as
to promote those variants of the evolving social order that permit at least the
minimum of liberty and justice without which human society is degraded to
merely animal existence."[27]

Before exploring the theoretical and practical development of Burnham's perspective, it may be interesting to note the reaction to *The Managerial Revolution* of Max Nomad and Selig Perlman (both of whom had earlier
presented ideas similar to those elaborated by Burnham). Nomad put this
entry into his *Skeptic's Political Dictionary*:

> MANAGERIALISM—The theory that the office-holder and manager,
> and not the worker, is going to take over the inheritance of the doomed
> capitalist. First briefly hinted at by Michael Bakunin, later developed by

the Polish revolutionist Waclaw Machajski, subsequently presented to the American public by this writer [i.e., Nomad], it became the subject of a best-selling book by an author who gave no credit to his predecessors. He was a teacher of ethics.[28]

Burnham later responded to this, in a fashion, by mentioning (in his 1959 introduction to a reissuing of his book) that "many of the elements had been treated by Max Weber, Vilfredo Pareto, Messrs. Adolf Berle and Gardiner Means, the romantic anarchist, Makhaisky, and the eccentric ex-Trotskyite Bruno Rizzi."[29]

Perlman, on the other hand, raised a more substantive objection. In his 1928 classic *A Theory of the Labor Movement* he had argued—as Burnham now did—that the working class lacked the capacity to take political power and become a ruling class, but he insisted that Burnham "underestimates owner-ship," adding: "It is the industrial politician or businessman who decides if the technician's plan is too perfect, and so on." Perlman's criticism has been sup-ported by later scholars who argue "ownership and control are interwoven in American industry." While "it is evident that the capitalist class has been trans-formed over the past century by the rise to economic dominance of the large corporation, so that the structure of ownership or possession has become more impersonal than it used to be in the days of the individual capitalist entrepre-neur," according to T. B. Bottomore, the fact remains that "a few large share-holders are normally able to exert effective control, and that the top managers themselves are usually substantial shareholders." Perhaps a recognition of this fact inspired Burnham's 1959 reformulation: "the capitalist era, in anything like the *traditional* meaning that we derive from the eighteenth and nineteenth centuries, is drawing to a close." The irretrievable passing of *laissez-faire* capi-talism is a fact that few would deny. And Burnham, no less than Selig Perlman, had concluded that modern corporate capitalism interlocked with the modern interventionist state was a more preferable variant of managerial society than totalitarian Communism in the form of the Stalin regime in the USSR (which represented the ideal of—and issued orders to—ideologically and often mate-rially powerful Communist parties throughout the world).[30]

Critique of Democracy

Brian Crozier has expressed the view of many that "the most important of Burnham's works is *The Machiavellians* (1943). It is the key to everything he wrote subsequently." Editor of *The Economist*'s confidential weekly *Foreign Report* from 1954 to 1964, Crozier commented in a 1969 study that "*The Machiavellians* is as fresh as the day it was written: a deeply apposite textbook for our age." Ostensibly a study of the political ideas of Machiavelli, Mosca, Sorel, Michels, and Pareto, it is an exposition of political philosophy in which, in the words of one of his later admirers, Burnham sets forth his own "analytical principles so plainly—almost brutally—that it takes a stern mental effort to adjust to them; in order to grasp them you have to resist the normal temptation to import all the 'values' he has eliminated." (This admirer, Joseph Sobran, worked with him on the conservative weekly *National Review* and also recalled: "Burnham was interested in the logic of power. His method was to look at everything in the world from its power-value. This made the moralist in me squirm, especially since he regarded even morality under the same aspect. At times, with a few mild critical questions, Jim could make me feel like a sentimental, attitudinizing liberal.")[31]

"'Democracy' is usually defined in some such terms as 'self-government' or 'government by the people,'" Burnham wrote. "Historical experience forces us to conclude that democracy, in this sense, is impossible." He believed the demand for this impossible democracy was a mask for the creation of a despotic form of managerial society which in this book he termed Bonapartism. "Mature Bonapartism is a popular, a democratic despotism, founded on democratic doctrine, and, at least in its initiation, committed to democratic forms. If Bonapartism, in fact, rather than in theory, denies democracy, it does so by bringing democracy to completion. . . . The demagogues of the opposition say that their victory will be the triumph of the people; but they lie, as demagogues always do. . . . The Marxists and the democratic totalitarians claim that freedom can now be secured only by concentrating all social forces and especially economic forces in the state which, when they or their friends are running it, they identify with the people." According to Burnham, their glowing arguments and programs are simply myths employed in "a contest for control over the despotic and Bonapartist political order which they anticipate. The concentration of all social forces in the state would in fact destroy all possibility of freedom."[32]

Against this notion of *self-government* or *government by the people*, Burnham articulated another conception: "a political system in which there exists 'liberty': that is, what Mosca calls 'juridical defense,' a measure of security for the individual which protects him from the arbitrary and irresponsible exercise of personally held power." Related to this, he argued, was the importance of the right of opposition. He noted "the primary object, in practice, of all rulers is to serve their own interest, to maintain their own power and privilege. There are no exceptions. No theory, no promises, no morality, no amount of good will, no religion will restrain power. . . . Only power restrains power. That restraining power is expressed in the existence and activity of oppositions." But his conception of such an opposition had little to do with the Marxists, "totalitarian liberals," and Bonapartist demagogues whom he detested. "When an opposition exists, this means only that there is a division in the ruling class; if an 'out-elite' replaces a governing elite, this is only a change in the personnel of the rulers. The masses remain still the ruled." Yet this is in the interest of the masses, too, because it preserves at least a minimum of liberty (which is beneficial to them no less than to the elites) and generates at least some responsiveness to their needs among the contending factions of the ruling class. "Political freedom is the resultant of unresolved conflicts among various sections of the elite."[33]

Burnham perceived this balance of liberty being jeopardized by the challenge of Bonapartist advocates of impossible democracy (government by the people) and by the fuzzy-mindedness of many opinion-molders and decision-makers in the face of that challenge. He concluded *The Machiavellians* with these words:

> It is probable that civilized society will, somehow, survive. It will not survive, however, if the course of the ruling class continues in the direction of the present, and of the past forty years. In that direction there lies destruction of rulers and ruled alike. But, during the monstrous wars and revolutions of our time, there has already begun on a vast scale a purge of the ranks of the ruling class. That purge, and the recruitment of new leaders which accompanies it, may be expected to continue until they bring about a change in the present course. Though the change will never lead to the perfect society of our dreams, we may hope that it will permit human beings at least that minimum of moral dignity which alone can justify the strange accident of man's existence.[34]

Anti-Communism

Burnham continued to teach philosophy at New York University (one of his students remembered him as a "superior teacher" whose lectures were characterized by "brilliance" and an infectious "intellectual excitement"), and for a time he continued to be associated with the "non-Communist left" through his involvement with the increasingly deradicalized magazine *Partisan Review* and the right-wing Social Democratic *New Leader*. Yet his one-time cothinker Dwight Macdonald mused that Burnham now represented a new political type. Macdonald labeled it "Conservative Liberalism." This was an orientation which "holds fast to progressive *values*: materialism, irreligion, scientific method, free development of the individual," while at the same time embracing "reactionary concepts," such as "seeing human nature as evil, history as either cyclical or without pattern, democracy as unattainable under any circumstances, class rule as inevitable, and man helpless to make any major improvement in society through conscious effort."[35]

Regardless of Burnham's precise location on the political spectrum, a decided shift was taking place in his involvements in the final years of the 1940s. In 1947 his book *The Struggle for the World* appeared, whose fundamental thesis was this:

> The discovery of atomic weapons has brought about a situation in which Western Civilization, and perhaps human society in general, can continue to exist only if an absolute monopoly in the control of atomic weapons is created. This monopoly can be gained and exercised only through a World Empire, for which the historical stage had already been set prior to and independently of the discovery of atomic weapons. The attempt at World Empire will be made, and is, in fact, the objective of the Third World War, which, in its preliminary stages, has already begun.... The present candidates for leadership in the World Empire are only two: the Soviet Union and the United States.[36]

The book was enthusiastically embraced by Henry Luce, the *Time-Life-Fortune* mogul who had already proclaimed the dawn of "the American Century." As Luce's biographer notes, *The Struggle for the World* "was the first of the mailed-fist shockers to bring the American Century into martial postwar focus and to call for fast US preparation not only for war with Russia but for assertion of world leadership." Condensed in *Life* magazine, it was given big play in *Time* as well, which asserted: "Only one defense of Burnham's book can be made: it is—chillingly—true." Burnham's erstwhile comrades, on the other hand, responded bitterly. "Professor James Burnham once informed us, with a straight-faced solemnity, that for him 'socialism is a moral ideal,'" recalled Socialist Workers Party leader James P.

Cannon, in an article entitled "The Treason of the Intellectuals" (in *The Militant*, May 24, 1947). "Today, with the force-worshipping mentality of a fascist and the irresponsibility of an idiot shouting 'fire' in a crowded theater, he incites the power-drunk American imperialists to convince the world of their benevolence by hurling atomic bombs." It seemed as if Burnham's previous Trotskyism had been turned inside-out.[37]

The Struggle for the World was hardly a piece of abstract theorizing. The book originated as an internal memorandum for the Office of Strategic Services, the wartime predecessor of the Central Intelligence Agency. Burnham was employed by both, serving as a consultant to the CIA's covert-action staff from 1948 to 1952. In early 1953 he was brought in "to assist with AJAX, Kim Roosevelt's operation to save the Shah of Iran from Dr. Mossadegh and his Tudeh (Communist) supporters," recalls CIA veteran Miles Copeland. "Frank Wiesner, our boss, decided it needed 'a touch of Machiavelli' to ensure what emerged in Iran *after* the [US-sponsored] coup would make some kind of sense. *The Machiavellians* being fresh in his mind, Kim Roosevelt immediately thought of Jim Burnham, who, he said, would 'lend credibility' to the operation." Burnham was also a regular lecturer in the early 1950s at the National War College, the Air War College, the Naval War College, and the School for Advanced International Studies. *The Struggle for the World* was credited at the time (by *Life, Time, Newsweek,* and *Christian Century*) as being an influence in the development of the aggressively anti-Communist Truman Doctrine. Two sequels—*The Coming Defeat of Communism* (1950) and *Containment or Liberation?* (1952)—were sharper critiques of the "containment" strategy that had been developed by State Department officer George F. Kennan. "At the time of the Korean war," writes John P. Diggins, "his writings had considerable influence in the State Department, the Pentagon, and the Central Intelligence Agency, especially among those officials who wanted to oppose the policy of containment with a new strategy of 'liberation-rollback.'"[38]

Burnham was prepared "to put his whole career on the line to accomplish an important task," as friend Ralph de Toledano put it. An example from 1950 or 1951 involved Burnham's effort, with Toledano and Karl Hess (both *Newsweek* journalists), to reach out "to New York mobster Frank Costello, who out of patriotism, they hoped, might supply them with professional help." Costello had, after all, responded to a similar appeal from Cardinal Francis Spellman in helping fight Communists in Italy. Burnham's target involved the US Communist Party, allegedly receiving material aid from the USSR. While this new scheme didn't work out, Toledano believed Burnham was involved in similar efforts, based on "little hints in conversation that didn't quite light up a dark corner."[39]

In 1950 Burnham played a central role in helping organize—with an international array of anti-Communists that included Sidney Hook, Arthur Schlesinger Jr., Melvin J. Lasky, Franz Borkenau, Arthur Koestler, Ignazio Silone, Stephen Spender, and other rightward-shifting leftists—the Congress for Cultural Freedom. Christopher Lasch has commented that "no gathering of the congress was complete" without Burnham, who undoubtedly was aware that this international anti-Communist alliance of moderate socialist, liberal, and ex-leftist intellectuals, with all of its international gatherings and array of publications, depended on secret funding from the Central Intelligence Agency. At the founding conference, Borkenau expressed views coinciding with those of Burnham and many others (summarized by Hugh Trevor-Roper for the *Manchester Guardian*), "that he was a convert from communism and proud of it; that past guilt must be atoned for; that the ex-Communists alone understood communism and the means of resisting it; that communism could only mean perpetual war and civil war; and that it must be destroyed at once by uncompromising frontal attack." In 1951, a US affiliate, the American Committee for Cultural Freedom was formed, by Burnham in conjunction with some of the most prominent US intellectuals, which—as Lasch has put it—"represented a coalition of liberals and reactionaries who shared a conspiratorial view of communism and who agreed, moreover, that the communist conspiracy had spread through practically every level of American society."[40]

It was in this period that Burnham effected his final break with the "non-Communist left" and with modern liberalism. As early as 1948, he had appeared as a friendly expert witness on Communism before the House Committee on Un-American Activities, urging that the US Communist Party be outlawed, although commenting: "It is unfortunate that Communism is referred to as the 'left wing.' It is actually the most 'right wing.'" Burnham's unequivocal defense of anti-Communist legislation and Congressional investigations of "un-American" activities in general (advanced most elaborately in his 1954 book *The Web of Subversion*) was capped by his defense of Senator Joseph McCarthy in particular. He angrily resigned from *Partisan Review* and also helped initiate a heated controversy in the

American Committee for Cultural Freedom on this issue. There is also indication that Burnham's defense of McCarthy—at a time when the Senator from Wisconsin was attacking the US State Department and the Central Intelligence Agency for allegedly harboring "Communists"—resulted in his dismissal from the CIA.[41]

He went further and testified against the Independent Socialist League (which was Max Shachtman's renamed Workers Party that Burnham had helped found in 1940) when it sought to get itself removed from the Attorney-General's "subversive list." Shachtman later recalled: "I must say it was a shock. . . . We just didn't expect a man of his type, this suave, above-the-battle, academic, political man to descend to this sewage of the government's attempt to gag and outlaw a tiny little left-wing propagandist society." But, of course, Burnham was hardly "above the battle." He had broken fundamentally with his left-wing past (burning all of his correspondence with Trotsky in an incinerator behind his apartment) in order to commit himself totally to the US "struggle for the world." Ironically, Shachtman himself and a section of his followers would drift far enough to the political right by the 1960s and '70s to become allies in this struggle— without, however, shedding at least some elements of their earlier socialist outlook. One participant-observer later commented that "their world-view was consistent with George Orwell's *1984*, Hannah Arendt's *Origins of Totalitarianism*, or James Burnham's *Managerial Revolution*."[42] Nonetheless, the dramatic change in his political trajectory stunned many as the 1940s shaded into the 1950s.

Burnham's metamorphosis was described, while obviously still in progress, in his own 1948 comments to André Malraux. In discussing "the broad movement of American intellectuals away from Communism," he made an astonishing admission: "No doubt the Marxists are right, in part, when they scornfully say this is a response to the mounting 'imperialist' pressures. But," he added, "it is also deeper than that." The truths which he felt he had identified in *The Managerial Revolution* and *The Machiavellians* were no less essential for explaining the intellectual shift. Nor was Burnham sure that his left-wing commitments had led him down a blind alley. "In spite of my present rejection of Communism," he said, "a rejection which I believe to be final and—one might say—absolute, I nevertheless often feel that *the experience of Communism* may have been a necessary phase in the moral development of our generation." The most effective anti-Communists might be the ex-Communists; one cannot get at certain elemental aspects of the truth of the epoch, he suggested, without having "lived *through* Communism." And yet he also confessed to a profound self-doubt: that "perhaps like the smug boast of a reformed drunk, this is a self-protective illusion of those of us who have ourselves been through Communism." Those on the political Right may have been, all along, the more sober analysts: "If our eyes remain bleary, it may be that the sights can be accurately taken only by those who, by nature or luck or even moral coarseness, were immune to the disease."[43] Elsewhere in his discussion with Malraux, he offered a disturbing analogy meant to illustrate the post-War situation, but which was just as much autobiographical:

> I have been reminded of a documentary movie that I saw recently. It showed a strange species of crab at the point in its development when it must totally rid itself of its old shell in order to grow the new shell without which it cannot live. The process was painful in the extreme, tortuous, slow, and in fact grotesque. The old shell was dead, but it clung nevertheless to the living flesh at a thousand points. Finally, when at last the attachments were broken, there came the most dangerous moment of all, when the old armor was gone and the new not yet gained, and the crab stood alone, exposed to all its enemies on the sea floor.[44]

When Burnham had finally gained his own "new armor" after a painful and lonely period of crisis, he was aligned with those who had all along been immune to the disease of believing in a socialist future. Yet his new comrades, far from mocking Burnham for his earlier illusions, embraced him as one of their most clear-sighted theorists.

Conservative Master-Thinker

In 1955 Burnham joined with William F. Buckley Jr. and a varied assortment of right-wing anti-Communists (traditionalists, libertarians and hardened ex-leftists) to establish the conservative weekly *National Review*. "Beyond any question," Buckley later wrote, "he has been the dominant influence of this journal." Former *National Review* staffer Garry Wills remembers: "Only Burnham, of those involved day to day in the magazine's direction, was secure enough not to challenge Bill's authority. But, of course, Burnham most completely shared Bill's concept of the journal's mission. Burnham, the student of power, saw *National Review* as a particular pressure point meant to have some real impact on the over-all strategic stance of America." More was involved here than simply a meeting of the minds between Buckley and Burnham. The former Trotskyist was a profound influence on the younger man, who wrote to him in 1978: "With the death of my father, no one else came near to occupying the same role in my life as you have done: as advisor, mentor, friend, companion."[45]

Burnham's general orientation in this last phase of his career is laid out in his incisive 1964 work, *The Suicide of the West*. One critic later commented that this leftist-turned-rightist "attacked the idea of a collectivist society with the weapons of nineteenth century liberalism," but this misses the power of Burnham's perspective, which goes well beyond the frontiers of all liberal ideology. "Liberalism is not equipped," he argued, "to meet and overcome the actual challenges confronting Western civilization in our time." He identified what he considered the three most crucial challenges: "first, the jungle now spreading within our own society, in particular in our great cities; second, the explosive population growth and political activization within the world's backward areas, principally the equatorial and subequatorial latitudes occupied by non-white masses; third, the drive of the communist enterprise for a monopoly of world power." He insisted that "liberalism cannot either see or deal with the domestic jungle and the backward regions—the two challenges are closely similar. Liberalism is unfitted by its rationalistic optimism, its permissiveness, its egalitarianism and democratism, and by its [feelings of] guilt." What's more, "the challenge of communism is from the Left; and all the major challenges that now bear crucially on survival come from the Left. But liberalism . . . is unable to conduct an intelligent, firm and sustained struggle against the Left. Liberalism can function effectively only against the Right." In his elaboration of this point, we can find echoes from his earlier writings:

> The secular, historically optimistic, reformist, welfare-statish, even plebiscatory aspects of liberalism are all present in communism. . . . What communism does is to carry the liberal principles to their logical and practical extreme: the secularism; the rejection of tradition and custom; the stress on science; the confidence in the possibility of molding human beings; the determination to reform all established institutions; the goal of wiping out *all* social distinctions; the internationalism; the belief in welfare state carried to its ultimate form in the totalitarian state. The liberal's arm cannot strike with consistent firmness against communism, either domestically or internationally, because the liberal dimly feels that in doing so he would be somehow wounding himself.[46]

This was the basic orientation of *National Review*. Although it was seldom stated so clearly, so was Burnham's uncompromisingly antidemocratic elitism. The poet Carl Sandburg's glowing hymn of the 1930s *The People, Yes* seemed as absurd to him as various intellectuals' later despair over the alleged limitations of "the American people." As he explained in a 1975 column in *National Review*, "it does not make much sense to blame (or to praise) 'the people' as an undifferentiated entity. 'A people' becomes historically significant through its articulation into institutions and its expression through leaders and an elite." Similarly, Burnham's tough-minded defense of the United States as an imperial power in the global political economy was essential to the magazine's orientation. As he explained in 1971:

> Now it is obvious, as well as confirmed by historical experience, that carrying out the imperial responsibilities requires certain characteristics in the imperial citizens, or at least in the leading strata; confidence in both their rights and their ability to perform the imperial task; resoluteness; perseverance; a willingness to assure the strength—that is, the military force—to fulfill the task; and finally (it must be added) a willingness to kill people, now and then, without collapsing into a paroxysm of guilt.[47]

In fact, Burnham's regular column in *National Review* was entitled "The Third World War" (renamed "The Protracted Conflict" a few years later), and his introduction to a 1967 collection of those columns, *The War We Are In*, stressed that "one thing the Cold War has not been is 'cold.' From the very beginning . . . there have been fighting and bloodshed." That "there should be shooting and killing" in this war, he mused, was hardly a distinctive quality of the Cold War. What was distinctive was "its multi-dimensional, indeed omni-dimensional nature." Burnham outlined the realities of the Cold War in "the last decade and the next" with his usual lucidity: "It is conducted, through shifting emphases, along every social dimension: economic, political, cultural, racial, psychological, religious as well as military; and the military dimension comprises every sort of guerrilla, terrorist, paramilitary, partisan and irregular combat as well as fighting by conventional forces." This is, of course, a policy recommendation as well as a description. In the 1970s, he also articulated what would become a touchstone of later US policy: the need to distinguish between "authoritarian" and "totalitarian" regimes.[48]

Burnham's previous Marxism is clearly linked to the nature of his anti-Communism. The "omni-dimensional" nature of the Cold War, he explained, was necessitated by the comprehensive nature of the Marxist critique of capitalism: "Existing non-communist civilization expresses essentially the exploitation and corruption of class society; it cannot be reformed, but must be overthrown and destroyed, so that the new communist man can build in its place the new classless communist society." His break from the Marxist analytical method also shaped his critique of liberal foreign policy perspectives, which were based on the notion of "belly-communism" (i.e., "since bad economic conditions breed communism ... we will be able to prevent communism or eliminate it by improving the economic conditions"). Burnham argued that this was a false notion deduced from faulty ideology: "from a vague economic determinism inherited both from classic laissez-faire doctrine and from the 'vulgar Marxism' that entered the American thought stream through Lincoln Steffens, Charles Beard, Vernon Louis Parrington and Gustavus Myers." In fact, "the primary active cause of communism is communists," and the only way "to stop communism or get rid of it" would be by defeating communists throughout the world—not "by 'avoiding confrontation' abroad and granting them freedom to operate at home." Burnham's embrace of the systematic elitism of "the Machiavellians" was just as crucial a factor in his latter-day Cold War orientation: "The primary passive cause, or condition, for the advance of communism—and of subversive revolution more generally—is the failure of the governing elite to supply firm leadership and a clear, coherent policy, the failure to give the masses the impression that the elite knows where it is going and is prepared to take the necessary steps to get there."[49]

The orientation Burnham articulated helped provide an ideological focus long lacking for US conservatives. "America—a conservative country without any conservative ideology—appears before the world a naked and arbitrary power," C. Wright Mills had commented in 1954, and as late as 1962, Mills could still assert: "The ideological and intellectual functions performed by nineteenth-century conservatism are now usually performed by liberalism. In fact, there is no half-way coherent conservatism that is not a variety of liberalism, a restatement of Edmund Burke, or mere eccentricity." Even the early *National Review* struck many as not providing a coherent ideology, reflecting instead "a crude patch-work of special interests," in the words of Dwight Macdonald, who added: "To be simply anti-liberal is not to be a conservative." Yet as time passed, the influence of Burnham became increasingly pronounced in the magazine, as did its intellectual and political impact.[50]

Intellectual historian George Nash has suggested that "if *National Review* (or something like it) had not been founded, there would probably have been no cohesive intellectual force on the Right in the 1960s and 1970s." This is a particularly decisive achievement, for as Nash notes: "In 1945 'conservatism' was not a popular word in America, and its spokesmen were without much influence in their native land. A generation later these once isolated voices had become a chorus, a significant intellectual and political movement which had an opportunity to shape the nation's destiny." Their influence was reflected at a 1980 banquet for *National Review* attended by six-hundred luminaries, including foreign policy architect Henry Kissinger and CIA director William Casey, as well as such prominent politicians as New York Mayor Ed Koch and Senator Alfonse D'Amato. The banquet celebrated the Presidential victory of Ronald Reagan, which was seen as the culmination of the conservative triumph."[51]

Burnham was now unable to savor the triumph, however, because in late 1978 he had been incapacitated by a stroke. Nonetheless, in 1983 President Reagan awarded Burnham the Presidential Medal of Freedom, the nation's highest civilian honor. The accompanying citation read: "As a scholar, writer, historian and philosopher, James Burnham has profoundly affected the way America views itself and the world. Since the 1930s, Mr. Burnham has shaped the thinking of world leaders. His observations have changed society and his writings have become guiding lights in mankind's quest for truth. Freedom, reason and decency have had few greater champions in this century than James Burnham." Burnham died in 1987, only a few years before the close of the Cold War which his admirers felt had been "won" through the application of his strategic perspectives.[52]

Indeed, the "new world order" which US policymakers seek to consolidate is that envisioned by this ex-revolutionary turned conservative master-thinker, which prioritizes the security of privileged elites. While many liberals and conservatives alike have proclaimed "the West's" victory in the Cold War to be a victory for "democracy," one is entitled to wonder whether they share Burnham's view that our "democratic" elitism is all well and good, but that genuine democracy (or "democratism"—rule by the people) is neither possible nor desirable, being inconsistent with human dynamics, corporate realities, and imperial responsibilities.

Comments of *National Review* associates in defense of their mentor, shortly after he died, help to illuminate aspects of his intellectual contribution no less than his personality. More than one took offense at the comments of Irving Howe, the editor of the moderate socialist journal *Dissent* (and an ex-comrade from Trotskyist days), who had once written that Burnham "has always been a cold-blooded snob, first as a Trotskyist, then as a herald of the 'managerial revolution,' and lately as geopolitical strategist in charge of World War III for the *National Review.*" Jeffrey Hart responded tartly that "nothing could be further from the truth. In fact, on his vacations, Burnham liked to take long automobile trips with Marcia [his wife], both viscerally and intellectually loving the ordinary life of the United States, fascinated by such things as families living in new sleep-in vehicles, and finding surprise and beauty in places such as Houston and Tucson."[53]

C. H. Simonds also recalled:

> Those in the know awaited with particular excitement his return from the periodic rambles to the hinterlands he took with Marcia, soaking up his country, conversing with mandarins and mechanics, and—always—observing and analyzing. His meditations on matters great (blue-collar conservatism in the heartland—he was the first to notice it) and small (the clothesline as a vanishing indicator of status) freshened the sometimes-hermetic atmosphere of East 35th Street [where the *National Review* offices were located].

Linda Bridges added that "you knew Jim had put in his time with the workers in his Trotskyist days."[54]

And yet there were some erstwhile comrades who questioned the quality of this "time with the workers." Morris Lewit, an aging working-class Trotskyist, later recalled a discussion which took place when James P. Cannon and he visited Burnham's pleasant country home in Connecticut during the 1930s:

> Burnham said, "Well the workers have no prejudices against Blacks." So I said, "No, there are prejudices against Blacks." For him it was a revelation. He idealized the working class. An intellectual, you know, who wanted to have a socialist revolution. I disappointed him . . . He was involved in abstractions and knew nothing about the working class. That you could see. And as a consequence he idealized [the working class], and couldn't stand the reality of it. Comes the revolution it will be a different working class, but it will have to go through struggles and learn something. . . . He was a naive intellectual, [who] could write abstract articles. . . . He entered without any experience in life. No wonder he's ended up all the way on the right.[55]

That Burnham had been naive about the actually existing working class during his Trotskyist days, of course, would obviously be less upsetting to his right-wing associates than the accusation that he was a "cold-blooded snob."

Priscilla Buckley acknowledged that Burnham's "cool exterior . . . led many to believe that he was cold." But she insisted: "There was nothing cool in the Jim Burnham I knew." It is possible, of course, that their similar social backgrounds contributed to the flourishing of an obviously warm friendship. It is certainly the case, in the last decades of his life, that he felt none of the agonizing inner conflicts which had torn him when he was part of the Socialist Workers Party. "That he stuck with *National Review* to the end of his life," notes Linda Bridges, "may say that he finally had found the appropriate means to his end."[56]

Recalling tensions between Burnham and another *National Review* editor Frank Meyer, Garry Wills remembered: "When Frank was feeling particularly exercised over some policy of Burnham's, he would take off the shelf Orwell's *Shooting an Elephant* and read to visitors its attack on Burnham's 'power worship.'" Joseph Sobran, however, believes that Orwell was mistaken "when he accused Burnham of worshipping power. Jim didn't worship it; he did unsentimentally respect it, and he came to terms with it in his own way, without compromising his honor. Later, Orwell more perceptively saluted Jim's vision and courage, and made the geopolitics of Jim's early books the premise of *1984*."[57]

Yet this may be a more dubious honor than Burnham's defender suspects. Literary critic Paul Siegel has suggested that George Orwell did more than use Burnham's geopolitics in his antitotalitarian novel *1984*. The forbidden theoretical work that Orwell's hero Winston Smith begins to read—often taken to be modeled after Trotsky's *Revolution Betrayed*—is thematically and stylistically much closer to Burnham's own *Managerial Revolution*. And the sinister Inner-Party man in the novel, O'Brien, "in his adoration of power, in his unquestioning acceptance of power," is, Siegel suggests, modeled on Burnham himself! "For to Orwell the oppressor is always the same, whatever the oppressive society calls itself." As Orwell put it: "The real question is not whether the people who wipe their boots on us during the next fifty years are to be called managers, bureaucrats, or politicians: the question is whether capitalism, now obviously doomed, is to give way to oligarchy or to true democracy."[58]

Chapter Ten

DENNIS BRUTUS

Poet as Revolutionary (1924–2009)

Losing Dennis, for many of us, is like losing a member of our family.[1] Activists all around the world know him and have loved him as a wonderful poet, seemingly tireless activist, comrade, and friend. He was incredibly important for me—as I believe he must have been for many—because he took various individuals that he met very seriously, validating them, encouraging them to realize the potential he could see in them, in some cases as poets and cultural warriors, in some cases as radical activists and revolutionaries.

This dear friend has left behind the riches of his poetry, particularly well represented in the two most recent volumes of his work. One is a very beautiful collection of poetry, plus photographs and an interview, *Leafdrift*. The second, *Poetry and Protest: A Dennis Brutus Reader*, is a more ambitious compilation—an important source not only for all those wanting information about earlier antiracist and global justice struggles and the South African freedom movement in particular, but also for all those who will draw inspiration from Dennis's efforts in order to participate effectively in future struggles.[2]

Dennis Brutus became politically active in South Africa in part through a cluster of revolutionary socialists influenced by the ideas of Leon Trotsky, but he later moved—in part through its development and promotion of the historic "Freedom Charter"—into the orbit of the more sizeable African National Congress (ANC), associating with the militants of the South African Communist Party (SACP) who were so influential in its ranks. Arrested in 1963, then shot while attempting to escape, he survived to break rocks with

Nelson Mandela and other imprisoned revolutionaries on the notorious Robben Island. Released in 1965, he was able to leave South Africa a year later—becoming prominent first in Britain and then in the United States in international antiapartheid efforts.

Many of us in the United States first became aware of Dennis Brutus in the 1970s, as an eloquent spokesman in exile against the system of racial separation and white domination afflicting his homeland. Not only a fine poet, Brutus was also a sophisticated organizer—helping to put together and lead a powerful movement (SANROC—South African Non-Racial Olympic Committee) to have the all-white teams of the apartheid regime excluded from the Olympic Games.

He explained in verse and prose the necessity of opposing the regime and the system that had—for example—gunned down peacefully protesting men, women, and children in Sharpeville in 1960:

What is important
about Sharpeville
is not that seventy died:
nor even that they were shot in the back
retreating, unarmed, defenseless
and certainly not
the heavy caliber slug
that tore through a mother's back
and ripped through the child in her arms
killing it
Remember Sharpeville
bullet-in-the-back day
Because it epitomized oppression
and the nature of society
more clearly than anything else;
it was the classic event
Nowhere is racial dominance
more clearly defined
nowhere the will to oppress
more clearly demonstrated
what the world whispers
apartheid with snarling guns

the blood lust after
South Africa spills in the dust
Remember Sharpeville
Remember bullet-in-the-back day
And remember the unquenchable will for freedom
Remember the dead
and be glad[3]

He told us about the meaning of the Soweto student uprising of 1976:

Understandably
there are many versions
of what really happened;
reporters of course, their stories,
but, better stories of students
those who were there just then
when it happened;
they say they were confused,
that they were scared of dying,
that there was so much happening:
but one, when I pressed him, tried,
haltingly, with much uncertainty:
"How many?" I demanded, "at least guess!"
but he backed away from figures
claimed he could not, would not guess
then began, again, haltingly
(also, partly, trying to explain)
why he could not say with certainty
how many students were killed in Soweto
on that June sixteenth day:
"When they had filled that church floor
with corpses
when they had filled all classrooms
with corpses
they laid corpses outside along fences
or grassy verges
or by pavements, sidewalks, street edges:

each corpse had on its forehead
a strip of bandaid imprinted with a number
those numbers were indistinct:
there were four numbers
it was hard to say what they were
but there were four numbers"
that is what he could say for certain
He was Sietsie Mashanini—
a student who escaped from Soweto
in Soweto on June 16, 1976
it was on that day Hector Peterson died
(13-year old first one shot his image
that is carried on posters)
on June 16
in Soweto
Soweto[4]

He told us about the vision of a new South Africa:

This is a land
so vibrant and alive
that laughter will come bursting through
as imperious as the sun
and the spirit will survive
Resilient as the soil.[5]

When conservatism's shining "champion of freedom" and "great com-municator" Ronald Reagan became president of the United States, Dennis Brutus became a cause célèbre as the US government—in deference to its white-racist and staunchly anti-Communist ally on the African continent—sought to deport the activist back to a South African prison. More than once, with many others, I had the opportunity to hear him explain his case, focus-ing on the realities of the brutal apartheid system. And many of us sometimes had an opportunity to linger over the poignancy of his poetic works. I loved listening to him, always, whether he was reading poems or giving talks. And he was obviously a revolutionary militant, as he explained in 1975:

I am a rebel and freedom is my cause:
Many of you have fought similar struggles
therefore you must join my cause:
My cause is a dream of freedom
and you must help me make my dream reality:
For why should I not dream and hope?
Let us work together that my dream may be fulfilled
that I may return with my people out of exile
to live in one democracy in peace.
Is not my dream a noble one
worthy to stand beside freedom struggles everywhere?[6]

Dennis won his battle against the Reagan administration, and in the wake of that victory he accepted an offer to be the chairperson of the Department of Africana Studies at the University of Pittsburgh in 1985. It was astonishing to me that this great spokesman for freedom was coming to live in my hometown.

Some of us who were "normal" day-to-day activists initially felt some reticence about approaching such an imposing presence—but Dennis, a seasoned activist himself, had no taste for holding aloof from the likes of us, rubbing elbows with increasing numbers of us at meetings, picket lines, rallies, and more.

Dennis did not hide his misgivings over compromises with the system of the global capitalism that so many of his ANC comrades, once partisans of socialism, were now making as the apartheid regime was collapsing and they themselves were assuming the reins of power.[7] As he put it in an angry poem written at 3:05 a.m. in 2000:

Forgive me, comrades
if I say something apolitical
and shamefully emotional
but in the dark of night
it is as if my heart is clutched
by a giant iron hand:
"Treachery, treachery" I cry out
thinking of you, comrades
and how you have betrayed
the things we suffered for.[8]

While some of his erstwhile comrades, now with government portfolio, testily mocked him as "Dennis the Menace" and accused him of being an "outsider," Dennis's many years on the Left helped him to place into perspective the disappointments associated with the conservative shift in ANC policy—which constituted a post–Cold War capitulation to the pressures from the multinational corporations and governmental superpowers dominating the global capitalist economy. It was the new variant of what such Marxists of the past as Lenin and Luxemburg had analyzed as imperialism, and which in its new form has been hailed as "globalization."

He turned his energies to help build "a globalization from below" of protest and struggle. Globalization from above "adds up to a systematic determination to concentrate power and wealth in the hands of a minority and to reduce the rest of us to beggars and even superfluous people because they no longer need us," he wrote in the forward to my book *Marx, Lenin, and the Revolutionary Experience*, but his indignation was tempered because "things are lively these days, and I continue my cautious optimism," pleased with the "increasing number of activists, especially young activists, making their voices heard" in protests around the world. He added: "A better world is possible, but it can be brought into existence only through an intensification of our efforts and a systematic evolution from protest to resistance, and from resistance to radical social change that will give masses of people the possibility of a decent life and control over their own situations. In order to struggle in the present for a better future, we need to comprehend the efforts and the lessons of the past." Specifically, he urged that "thoughts of the giants of the past—whether Karl Marx or Rosa Luxemburg or Antonio Gramsci—[be] connected with . . . [global justice] actions of Seattle, Prague, Washington, and Genoa."[9]

Just as he had been a leading activist in the struggle against apartheid, he became known to millions worldwide in the global justice movement. "His passion for justice in our native African continent has now long extended to the whole world where the abyss between rich and poor countries grows instead of closing," commented his friend Nadine Gordimer. "Dennis's passion is the real face of globalization."[10]

Dennis was incredibly accessible to a broad range of us who were activists in Pittsburgh, and relationships developed that had meaning for all concerned. He spoke at socialist forums that I helped to organize in Pittsburgh, and he gave me incredibly meaningful encouragement as I sought to develop a body of Marxist writings that would be helpful to activists of today and tomorrow—all the while urging me and others to do this in a way that was open, nondogmatic, and framed in terms to which those unfamiliar with left-wing jargon could connect.

In the wake of the World Social Forum in Porto Alegre, Brazil, to which he had journeyed in 2002, Dennis initiated the organization of an ongoing Pittsburgh Social Forum in which many of us became involved for a couple of years, and some of us followed him to future World Social Forums in Brazil and India.

One of the striking features in the way he communicated—in his political talks at various events—was his consistent avoidance of what I have seen less effective left-wing speakers do, and have sometimes done myself: try to fit the entire revolution into one presentation (which means unloosing an avalanche of quickly made points that inundate the listeners and make it impossible for them to absorb, let alone reflect on, what is being said).

In a typical Dennis Brutus talk, he would speak slowly, clearly, and eloquently, letting you know at the very beginning that there were three or four specific points he wished to make, telling you what they are at the beginning of his comments. Then he would visit each point in turn, using a memorable example, image, statistic, with spare but telling rhetoric. This coincides with aspects of his poetry. As he explains in his interview with Lamont Steptoe: "So you can see I'm shooting for the minimum. Always as compact as I can make it."[11]

There is an Asian influence here, which he discussed in an earlier collection, *China Poems*:

> The trick is to say little (the nearer to nothing, the better) and to suggest much—as much as possible. The weight of meaning hovers around the words (which should be as flat as possible) or is brought by the reader/hearer. Non-emotive, near neutral sounds should generate unlimited resonances in the mind; the delight is in the tight-rope balance between nothing and everything possible, between saying very little and implying a great deal.[12]

An illustration from that volume:

Not in my hands
is the clay
of my life[13]

There were other qualities of this man that I was able to see during an unfortunate experience. He had invited me to participate with him in a conference on Latin America and revolutionary struggles sponsored by Larry Robin, of Robins Bookstore in Philadelphia—but when I got there, I found he had just thrown out his back and was in agony.

A wheelchair was commandeered, and I pushed him along Philadelphia sidewalks to a hospital and then to the office of a doctor. At various points, only slightly under his breath, there were mutterings that turned out to be poetry—elements of poems that he was playing with, almost like breathing.

Nor would he tolerate being away from the conference for very long, and I wheeled him into a session—Dennis looking quite disheveled, still in pain, but insistent on being there—and it seemed to me then that revolutionary politics, too, was almost like breathing to him.

When I returned with him to Pittsburgh and insisted on cleaning his apartment for him while he was laid up, I gathered together—to toss into a big garbage bag—various scraps of paper, old envelopes, napkins, among pizza boxes in the kitchen, only to discover with horror what Lamont Steptoe comments on in his interview: "Dennis, you write on scraps of paper, envelopes, napkins."[14] I had come close to destroying many unpublished poems by an internationally renowned poet! I humbly piled the scraps onto the corner of the table.

The poems and the politics were inseparable from his daily life, and he asked me to attend a poetry reading on his behalf, sponsored by the Carnegie Library, on the struggles against censorship. The poems he selected were from a wonderful little booklet of his poems (this one edited by Gil Ott) from Lamont Steptoe's publishing project, *Airs and Tributes*, most of which cannot be found in the two recently published volumes. He made selections, patiently explained the poems to me so that I could explain them to the audience, and sent me on my way. The one I loved the best was "For Ruth First," the heroic South African Communist (portrayed by Barbara Hershey in the fine film "A World Apart," which among other things depicts the imprisonment she described in her book *117 Days*). Dennis knew Ruth First and her husband Joe Slovo well and once described to me an argument between the three of them in which she and he were aligned in a criticism of the 1956 Soviet invasion of Hungary in the face of Slovo's intransigent defense. (Dennis noted that Slovo mellowed in later years.)[15] His friend Ruth First was assassinated in 1982 by letter bomb while in Mozambique, sent courtesy of the racist apartheid regime:

They would come again
you wrote
you knew
but what they did not know
was that your spirit would live on
in thousands willing to fight for freedom
in thousands willing to die for freedom
that you might be gone
but that you would come again.
They would come again
you wrote
because you knew
they could not rest
and would not let you rest
—dear restless spirit—
until, finally, shattered
in a bomb-wrecked office in Maputo
your bloody corpse rested.[16]

Dennis's own "dear restless spirit" endured, although twenty-seven years later he was brought down by cancer, after having returned to his African homeland in 2006–2007. Even in his final days, surrounded by friends and family, hoping perhaps to get to Copenhagen to protest against capitalist-generated global warming, agitating against Israeli injustices against the Palestinians, calling for reparations from the big corporations implicated in apartheid and slavery, continuing to rail against the elitist and profiteering globalization from above, beckoning people to the struggle, pressing for a socialist future in which the free development of each would be the condition for the free development of all, and generously sharing his wonderful poems.

An interviewer once asked him, "How would you like history to remember you?" Dennis answered: "I don't care." He explained to me, later, that what counts for him are not nostalgic memories that romanticize who he is, but rather the struggles of today and tomorrow, "the thousands willing to fight for freedom," that can make a difference in the lives of those who remain.

South African Archbishop Desmond Tutu once asserted (in comments on the back cover of *Poetry and Protest*) that the antiapartheid struggle "had

none more articulate and with all the credibility and integrity so indispensable than Dennis Brutus to plead our cause." This could be said also of his
role in the struggle for global justice—except that the notion of "pleading"
seems off. Perhaps it is more accurate to say that, now as before, he eggs us
on, helps us understand more deeply, encourages us to connect with each
other, and to move forward.

Chapter Eleven

REVOLUTIONARY PATIENCE

Daniel Bensaïd

Daniel Bensaïd (1946–2010) was one of the most respected theorists to emerge from the 1960s radicals of Western Europe. Always inclined to think "outside the box," waving aside venerable dogmas and shrugging off standard formulations, he found fresh ways, energized with the aura of unorthodoxy, to express and apply truths from the revolutionary Marxist tradition. Sometimes his creativity could provide insights that opened fruitful pathways of thought and action. "We were young people in a hurry, as is inevitably the case," he writes near the start of his memoir, *An Impatient Life*.[1] "As if we had to make up for the wasted time of the 'century of extremes,' as if we were afraid of missing our appointments, in politics and in love." In the end, "we had to learn 'the art of waiting,'" he muses, yet the author remains an unbowed militant: "We have sometimes deceived ourselves, perhaps even often, and on many things. But at least we did not deceive ourselves about either the struggle or the choice of enemy" (18–19, 10). This substantial volume is a parting gift, sharing memories of what he had seen and done, offering a piece of his mind, exploring the meaning of it all—as befits the image, snapped a few years before his premature death, of the gaunt, frail man whose keen intelligence shines out from his now-bespectacled eyes.

Yet a photograph from 1948 reveals an adorable two-year-old with long curly hair toddling toward us. We see a boy at ages five, nine, and fourteen, with bright and impish eyes, destined to appear (in half a dozen photos from the 1970s) as a buoyant, handsome, charismatic activist of the famed "Generation of 1968." Daniel was centrally involved in the revolutionary student-worker upsurge that shook France and almost brought down the government of Charles De Gaulle.[2] Out of this experience was born the militant Ligue Communiste Révolutionnaire (LCR), which powerfully impacted the global far-Left and became a central component of the Fourth International (a network of comparatively small revolutionary socialist parties and groups founded by Leon Trotsky and other dissident-Communists over three decades before).[3] In the late 1960s and early 1970s, Bensaïd and his comrades were intimately connected with currents in Latin America, utilizing the perspectives of Che Guevara and other revolutionary warriors and generating some of his most searching reflections.[4]

The exciting years of upsurge gave way to disaster, disappointment, defeat. It was during this in-between period that I fleetingly met Bensaïd, at a 1990 World Congress and at a 1991 meeting of the International Executive Committee of the Fourth International, as I represented the smallest one of three US Trotskyist fragments identifying with this "world party of socialist revolution." It was obvious that his experience was incomparably richer than mine, and that he had earned profound respect from the other comrades who, with him, made up the inner circle of the Fourth International's leadership.

A friend who read this book before I did warned that Bensaïd was quite a name-dropper, and there are certainly scores of names that flow from these pages. But I came upon his description of the cluster of comrades from the 1980s whose labors maintained "the bonsai Comintern" that was the Fourth International: a dozen names of people—many now dead—whose strengths and weaknesses and life-energy had been essential to the world movement to which I was committed. I knew these people, they were important to me, and I felt grateful that their names with brief descriptions are shared with the readers of this book.

History is the lives of innumerable people, not abstractions, and the history of our revolutionary socialist movement is nothing without the amazing number of names (with all-too-brief descriptions) that Bensaïd weaves into his narrative. Distinctive features of this volume include (with a list of abbreviations) twelve pages of descriptions of left-wing organizations, plus extensive footnotes providing information on the dozens upon dozens of activists he mentions—together with the main narrative, making this an essential source on the international Left and on world Trotskyism.

Youth Radicalization

Daniel was born into a working-class family that moved from Algeria to France shortly before his birth—the father a Sephardic Jew, the Gallic mother inclined to self-identify as Jewish. They saved enough money to start a bistro with a predominantly left-wing working-class clientele. Their clever and inquisitive son ascended into the ranks of university students while also, quite naturally, drifting into the youth group of the French Communist Party. But like many of his comrades of the time (influenced by Trotskyists doing "deep-entry" work in the group), partly under the impact of Algeria's anticolonial revolution and the tepid response to this by the French Communists, he came to the conclusion that it would be wrong to "confuse the revolutionary project with Stalinism."

Rejecting the intellectual "ravages of a positivist and authoritarian Marxism" (almost in the same breath he characterizes it as "a glacial Marxism without style or passion"), they turned to heretical texts—Herbert Marcuse, Wilhelm Reich, Lucien Goldmann, Jean-Paul Sartre, Simone de Beauvoir, Frantz Fanon, Che Guevara, Daniel Guerin, Henri Lefebvre, Ernest Mandel. Bensaïd adds that for him and many of the young radicals, too, "Lenin was all the rage" (79, 80, 81), but this was a Lenin having little in common with the immense leaden statues worshiped by older, disapproving Communist Party comrades. The intellectual rebellion quickly culminated in mass expulsions from the mainstream Communist movement, with many of the young rebels (the spirited Bensaïd no less than others) gradually recruiting themselves to a maverick variant of Trotskyism.

This historical moment was one of a youth radicalization sweeping through Europe and other continents. In France, the young Trotskyists-in-the-making were caught up in the swirl—along with anarchists and Maoists and activists without clear labels—of students pushing for radical educational reforms and sexual freedom. The wondrous days of May 1968 saw huge demonstrations, endless meetings, student strikes and school occupations. Struggles for educational transformation blended into a more general antiauthoritarianism, opposition to imperialist wars, romantic identification with "third world" insurgencies, and the rights of the working class. This last element took on special meaning as many workers—to the horror of Stalinist and moderate-socialist trade union bureaucrats—threw their support to the "crazy" students and began organizing militant strikes, matching the student barricades and street battles against brutal police repression. The question of power was being posed—the overturn of the old order seemed on the agenda.

It soon became apparent, however, that the May uprising had neither the strategic vision nor the organizational coherence nor sufficiently deep popular roots to bring on the thoroughgoing revolution that the young radicals dreamed of. This was, many agreed, simply a "dress rehearsal."

Struggle, Violence, Principles

As the newly crystallized LCR grew, Bensaïd and its other leaders felt that "history was breathing down our necks." If May 1968 was the dress rehearsal for revolution, these revolutionary militants had a responsibility to see that an actual revolution would, indeed, be produced. "We were in a hurry," he writes, and with others he developed theoretical reference points of "an (ultra-) Leninism, dominated by the paroxysmic moment of the seizure of power" (90). But it had taken the Bolsheviks decades to develop experience and revolutionary seasoning in prerevolutionary Russia that would be sufficient for the 1917 revolution. As Bensaïd describes it, the group and its young cadres were far from that. Nonetheless, their most respected revolutionary Marxist mentor, Ernest Mandel, was assuring them that "revolution is immanent," and both in the LCR and the Fourth International they felt a responsibility to make it so. It was a time of "hasty Leninism," whose "fearsome burden" he poignantly describes:

> Our feverish impatience was inspired by a phrase from Trotsky that was often cited in our debates: 'The crisis of humanity is summed up in the crisis of revolutionary leadership.' If this was indeed the case, nothing was more urgent than to resolve this crisis. The duty of each person was to contribute his or her little strength, as best they could, to settle this alternative between socialism and barbarism. It was in part up to them, therefore, whether the human species sank into a twilight future or blossomed into a society of abundance. This vision of history charged our frail shoulders with a crushing responsibility. In the face of this implacable logic, impoverished emotional life or professional ambition did not weigh very heavy. Each became personally responsible for the fate of humanity. (109)

In North America, in Asia, and especially in Latin America there was also such "hasty Leninism." A substantial minority in the Fourth International fiercely opposed the course which Bensaïd and others advocated—initially calling for a continent-wide strategy of rural guerilla warfare in Latin America (a perspective soon "modified" to include urban guerilla warfare as well), with similar impulses theorized for elsewhere. This led to a factional battle in the Fourth International, with a substantial minority projecting a more patient orientation grounded in classical Marxism. A prestigious former secretary of Trotsky's, Joseph Hansen, labeled his 1971 oppositional polemic "In Defense of the Leninist Strategy of Party-Building" (which can be found online, as can some of Bensaïd's writings, through the Marxist Internet Archive).[5] After several years of experience, most of the "hasty Leninists" would more or less swing over to Hansen's position.

But Bensaïd, a dedicated representative in Latin America from the Fourth International's "center," is compelled to share haunting memories: "Our comrades were young and intrepid, full of confidence in the socialist future of humanity. Three years later, half the people I met at these meetings had been arrested, tortured and murdered" (132). It becomes a poetry of horror:

We were running headlong into an open grave. . . .
So many faces wiped out.
So many laughs extinguished.
So many hopes massacred. (134–35)

He draws the lessons: "It was clear that we were on the wrong path. . . . Armed struggle is not a strategy. . . . The armed struggle we voted on at the 9th World Congress [1969] was an ill-timed generalization." Bensaïd emphasizes that "weapons have their own logic," elaborating:

> Buying and storing and looking after weapons, renting safe-houses and supporting underground activists is an expensive business and needs money. To obtain this, you have to rob banks. And to rob banks, you need weapons. In this spiral, an increasing number of militants are socially uprooted and professionalized. Instead of melting into a social milieu like fish in water, their existence depends ever more on an expanding apparatus (141–42).

Marx, Luxemburg, Lenin, and Trotsky had envisioned revolutionary cadres facilitating the self-organization, self-activity, and revolutionary consciousness of various working-class and oppressed sectors. Central to this was the building reform struggles for democratic rights and economic justice, creating a movement "of the great majority, for the great majority" that would culminate in "winning the battle of democracy" and bringing a transition from capitalism to socialism. For revolutionaries—Bensaïd tells us—such a working-class implantation also provides "a reality principle" to counterbalance "leftist temptations." He and others, including seasoned guerrilla fighters, "drew the conclusion of a necessary return to more classical forms of organization and the primacy of politics over military action, without which the logic of violence gets carried away and risks becoming uncontrollable" (161, 163).

A strength in Bensaïd's searching exploration of violence, to which he devotes a full chapter, is his understanding that violence is at the very core of capitalism and all forms of class society, quoting poet André Suares: "Wealth is the sign of violence, at every level" (153). He shows that the violence of the status quo is intensifying: "the tendency to a privatization and dissemination of violence is accelerating. Ethnic cleansing and religious massacres are proliferating. The world is collapsing into the hyper-violence of armed globalization" (165). Yet he sees the contamination of violence manifesting itself again and again in struggles against oppression and exploitation—liberators can become criminals, in some cases devolving into common gangsters, in the worst cases bringing in their wake the gulag and the killing fields. Surveying revolutionary experience for over a century, he concludes: "Violence and progress no longer marched together, at the same pace, in the supposed direction of history" (164). He insists on the need for a practical-ethical regulation of violence in the perspectives of revolutionaries. He finds it in Trotsky's 1938 classic *Their Morals and Ours*:

> The "great revolutionary end" thus necessarily spurns "those base means and ways which set one part of the working class against other parts, or attempt to make the masses happy without their participation; or lower the faith of the masses in themselves and their organization, replacing it by worship for the 'leaders.'" (165)

Exhaustion and Affirmation

Exhaustion can afflict a revolution, a struggle, an activist, an idea. A variety of such things are traced for the twentieth century's final decades. Bensaïd's own intensely activist organization, the LCR, was able to endure, weather more than one storm, making important contributions to liberation struggles. Yet, "we had worked wonders, exhausting ourselves in running faster than our own shadow" (178). He describes excellent comrades finally asking, "what it's all about" and falling away.

Amid all of this, there appears a fleeting pen-portrait of an important mentor to innumerable Fourth Internationalists, Ernest Mandel—"a tutor in theory and a passer between two generations . . . who set out during the 1950s to conceptualize the new features of the era, instead of piously watching over the political legacy of the past. . . . This daily contact with Ernest was a wellspring of knowledge and a permanent initiation into the foundations of Marxism" (259). As time went on, there was a partial exhaustion of the relationship between Mandel and "the Generation of '68"—a relationship always inspiring "more in the way of respect than affection," and "rarely reciprocal and egalitarian." Bensaïd saw him as at least a partial prisoner of a belief in "the emancipating powers of science and the historical logic of progress," elaborating: "Ernest was an exemplary case of stubborn optimism of the will tempered by an intermittent pessimism of reason: for him, permanent revolution would win the day over permanent catastrophe. And the socialist prophecy would (almost) always defeat barbarism" (260). Yet for many of Mandel's political children, this seemed increasingly inadequate for the realities they were facing.[6]

This shifting mood went far beyond the ranks of the Fourth International. Wearying leftists with an ambitious bent began proclaiming a set of "farewells"—to Marxism, to the working class, to the passionate logic of revolutionary struggle. Sanctuary could be found, sometimes with considerable comfort and impressive careers, in the power structures which their younger selves had militantly confronted. Among "third worldists" and Maoists who had once enthusiastically proclaimed that "the wind is blowing from the East," there was a growing conviction that "it was the west wind that now prevailed over the east" (181), blowing ever stronger thanks to the Reagan and Thatcher Revolutions. Some activists migrated from revolution to reformist politics, and some (perhaps frightened by totalitarian impulses they discovered in themselves) veered more sharply to the right.

This reflected a deeper exhaustion—of Maoist China's revolutionary élan, of the Central American revolutions, of many hopeful aspects of the Cuban Revolution, and finally of the so-called "bureaucratized workers' states" of the Communist Bloc and the USSR itself.

The collapse of Communism was soon accompanied by other exhaustions impacting on Bensaïd and his comrades. In the 1980s, the LCR had been joined by the large, growing, vibrant Mexican and the Brazilian sections as "the big three" in the Fourth International, seeming to promise much in the rebuilding of the global left. Yet the Mexican organization, "with wind in its sails," had insufficient theoretical grounding and organizational strength to prevent success from corrupting some of its most prominent militants—soon leading to betrayal, demoralization, and fragmentation. The Brazilian comrades, with whom he worked closely for many years, had thrived as an integral part of the glorious and multifaceted working-class upsurge that finally pushed aside the military dictatorship. In the form of the massive Workers Party headed by the working-class militant Lula, the insurgents finally won the presidency of the country. But a majority of the comrades found themselves pulled along into the new reformist trajectory and even neoliberal policies of the Lula regime, with a dissident fragment expelled and others splitting away amid exhausted hopes. (There was, obviously, no time for Bensaïd to offer a balance-sheet on the LCR's 2009 decision to dissolve into a broader New Anticapitalist Party.)[7]

Many activists, not inclined to join the well-heeled legions of the status quo, sought more resources to help them endure the new realities. Those who were Jewish (as he was) felt a need to explore the meaning of that identity and its complex and often horrific history. In such explorations, while in no way turning away from this identity (and joining in "not in my name" protests against Israeli oppression of Palestinians), Bensaïd affirmed his rejection of "the Chosen People" concept—having no desire "to feel chosen in this way, whether to share the blessings of this election or to bear the crushing responsibility according to which Jews are supposed to be better than common mortals" (283). Some, in this troubling period, explored new pathways of spirituality and even mysticism (as he did), as a means to transcend the "instrumental rationality [that] has stubbornly set out to empty time of its messianic pregnancy, to dissolve the surprises of the event with the regularity of the clock" (288). There is need for transcendence, "when revolution becomes the name of the inconstant event that has refused to arrive, or—still worse—has appeared in the form of its own rebuttal" (290). Such transcendence of "practical" and "instrumental reality" can open the way "to a new representation of history" (291). He insists that "the ancient prophet was neither a divine, nor a sorcerer, nor a magician. He or she was someone who switched the points of the present into the unknown bifurcations of the future" (290).

Yet, for Bensaïd, revolutionary Marxism remained the essential ingredient in his identity as a political person. A remarkable chapter in the book—"Spectres in the Blue House"—focuses on the final, Mexican years of Trotsky's exile, eloquently tracing the revolutionary's meaning for his time and for ours. "From Marx to Trotsky," Bensaïd writes, "permanent revolution . . . welds together event and history, moment and duration, rupture and continuity" (307–8). Marx is primary. In some ways the most powerful chapter is "The Inaudible Thunder," offering an elegant explication of the three volumes of Marx's *Capital*—"inescapable, always uncompleted, constantly recommenced, it is an unending project" (303). The profound influence on Marx of the philosopher Hegel accounts for this chapter's title: "the still inaudible thunder of Hegelian logic" challenges the "instrumental rationality" used to "explain" and justify the capitalist status quo (312).

Marx's method shatters such ideological facades, providing an in-depth analysis of "generalized commodity production" revealing the exploitation and mutilation of human labor and creativity at the system's very heart. His intricate exploration of the "capital accumulation process" reveals the impact of bending society and culture and the environment to the voracious and destructive need for maximizing profits more and more and more, forever. "The important thing," Bensaïd insists, is "not to bend, not to give in, not to submit to the proclaimed fatality [inevitability] of the commodity order" (313).

The very nature of this system is such that "the world still has to be changed, and still more profoundly and more urgently than we had imagined forty years ago. Any doubt bears on the possibility of succeeding, not on the necessity of trying" (313). Inaction in the face of doubt is not a choice. Given the dynamics of capitalism, the oppressed and exploited majority does not have the option of "not playing the game," and for revolutionary activists "the only compass in this uncertain work is to take the part of the oppressed, even in defeat if need be" (306–7).

The serious scholar in Bensaïd compelled him to note—in *Marx for Our Times*—that "the research program inspired by Marx remains robust" (to which numerous academics would surely give an appreciative nod), but the serious activist is compelled to insist: "it only has a genuine future if, rather than seeking refuge in the academic fold, it succeeds in establishing an organic relationship with the revived practice of social movements – in particular, with the resistance to imperialist globalization."[8]

"Knowing oneself to be mortal—we all do, more or less—is one thing," Bensaïd muses in the memoir's penultimate chapter. "Something else is to experience this and really believe it" (315). Seeing his own impending death as the book comes to a close, and impelled to pass his torch to us, he conveys multiple insights:

> Revolts against globalised injustice are multiplying. But the spiral of re-
> treats and defeats has not been broken. Number and mass are not enough,
> without will and consciousness. . . . A resistance without victories and per-
> spectives of counter-attack ends up being worn out. There is no victory
> without strategy, and no strategy without a balance of forces. . . . Is it pos-
> sible to be truly democratic without being truly socialist? . . . Today's po-
> litical landscape is devastated by battles lost without even being fought. . .
> (324, 326, 327)

Chapter Twelve

CONCLUSIONS ON COHERENCE AND COMRADESHIP

Recent discussions with European comrades, whom I have known for many years and whose experience in the struggle goes back many more years, have stirred a desire in me to draw together some political thoughts long swirling and at least partially coming together in my mind.[1]

Working in Europe during the period from mid-January to mid-April of 2019 took me away from a political earthquake and aftershocks hitting my organization in the United States, the International Socialist Organization (ISO). Regarding aspects of both the earthquake and the aftershocks, I have formed only tentative and partial judgments. An impending dissolution of the group seems likely. (A vote to dissolve was actually taken on March 29, 2019.) What I have written is not a commentary on these recent specifics. Yet they have deepened my desire to draw together longer-range thoughts, and they find reflection in what I have to say here.

The gist of what I am reaching for involves several things.

1. I feel compelled to continue the work, in which I have been engaged for some time, of seeking to identify aspects of the nature of the revolutionary approach, organization, and politics that are needed at the moment of history in which we find ourselves.

2. I am concerned that the proliferation of elitist manipulations (even when based on the best of intentions and cleverest of analyses), cropping up within diverse revolutionary as well as reformist currents, have generated confusions and disillusionments that are ob-

stacles to engaging with the tasks we face.

3. I am haunted by the challenge posed by the fact that the approach many of us have been following—working to bring the necessary mass revolutionary consciousness and organized force into being—has not brought the hoped-for result. In such places as Brazil and Greece, which seemed for many of us to be exciting experiences to emulate (involving the creation of powerful mass socialist movements), it turned out that what we saw as revolutionary promise would culminate in humiliating disaster.

I believe it is crucial to be wrestling with these and related questions, given the nature of the present period. We are facing questions of life and death, as the crises of global capitalism seem to be deepening and pushing massive numbers of people into greater hardship, turmoil, and calamity. It is an open question as to whether climate change, in upcoming decades, will be tipping into something increasingly deadly for many millions of people. Economic inequality and crisis seem to be intensifying—austerity, poverty, joblessness and semijoblessness, lower incomes for all but the wealthy and their minions, degradation of living standards and conditions, and multiple insecurities.

In reaction, we see around the world the rise of an antihumanist Right, fake-populist authoritarians, with even worse elements beginning to mobilize to offer their own horrific "solutions" (with multiple bigotries—racism, misogyny, homophobia, and more) to the terrible problems that are shaping up. At the same time, a deep and long-term process of radicalization—in the best sense—is also becoming manifest in multiple ways. In the United States this has been reflected in the Occupy movement, the Black Lives Matter movement, the million-woman mobilization against Trump, the #MeToo movement, the growing strike-wave spearheaded by teachers, and the amazing impact of the Bernie Sanders campaign, and the accompanying mushrooming of Democratic Socialists of America. Things are incredibly complex, fluid, horrible, hopeful . . . yet-to-be-determined. What we do and fail to do—each and every one of us—makes a difference. All the vibrant, interactive specks of humanity, all of us, are part of the amazing equation whose solution is not yet clear.

In order to help deal with such realities, we need to face, and move beyond, the long-term crises afflicting the Left—that segment of the political spectrum that is defined as favoring rule by the people, with liberty and justice (social justice, economic justice) for all. And we need to wrestle with the age-old question of *what is to be done*. For many on the revolutionary Left, there is a need to move beyond the shambles in which we find ourselves in order to do what we need to do. There is much good, over time, that we have contributed to struggles for human liberation, but we must learn from limitations and recent failures if we are to do more.

The God That Failed—or Not

Over the years, I have seen crises, unravelings, implosions, explosions, and quiet disintegrations of many organizations on the Left. I have sometimes witnessed such things from the inside: Students for a Democratic Society, Socialist Workers Party, Socialist Action, the Fourth Internationalist Tendency (the only one here that intended to go out of existence at the appropriate time, and did), the Labor Party emerging from its more accurately named predecessor Labor Party Advocates, Solidarity, Committees of Correspondence, and the Green Party.[2]

Varied critics have cited one or another demise as the inevitable consequence of embracing or failing to embrace a truly revolutionary program, the absence or presence of certain organizational structures or policies, the wickedness of specific leaders, the absence or presence of Leninism, etc. Looking back on almost six decades of experience, it seems to me that the complexity of factors cannot be reduced to any single or simple cause—one must look at the multiple specifics in each case to comprehend what actually happened in each case. (This is something I have tried to do in my two essays on the SWP in *Trotskyism in the United States* and in my reviews of books by Peter Camejo, Leslie Evans, and Barry Sheppard in my collection *Left Americana*.) At the same time, I have seen certain patterns common to many of these experiences.

Often members and supporters are inclined to idealize or even deify (unconsciously, of course) the specific organization: it will live forever, manifesting in itself, and at a future glorious time bringing into the world all that is good. But—consisting exclusively of mortal creatures—no organization can live forever, and for the same reason no organization can manifest in itself all that is good. Organizations *can*, if their members operate intelligently, help to create a better world—but if they aspire to do more than they can possibly do, profoundly debilitating results are inevitable.

Related to this tendency toward idealization or deification, members of the organization can make a variety of mistakes. One mistake is to approach the organization uncritically, as a "beloved community," an affinity group that validates one's own goodness or superiority—rather than as something that can and must be utilized to accomplish real-life practical goals that will actually contribute to meaningful change and, ultimately, a better world. Another mistake is to allow an exasperated or dismissive or contemptuous or condescending attitude toward those not adhering to the organization (especially if they are in different and competing organizations).

Connected to this is the illusion that the organization must do more than it actually can do—and in this, falling prey to a sort of magical thinking that (abracadabra!) in *some way,* or *some how,* the organization will be able to *do what must be done* to create a beautiful (perhaps socialist) future, even though an objective analysis would reveal that the actual members of the organization lack sufficient resources, knowledge, or expertise to make this so. At best, the organization can be part of a process preparing consciousness, experiences, and conditions, and in this help to bring together the massive and diverse forces that will actually be capable of doing what must be done. This should mean being more respectful of, and inclined to learn from, those who are not in one's organization—and also avoiding unrealistic actions that will isolate, demoralize, disappoint, and exhaust the organization's membership.

The organization's inability to live up to some members' idealized or deified conceptions may, at decisive moments, feed into feelings of betrayal, disillusionment, and bitterness. While such feelings have often been justified by truly negative practices or policies within the organization, such negative dynamics are hardly to be found only in organizations on the Left. One could almost say they are inseparable from the human condition. Still, the traumas suffered have sometimes become as debilitating as the previous idealization and deification, in regard to aspirations and efforts to change the world for the better.

There are two concluding notions that occur to me as I seek to relate these reflections to the struggles against oppression and for a society of the free and the equal.

One is that, since no organization existing today can possibly be the force we need to lead the struggle for such a future society, it is crucial to push against the idealization and deification of any organization on the Left. We must see our present organizations as part of a process—each organization may have strengths, but each is limited and must go out of existence, feeding into the future, richer, more massive organization that we need.

The second concluding notion is that organizational mistakes, frustrations, or failures must not be reduced simply to matters of psychology, sociology, ethics, tragedy, or comedy. They may have each of these dimensions—but they also have an essential and practical relevance to politics, economics, and human survival. Regardless of the fortunes of one or another currently existing organization, we must labor as best we can to learn from and build on our experiences in a way that can really, truly, practically advance the struggle for liberation.

This struggle for liberation was described by the young Karl Marx as overturning all conditions that make people oppressed, damaged, mutilated beings, prevented from realizing all that is wondrous within them as free (self-determining) and creative beings living in genuine community. But sometimes this struggle has been constricted by those seeking to advance it. The multiple identities of those who make up the rich tapestry of humanity are sometimes belittled in preference to an abstract, idealized, or deified understanding of *one* of these identities—*class*. There is a logic to doing that, since in our own capitalist society the great majority of people have become part of *the working class*, and in unity there is strength. But this can create a tangle that must be undone in order to help us make sense of what we need actually to do.

The Wondrous, Mundane, Multifaceted, Actual Working Class—All of Us

It is possible (and among certain socialist, communist, anarcho-syndicalist currents, it is the norm) to idealize and deify the working class. This can become a huge barrier to revolutionaries who wish to overcome multiple forms of exploitation—thinking of people as glorified abstractions instead of actual people.

Actual people have a variety of ages and cultural preferences, different genders and sexual orientations, different sets of biases and prejudices, different levels of knowledge and insight, various neuroses and other mental-emotional problems, divergent attitudes on multiple questions, and more. All of this is true of the working class, given that it is composed of actual people.

The classical definition of the working class is those who make a living (get enough money to buy basic necessities and perhaps some luxuries) by selling their *ability to work* (their *labor-power*) to an employer. Out of the labor-power, the employer squeezes actual labor in order to create the wealth that is partly given to the workers (usually as little as possible), with the rest of this labor-created wealth going to the employer. In the early decades of the Industrial Revolution in patriarchal and capitalist Europe, men were often considered the "real" workers (even though many women worked), and factory workers were often considered the "real" working class. But men and women, and many, many children too, were part of the working class the way we have defined it, and that was the case whether they produced goods or services, regardless of specific and proliferating occupations, skill sets, levels of income, levels of occupational pride, etc.

As a class, the immense collectivity of people just described have been oppressed and exploited in order to enrich the tiny and powerful minority that owns and controls our economy. But there are powerful and terrible forms of oppression that bear down—in multiple ways—on people through their nonclass identities, including race, ethnicity, gender, sexuality, religion, age, distinctive physical specifics, and more. Not only must fighting against such oppression be central to all that activists do in the struggle for human liberation, but the interrelationship of such forms of oppression, and of the struggles against them, must be understood.

In particular, the *class struggle* must be seen as involving determined, creative, uncompromising struggle against all forms of oppression. "Working-class consciousness cannot be genuine political consciousness unless the workers are trained to respond to all cases of tyranny, oppression, violence, and abuse, no matter what class is affected," Lenin once emphasized. He specified that this includes oppression around freedom of speech and expression, cultural freedom, the rights of religious minorities, the rights of racial and ethnic groups, the rights of women, of soldiers, of students, of peasants. He argued that such oppression must be seen by the worker (here Lenin was presumably speaking of male workers) as coming from "those same dark forces that are oppressing and crushing him at every step of his life." A revolutionary must be a "tribune of the people, who is able to react to every manifestation of tyranny and oppression, no matter where it appears, no matter what stratum or class of people it affects."[3]

Good as Lenin was, however, he had his limitations—not least of which is that he was a mortal human being who never said the last word on anything. An amazing collectivity of people have addressed these and related questions over the years, and their insights can be indispensable for those seeking to advance the struggle for human liberation. (Among those who have influenced me, in novels, nonfictional works, or both, are Simone de Beauvoir, Doris Lessing, Rita Mae Brown, James Baldwin, C. L. R. James, Malcolm X, Martin Luther King Jr., Ella Baker, Sheila Rowbotham, Alexandra Kollontai. There are many more.)

Also worth considering, in this regard, are the comments of someone I knew personally, and who became one of my mentors—a seasoned working-class intellectual named George Breitman, who put the matter this way half a century ago:

> The radicalization of the worker can begin off the job as well as on. It can begin from the fact that the worker is a woman as well as a man; that the worker is Black or Chicano or a member of some other oppressed minority as well as white; that the worker is a father or mother whose son can be drafted; that the worker is young as well as middle-aged or about to retire. If we grasp the fact that the working class is stratified and divided in many ways—the capitalists prefer it that way—then we will be better able to understand how the radicalization will develop among workers and how to intervene more effectively. Those who haven't already learned important lessons from the radicalization of oppressed minorities, youth and women had better hurry up and learn them, because most of the people involved in these radicalizations are workers or come from working-class families.[4]

The integration of such understandings as these into one's thinking, and into the very core of one's political collective or organization, is necessary, I believe, for anyone who genuinely wants to see a revolution. Yet simply doing that will not, by itself, bring a revolution. Which leads to further sets of reflections.

Aspirations and Realities

"You say you want a revolution," sang the Beatles in 1968. "Well, you know, we'd all love to change the world." *What kind of change* has been a focal-point of revolutionaries for generations. We have been told that Spartacus defined it as "a world without slaves." It is said that Jesus projected the Kingdom of God as something to exist "on earth as it is in Heaven"—which meant that all would be equal before their Creator, living in brotherhood and sisterhood, with all things in common, animated by the Golden Rule of each person treating all others as they themselves would want to be treated. Architects of, advocates for, and participants in various utopian projects in more recent centuries sometimes advanced very detailed plans that reflected—in one way or another—their distinctive communitarian ideals and aspirations.

Marx added three compellingly realist notions to the mix: (1) the actual possibility of this hoped-for cooperative commonwealth must be grounded in a serious, disciplined understanding of the realities of the present and an understanding of history (social sciences); (2) the dynamics of capitalism, despite their inherent destructiveness, have created technological possibilities providing the material conditions for a society of the free and the equal in which all might realize their full human potential for freedom, creative endeavor, and genuine community; and (3) the dynamics of capitalism have also created a complex but truly amazing force, increasingly global, of working-class majorities (those whose labor collectively creates the wealth—goods and services—through which society lives), majorities having the potential, if their vast numbers are drawn together through consciousness and organization, to bring to birth a new and better world.

Rosa Luxemburg brilliantly emphasized essential aspects of this realist standpoint, particularly in regard to a controversy arising among Marxist-influenced socialists. Some of her comrades argued the hoped-for future could only be brought about by a revolutionary mobilization of the working class to overturn the existing capitalist order and create a workers' democracy for the socialist reconstruction of society. Others insisted that this could be achieved more gradually, with the accumulation of reforms (in part secured through compromises with procapitalist liberals) that would over time transform a problematical capitalism into a harmonious socialism. Such differences continue to find expression today, including in what is now by far the largest socialist organization in the United States, the Democratic Socialists of America.

Luxemburg insisted that it is foolish to think one could simply choose different paths to socialism—one a quicker, more radical (but trickier, if spicier) path, the other a slower, more moderate (milder but less risky) path, as if one were selecting mild or spicy sausages at the market. The realities of capitalism make it impossible to compromise that system out of existence— the effort would involve an entanglement in and adaptation to capitalism, with an ultimate erosion and corruption of reformist achievements. The "mild" path could not actually lead to socialism, but only to a partially (and impermanently) "reformed" capitalism.

The reformist pathway to socialism is utterly unrealistic because of the nature of capitalism—its incredible dynamism and inexorably destructive dynamics. Luxemburg explored this in her classic *The Accumulation of Capital* (an irreplaceable contribution, whatever its imperfections). This text also decisively challenges, it seems to me, the notion that *any* conscious person can afford simply to withdraw from political activism, tending to interesting hobbies and one's own little garden, and let the deadly problems of the world unfold as they may. For committed political activists, such realities intensify the challenge—*what is to be done?*

Collectives and Cadres

Many adages from past struggles continue to resonate: an injury to one is an injury to all, in unity there is strength, if we fail to hang together we may be hanged separately, and so on. Such elemental notions are taken further by the evolving understanding—throughout their political lives—of such figures as Luxemburg, Lenin, Trotsky, Gramsci, Zetkin, and their many cothinkers. There will be no inevitable triumph of human rights, freedom, creativity, community, and a better future. Such things must be fought for, and they must be fought for against oppressive and exploitative elites that have immense resources and are powerful and well-organized. The oppressive elites can be overcome by the force of the majority, but only if that majority has the necessary consciousness and a high degree of organization.

Obviously, not every human being who is part of "the majority" has the same thoughts and values. Some are drawn to multiple forms of bigotry and/or fear and/or passivity and/or submissiveness, etc. Only a portion—a layer—of the working-class majority is at this moment inclined toward a revolutionary class-consciousness, commitment against all forms of oppression, and inclination to fight for a better world. Within this layer, there are some who have developed skills in actually fighting back, in analyzing what's what, and in waging effective struggles. Anarcho-syndicalists have referred to this as "the militant minority," and such a minority has sometimes been able to provide leadership in sustained struggles that result in victories. Many among those inclined to read a book such as this happen to be part of the *broad vanguard layer* of the working class.

Based on what has been said so far, it seems clear that this vanguard lay-er or militant minority must not substitute itself for the majority (let alone arrogantly claim that it *is* the majority). Rather, it must seek to win more and more individuals, more and more of the majority, to forms of consciousness and activity through which they too will either become part of the vanguard layer or increasingly conscious and active supporters of what that layer is reaching for—against all forms of oppression, and for a world in which the free development of each will become the condition for the free develop-ment of all.

Just as the entire working class or the entire majority of the population are not telepathically connected, thinking the same thoughts and automati-cally inclined to carry out the same actions, so those who are part of the van-guard layer do not all have the same thoughts and understanding, including about pathways that make sense and about what to do next. To be effective, individuals who are part of this layer must join together to pool their ener-gies, their ideas, their resources, their insights, their commitments. Without the development of such a collaboration of thinking and activism, without a political collective (in fact, a network of collectives), there can be no effec-tive plans of action that can be carried out to change the world.

Such collectives cannot be sustained, cannot grow, cannot carry out the broad array of educational, consciousness-raising, and practical political ac-tivities, without people who have developed the skills to make this so. The word *cadre* has been used as a tag for such people.

Such a person has developed the interactive blend of knowledge, under-standing, experience, and skills to do the things that must be done.

◊ How does one organize a meeting that is coherent and democratic and effective and has good practical results? How are those good practical results achieved, and how can various comrades be helped to make sure that they are achieved? How can one's specific collec-tive be sustained in order to ensure the development and effective-ness of its various comrades and the collective as a whole?

◊ How does one size up an actual situation in the community or the workplace, figure out the kinds of things that need to be done, and figure out how they can be done in order to realize a specific goal? How does one organize an educational forum, a picket line, a strike, a rally, a mass demonstration, an election campaign, a struggle for a specific reform, etc.?

◊ What can we learn from other struggles, at other times, from other places, that can help us be strong and effective in our own struggles? How can these be applied to our specific situations?

Not everyone can answer such questions—but a cadre is someone who can answer some of them and can help create collaboration in which further answers can be developed and tested in practical action. A cadre is someone who can help ensure that the collective can be what it must be, who can help others see the need to become part of the collective, and who can help members of the collective (and even people who are not members of the collective) become cadres in the sense that is suggested here.

With the proliferation of cadres, with more and more and more of us developing as cadres, we can see the growth of a mass movement that is capable of being effective in the fight against all forms of oppression, forging pathways in the struggle for a better world of the free and the equal.

As we seek to realize such goals, we necessarily come to additional and interrelated sets of reflections—on structures and strategies.

Democratic and Revolutionary Structures

There are two fundamentals that must be of concern to revolutionary activists. One involves the organizational forms and policies through which we *structure* our collective efforts. Another involves the actual purpose of that structure: getting from the "here" of our present-day realities to the "there" of our hoped-for socialist goals—*strategy* being the term often used to refer to that specific and practical pathway. As has been suggested already, it would seem that the effective approach to developing both structure and strategy must be democratic and revolutionary.

Focusing on the matter of organizational structures for a moment, it occurs to me that the old and much-maligned and sometimes grotesquely distorted term *democratic centralism* continues to make a considerable amount of sense. I am absolutely opposed to the follow-the-leader interpretation which tells us that some central authority (the wise leader, the top cadres, the central committee or whatever) should be the brain that does the thinking and gives the orders—after which we should "democratically" discuss it all and then carry it all out as disciplined little soldiers. That is the opposite of the actual democratic centralism I believe in—a phony "Leninism" associated with pretentious clowning and the organization falling flat on its face (to paraphrase Lenin's *Left-Wing Communism: An Infantile Disorder*).[5]

Democratic centralism was not quite the hallmark of Leninism that many make of it. Use of the term has been found in the German workers' movement of the 1870s, and it seems to have been introduced in a positive way into the Russian Social Democratic Labor Party around 1905 by the Menshevik faction, although the Bolsheviks embraced it as well. It seems to me to involve a democratic common sense for any serious organization, and at the same time its implementation necessarily involves a reasonable flexibility.

If the organization has a full, democratic discussion regarding *actions to be taken* and makes a decision (determined by majority vote)—then the organization *carries out* the decision that was democratically decided upon. If the decision is to support a strike action, or an antiwar action, or an antiracist action, then no comrade is to work against the action. On the other hand, if a majority of comrades in the organization have a specific position regarding a philosophical question, or an understanding of history, or a specific political analysis, there is no reason why dissident comrades cannot openly, publicly state their own views, if they have them. Nor are they prohibited from expressing disagreements with the leadership or with majority decisions on other matters as well, even publicly. But if the collective decides to *do* one thing, it is not acceptable for dissident members simply to do the opposite. Only on questions involving basic revolutionary principles is there validity in breaking ranks (Lenin himself did this at certain decisive points)—but this is generally an indication that a political break may be in the offing.

Related to this mode of functioning is the elective principle in regard to selection of leaders (with no mandatory slates chosen by "outgoing" but actually self-perpetuating leaderships). Full and critical-minded discussions must occur prior to national conventions of democratically elected delegates, where the basic decisions are made and leaders chosen. Leadership bodies, elected at the local and national level, are answerable to and replaceable by the membership.

Insights, experiences, and energies of *all* members are needed by the organizational collective. Individual members must be animated by the sense that this organization is *theirs*, collectively, and by the understanding that each and every comrade makes a difference. This is enhanced by collective decision-making and the collective testing out of the decision in practice, in action.

The democratic mode of functioning must, in repressive contexts, naturally be modified to help protect members and thwart the forces of repression. This has proved to be the case with organizations forced into underground work by vicious dictatorships, and those initiating armed struggle. But such restrictive organizational policies (problematical even when necessary) have also cropped up in less repressive contexts. The utilization of "security" precautions that dispense with transparency and accountability must be avoided as much as possible.

Experience has shown that the absence of openness, transparency, and democratic accountability can result in self-inflicted wounds, internal abuses, and victimization of some comrades by powerful but disoriented comrades. Organizational secrecy provides enhanced opportunities for dirty tricks and provocations on the part of the state's repressive apparatus. Especially damaging has been the separation of select cadres "in the know" from a majority of their comrades, because: (1) it can distort the political judgment of those "in the know," (2) it can narrow the involvement of the organization's active membership, and (3) it can weaken ties with the potential social base in the revolutionary process. Which brings us to questions of strategy.

Strategic Challenges

The democratic mode of functioning seems most consistent with the revolutionary strategic orientation of classical Marxism. This orientation was powerfully advanced by Marx and Engels in the *Communist Manifesto*. The actual struggles of the laboring masses of the exploited and oppressed are the essential element in the struggle for a better world, according to Marx and Engels. Revolutionary socialists have relevance only to the extent that they merge their ideas and energies with such struggles. Struggles at the workplace by trade unions, as well as struggles for human rights and for life-giving reforms through social movements must ultimately be combined with struggles for political power by the working class—"winning the battle for democracy" through a developing and triumphant labor party. The revolutionary-democratic triumph would set the stage for the transition to socialism.

This strategic perspective was enriched by later revolutionaries who embraced it: Luxemburg's reflections on reform and revolution and on the mass strike; Lenin's notions of revolutionaries as tribunes of the people fighting against all forms of oppression, plus the need for a worker-peasant alliance, and especially the centrality of the struggle for radical democracy in the fight for socialism; Trotsky's formulation of permanent revolution—highlighting the revolutionary internationalism shared by all being discussed here—and his insights on the obstacles and dangers of bureaucracy; Gramsci's profound contributions on cultural dynamics, the masses/vanguard interplay, and his utilization of the concept of hegemony. These and contributions from yet other twentieth-century Marxists have been invaluable for those seeking to develop strategic perspectives—how to develop practical pathways of struggle that can get us from the "here" of present-day capitalism to the "there" of a socialist future.

The compelling nature of such theoretical contributions poses its own dangers. One could spend one's entire life simply studying and discussing such things, with little time to spare for actual efforts to change the world. An alternative to such passive individualism is to form activist collectives dominated by leaders presumably grounded in Marxist theory, what my Uncle Adrian (a class-conscious worker) called "the words-of-wisdom guys," leaders who would call the shots regarding what the organization should do. This approach can involve greater or less sophistication, but it has proved, over time, to be problematical.

An obvious danger is for leaderships to mechanistically superimpose previously developed theoretical perspectives and experiences (a sort of tyranny of the past) on today's realities in ways that make no sense, given dramatically changed conditions. Another danger, even among sophisticated leaders, is to conclude that—as keepers of revolutionary Marxism's amazing truths—they must ride herd on the organization's membership, preventing deviations from that truth. After all, the hope for the future depends on that specific revolutionary collective (sometimes perceived as the party, or the nucleus of the future party) guided by this truth. This is strategically barren, not really helping us get from "here" to "there." Instead, the priority becomes maintaining the specific organization that is the keeper of truth.

Even among more sophisticated comrades and dynamic organizations there can be problems. Pierre Rousset recently reminded me of something he had pointed out when he was the director of the International Institute for Research and Education in Amsterdam, when I attended back in the 1980s. There is a fatal pattern among revolutionary organizations, not an iron law but a recurrent tendency. This tendency can even involve quite creative and insightful efforts (but flawed efforts) to use revolutionary theory for the purpose of developing genuinely revolutionary strategies. I want to try to describe this "fatal pattern" here, because it has implications regarding the interplay of revolutionary strategy and democratic organization.

A primary purpose of studying revolutionary theory is not only to comprehend the past and understand the present but to develop an understanding of how things are likely to play out in the future—or, to use a common term, *predictions*. The more sophisticated theorists, employing the best of Marxist social science, often base strategic orientations on an analysis of trends and tendencies in the present that point to likely outcomes in the foreseeable future. There are various plausible predictions that have been advanced over the years. Capitalist and Stalinist elites seemed likely to be swept away throughout Europe in the aftermath of the Second World War. A Third World War seemed likely, in the early years of the Cold War, between imperialist capitalism and the Stalinist degenerated workers' states. Experiences of the late 1950s and early 1960s suggested a wave of guerrilla wars culminating in triumphant liberation struggles throughout the Latin American continent. The dynamics of social struggles and economic problems in the United States from the 1960s through the 1970s indicated a deepening radicalization that would culminate in a class-conscious working class moving to center stage of the political arena in the twentieth century's final decades.

Strategic orientations developed and implemented on the basis of these predictions were disastrous failures. The social sciences lack the exactness of such natural sciences as mathematics, chemistry, astronomy, physics. (Even with these "exact sciences," there are multiple variables.) Social science can identify past patterns, current structures and dynamics, and possible developments, but it can hardly grasp all of reality's complexities. Far-reaching predictions are too weak a reed on which to forge coherent strategies, even when articulated by the most sophisticated "words-of-wisdom guys."

Strategic orientations are essential if one truly hopes to get from the capitalist "here" to the socialist "there." But strategies must be based on more than the abstract theory and prediction-connected analyses offered by the words-of-wisdom guys. Historical and political and economic developments impact powerfully, but in complex ways, on the essential and infinitely complex human factor. And it is this human factor that is the key to strategy—the incredible variables and possibilities in what people, masses of people, actually think, do, desire, and are inclined to try out.

A democratic collective process is needed by revolutionary activists. Naturally, we must understand trends and tendencies of history, of capitalism, and of our times. These impact on popular perceptions and moods and consequent political responses and struggles or inclinations to struggle. It is the vanguard layer's alertness to these popular responses, thanks to their connections with masses of people, that help generate struggles and suggest strategies that will make sense. A democratic process within revolutionary collectives provides the basis for our getting from "here" to "there." Our organizations must be structured and developed to enable such a revolutionary-democratic process to flourish.

And Yet...

The *problems* of how to get from here to there have hardly evaporated by virtue of any theoretical flourish that might be teased out from what I have written so far. A few years ago, I wrote that "Leninism is unfinished," and this is certainly true of revolutionary organization and strategy in general, and in more than one way. But we are faced with the question of just *how* the orientation represented by Lenin and his generation of revolutionaries relates to the fluid, complex, specific realities of today and tomorrow.

I want to conclude with additional brief reflections regarding strategy. We have broad strategic outlines whose validity can be demonstrated with serious reference to historical experience and current realities—but applying this to the specifics of now, as an *activist* orientation, must involve practical details. And the devil is often in the details.

As an exuberant young activist back in the 1970s and '80s, I advocated the creation of a labor party based on the trade unions—which would give the working-class a political voice of its own, greatly advancing class struggle and class-consciousness. I could point to our northern neighbor, Canada, a country similar to our own, as having exactly what I was advocating—in the form of the New Democratic Party. And in the province of Ontario, in 1990, the NDP ran a militant campaign with strong reformist demands, backed by strong and left-leaning unions conducting their own militant campaigns, and it was swept into power—just as an economic recession was beginning. And I learned a bitter lesson.

Apparently the NDP leaders had not expected to be swept into power, and they had no idea of what to do. They found themselves enmeshed in a capitalist state, grounded in a capitalist society, and they responded to the situation, in their new governmental positions, by managing that capitalist state and working to salvage the capitalist economy—implementing austerity measures and antiunion policies that were the opposite of what they had campaigned for (not to mention a betrayal of the socialist principles with which some of them had spiced their speeches). This hopeful model that I had pointed to seemed totally discredited.

More recently, triumphant new "broad parties of the Left" (far more substantial and radical than the NDP)—in Brazil, for example, and in Greece—crystallized and won decisive elections. And each in their own way, for their own specific reasons and in their own specific circumstances, then traveled along a similar trajectory. My friend John Riddell has, in an email response to an earlier draft of these reflections, appropriately noted that "even when the power of the masses is fully mobilized," global capitalism "has proved able to wall off the process, isolate it, undermine and strangle it." He pointed to Greece and Venezuela as examples, but of course there have been and, quite likely, will be others. This highlights the necessity of revolutionary internationalism—not as an abstract slogan or as a simple appeal for solidarity work, but as an essential element in developing a strategic orientation capable of interlinking revolutionary struggles and triumphs in a variety of countries.

It is time to bring these reflections to a close. This is not the place to take up the challenge of the recent experiences just referred to, which will require more detailed engagement than is possible in this conclusion. But it is essential that there be such critical engagement, analyzing what went wrong, what might have been done, and what must be done in the future. That is essential for anyone truly wanting to find pathways from the "here" of capitalism to a society of the free and equal.

What seems clear to me, also, is that this can best be done by serious activists in a collective and democratic manner, with revolutionary organizations helping to provide the kind of cohesion and comradeship that can enable us to struggle effectively for a better world.

NOTES

1. Lenin Studies: Method and Organization

1. Antonio Negri, *Factory of Strategy: 33 Lessons on Lenin* (New York: Columbia University Press, 2014), xxiii.
2. For further discussion of Lenin's relevance, and related matters, see Paul Le Blanc, "Ten Reasons for Not Reading Lenin," in V. I. Lenin, *Revolution, Democracy, Socialism: Selected Writings*, ed. Paul Le Blanc (London: Pluto Press, 2008), 3–80.
3. Roland Boer, *Lenin, Religion and Theology* (New York: Palgrave Macmillan 2013).
4. August H. Nimtz, *The Ballot, the Streets—or Both: From Marx and Engels to Lenin and the October Revolution* (Chicago: Haymarket Books, 2019).
5. Among the relevant memoirs available in English (though long out of print) are A. Badayev, *The Bolsheviks in the Tsarist Duma* (London: Martin Lawrence, 1929); C. Bobrovskaya, *Twenty Years in Underground Russia: Memoirs of a Rank-and-File Bolshevik* (New York: International Publishers, 1934); O. Piatnitsky, *Memoirs of a Bolshevik* (New York: International Publishers, 1935); F. F. Raskolnikov, *Kronstadt and Petrograd in 1917* (London: New Park, 1982); Alexander Shylapnikov, *On the Eve of 1917: Reminiscences and Documents of the Labour Movement and the Revolutionary Underground* (London: Allison and Busby, 1981)—although there is much material in Russian yet to be made available to anglophones. Relevant secondary works include Ralph Carter Elwood, *Russian Social Democracy in the Underground: A Study of the RSDRP in the Ukraine, 1907–1914* (Assen, Netherlands: Van Gorcum, 1974); Leopold Haimson, "The Problem of Social Stability in Urban Russia, 1905–1917," part I, *Slavic Review* 23, no. 4 (December 1964); Leopold Haimson, "The Problem of Social Stability in Urban Russia, 1905–1917," part II, *Slavic Review* 24, no. 1 (March 1965); David Mandel, *The Petrograd Workers and the Fall of the Old Regime: From the February Revolution to the July Days 1917* (London: Macmillan, 1983); David Mandel, *The Petrograd Workers and the Soviet Seizure of Power: From the July Days 1917 to July 1918* (London: Macmillan, 1984); Alexander Rabinowitch, *The Bolsheviks Come to Power: The Revolution of 1917 in Petrograd* (Chicago: Haymarket Books, 2009). On Gramsci, see Paul Le Blanc, *From Marx*

to *Gramsci: A Reader in Revolutionary Marxist Politics*, 2nd edition (Chicago: Haymarket Books, 2016); see also chapter 6 in this volume. On Lukács, see chapter 5 in this volume.

6. Daniel Bensaïd, "Leninism in the 21st Century," *International Viewpoint*, November 16, 2001; and Sebastian Budgen, Stathis Kouvelakis, and Slavoj Žižek, eds, *Lenin Reloaded: Toward a Politics of Truth* (Durham, NC: Duke University Press, 2007), 150–51. For valuable clarifications on Leninism, see Valentino Gerratana, "Stalin, Lenin, and 'Leninism,'" *New Left Review* 103 (May-June 1977): 59–71, and Robert C. Tucker, *Stalin as Revolutionary: 1879–1929* (New York: W. W. Norton, 1974), 313–29. Erik van Ree comments that Stalin's approach (culminating in the conceptualization of "Marxism-Leninism"), is "remarkable for its closedness," Zinoviev and Bukharin both objected to this hyphenated term, while Stalin embraced it as eliminating any "rift between Marxism and Leninism"—emphasizing "Lenin's Marxist orthodoxy." See Erik van Ree, *The Political Thought of Joseph Stalin: A Study in Twentieth-Century Revolutionary Patriotism* (London and New York: Routledge/Curzon, 2002), 255, 256, 257.

7. Gregory Zinoviev, "The Death of Lenin and the Problems of Leninism," *Communist International* 30 (1924): 9, 10; Nikolai Bukharin, *Lenin as a Marxist* (1925) in *In Defence of the Russian Revolution: A Selection of Bolshevik Writings, 1917–1923*, ed. Al Richardson (London: Porcupine Press, 1995), 255, 258.

8. For example, see E. H. Carr, *A History of Soviet Russia*, vol. 4, *The Interregnum, 1923–1924* (London: Macmillan, 1954), 320–23; and E. H. Carr, *A History of Soviet Russia*, vol. 5, in the first volume of *Socialism in One Country, 1924–1926* (London: Macmillan, 1958), 142–43,155, 303–5.

9. Tamás Krausz, *Reconstructing Lenin: An Intellectual Biography* (New York: Monthly Review Press, 2015), 351, 352, 356, 357, 360.

10. Negri, *Factory of Strategy*, 6, 21.

11. Budgen, Kouvelakis, Žižek, eds., *Lenin Reloaded*.

12. Within this field of Lenin studies, some (such as Carr and Lewin) focus on exploring texts and actions of Lenin, placing these carefully and interactively in their historical contexts, while others (such as Negri and Shandro) have a more abstract bent, reaching for generalizations that might have application in a variety of different contexts. Perhaps the most valuable works succeed in doing both (one thinks of Deutscher).

13. There are other figures from Lenin's own time whose contributions merit serious consideration—not simply Georg Lukács's 1924 classic *Lenin: A Study on the Unity of His Thought* (London: Verso Books, 2009), but also offerings by Leon Trotsky, Gregory Zinoviev, Lev Kamenev, Nikolai Bukharin, Anatoly Lunacharsky, M. N. Pokrovsky, Maxim Gorky, Clara Zetkin, and others too often dismissed as "hagiographers." Especially helpful will be the translation into English of works by Kamenev and Zinoviev, from whom many of us, unable to read Russian, have only fragments.

14. Substantial discussion of divergent and convergent perspectives of Lih and myself can be found in Paul Le Blanc, *Unfinished Leninism: The Rise and Return of a Revolutionary Doctrine* (Chicago: Haymarket, 2014), 95–114.

15. Joseph Stalin, *Problems of Leninism* (Peking: Foreign Languages Press, 1976), 3.

Also see Erik van Ree, *The Political Thought of Joseph Stalin: A Study in Twentieth-Century Revolutionary Patriotism* (London and New York: Routledge/Curzon, 2002). The following draws from Paul Le Blanc, "Reflections on the Meaning of Stalinism," *Crisis & Critique* 3, no. 2 (2016): 89–90.

16. V. M. Molotov and Felix Chuev, *Molotov Remembers: Inside Kremlin Politics*, ed. Albert Resis (Chicago: Ivan R. Dee, 1993), 131, 132, 133.

17. Georges Haupt and Jean-Jacques Marie, *Makers of the Russian Revolution: Biographies of Bolshevik Leaders* (Ithaca: Cornell University Press, 1974), 157.

18. Nadezhda Krupskaya, *Reminiscences of Lenin* (New York: International Publishers, 1979); Robert H. McNeal, *Bride of the Revolution: Krupskaya and Lenin* (London: Victor Gollancz, 1973), 267, 268; Leon Trotsky, *Diary in Exile: 1935* (New York: Macmillan, 1963), 33; Haupt and Marie, *Makers of the Russian Revolution*, 158.

19. Gregory Zinoviev, *History of the Bolshevik Party: From the Beginnings to February 1917: A Popular Outline* (London: New Park, 1973); Leon Trotsky, *My Life: An Attempt at Autobiography* (New York: Pathfinder Press, 1970); Leon Trotsky, *Portraits Political and Personal* (New York: Pathfinder Press, 1977); Isaac Deutscher, *Marxism in Our Time* (San Francisco: Ramparts Press, 1971); Ernest Mandel, *The Place of Marxism in History* (Atlantic Highlands, NJ: Humanities Press, 1996); Lars Lih, *Lenin Rediscovered: "What Is to be Done?" in Context* (Chicago: Haymarket Books, 2008); Lars Lih, *Lenin* (London: Reaktion, 2011); Lars Lih, "The Strange Case of the Closeted Lenin," *Links: International Journal of Socialist Renewal*, December 4, 2014; Lars Lih, "Lenin's Verdict on Kautsky in State and Revolution," in John Riddell, ed., *Marxist Essays and Commentary*, August 5, 2019, https://johnriddell.com/2019/08/05/lenins-verdict-on-kautsky-in-state-and-revolution.

20. Lih, *Lenin*, 13. Lih does not portray Lenin as a disciple or "loyal follower" of Kautsky, but see Charles Post, "Lenin Reconsidered," *International Viewpoint*, November 3, 2011, critically discussed in Le Blanc, *Unfinished Leninism*, 115–28.

21. This is touched on in Paul Le Blanc, "The Absence of Socialism in the United States: Contextualizing Kautsky's 'American Worker,'" *Historical Materialism* 11, no. 4 (2003): 126, 134–35. Also see Paul Blackledge, "Karl Kautsky and Marxist Historiography," *Science & Society* 70, no. 3 (July 2006): 337–59; and Paul Blackledge, *Reflections on the Marxist Theory of History* (Manchester, UK: Manchester University Press, 2006), 53–94.

22. Alan Shandro, *Lenin and the Logic of Hegemony: Political Practice and Theory in the Class Struggle* (Chicago: Haymarket Books, 2015), 196–97; Negri, *Factory of Strategy*, 53–54.

23. Krausz, *Reconstructing Lenin*, 138–39. Krausz doesn't provide documentation, but see Haimson, "The Problem of Social Stability in Urban Russia," and Paul Le Blanc, *Lenin and the Revolutionary Party*, new edition (Chicago: Haymarket Books, 2015), 189–207.

24. For valuable contextualization and discussion, see Michael Hardt, "Into the Factory: Negri's Lenin and the Subjective Caesura (1968–73)," in *Resistance in Practice: The Philosophy of Antonio Negri*, eds. Timothy S. Murphy and Abdul-Karim Mustapha (London: Pluto Press, 2005), and—with more critical

detail—Steve Wright, *Storming Heaven: Class Composition and Struggle in Italian Autonomist Marxism* (London: Pluto Press, 2002), 147–50, 152–75.

25. Negri, *Factory of Strategy*, xix, 45; Krausz, *Reconstructing Lenin*, 356; Shandro, *Lenin and the Logic of Hegemony*, 326. See initial (sympathetic yet critical) reviews of Shandro and Krausz in Paul Le Blanc, "Lenin's Revolutionary Marxism," *International Socialist Review* 97 (Summer 2015) and Paul Le Blanc, "Sorting Through Lenin's Legacy," *Links: International Journal for Socialist Renewal*, March 10, 2015.

26. Krausz, *Reconstructing Lenin*, 356.

27. Negri, *Factory of Strategy*, xix, 10, 11. Such developments caused him to suggest a reconceptualization, in Michael Hardt and Antonio Negri, *Multitude: War and Democracy in the Age of Empire* (New York: Penguin Books, 2005), xiv–xv, 106–7, but also see Trevor Blackwell and Jeremy Seabrook, *A World Still to Win: The Reconstruction of the Post-War Working Class* (London: Faber and Faber, 2005); Kim Moody, *Workers in a Lean World: Unions in the International Economy* (London: Verso, 1997); Ronaldo Munck, *Globalisation and Labour: The New "Great Transformation"* (London: Zed Books, 2002); and Paul Mason, *Live Working or Die Fighting: How the Working Class Went Global* (Chicago: Haymarket Books, 2010).

28. Krausz, *Reconstructing Lenin*, 360–62. Similar points have been made by contemporaries of Lukács—Adolf Sturmthal, *The Tragedy of European Labor, 1918–1939* (New York: Columbia University Press, 1943), 1–21, 32; Fritz Sternberg, *Capitalism and Socialism on Trial* (London: Victor Gollancz, 1951), 142–55. Such views are critically discussed in Le Blanc *Lenin and the Revolutionary Party*, 218–23.

29. Negri, *Factory of Strategy*, 13.

30. Krupskaya, *Reminiscences of Lenin*, 90.

31. Negri, *Factory of Strategy*, 5–6.

32. Negri, *Factory of Strategy*, 58.

33. Negri, *Factory of Strategy*, 59.

34. Negri, *Factory of Strategy*, 17, 20.

35. Negri, *Factory of Strategy*, 23, 32, 71, 73, 74, 77.

36. This coincides with the Hegelian notion of *Aufheben* (meaning cancel, preserve, lift up)—see Georg Lukács, *The Young Hegel: Studies in the Relations between Dialectics and Economics* (Cambridge, MA: MIT Press, 1976), 118, 275, 307, J. N. Findlay, *Hegel: A Re-examination* (New York: Collier Books, 1962), 44–45; Walter Kaufmann, *Hegel: A Reinterpretation* (Garden City, NY: Anchor Books, 1966), 24–25, 144, 180–82.

37. Negri, *Factory of Strategy*, 64, 66.

38. Negri, *Factory of Strategy*, 21, 22, 23, 24.

39. Marcel Liebman, *Leninism Under Lenin* (London: Merlin Press, 1975), 29–49; and Tony Cliff, *Lenin*, vol. 1, *Building the Party* (London: Pluto Press, 1975), 79–98, 168–83.

40. Raya Dunayevskaya, *Marxism and Freedom: From 1776 until Today* (Amherst, NY: Humanity Books, 2000), 167–76—this book first appeared in 1958. A capable elaboration of Dunayevskaya's argument is provided by Kevin Anderson,

Lenin, Hegel, and Western Marxism: A Critical Study (Urbana: University of Illinois Press, 1995).

41. Raphael Abramovitch, *The Soviet Revolution* (New York: International Universities Press, 1962), 210, 214, 216.

42. Krausz, *Reconstructing Lenin*, 360, 357, 355; Negri, *Factory of Strategy*, 337.

43. See Negri, *Factory of Strategy*, 260–64, 263–73; Krausz, *Reconstructing Lenin*, 209–278, 311–52; Shandro, *Lenin and the Logic of Hegemony*, 289–314. Also see: Lih, *Lenin*,154–205; Arno J. Mayer, *The Furies: Violence and Terror in the French and Russian Revolutions* (Princeton: Princeton University Press, 2000); and Paul Le Blanc, *Marx, Lenin and the Revolutionary Experience: Studies of Communism and Radicalism in the Age of Globalization* (New York: Routledge, 2006), 15–48, 77–151.

44. Krausz, *Reconstructing Lenin*, 367, 370; Negri, *Factory of Strategy*, 76–77.

45. Angelica Balabanoff, *My Life as a Rebel* (Bloomington, IN: Indiana University Press, 1973), 143–44. The role of those Mensheviks and Left Socialist Revolutionaries rallying to the Bolsheviks' revolutionary position is indicated in several accounts, for example Victor Serge, *Year One of the Russian Revolution* (New York: Holt, Rinehart and Winston, 1972), 73–74, 85–86, 359–60, and Rex A. Wade, *The Russian Revolution, 1917* (Cambridge: Cambridge University Press, 2000), 206–13.

46. Alfred Rosmer, *Moscow Under Lenin* (New York: Monthly Review Press, 1972), 46, 47, 48.

47. Negri, *Factory of Strategy*, 15.

48. Negri, *Factory of Strategy*, 37, 38, 41, 43.

49. Negri, *Factory of Strategy*, 38–39.

50. Negri, *Factory of Strategy*, 37.

51. Negri, *Factory of Strategy*, 79.

52. Negri, *Factory of Strategy*, 91. There are a number of studies corroborating Negri's charges of bureaucratization and reformism in the Comintern. See C. L. R. James, 1996. *World Revolution 1917–1936: The Rise and Fall of the Communist International* (Atlantic Highlands, NJ: Humanities Press, 1996); E. H. Carr, *Twilight of the Comintern, 1930–1935* (New York: Pantheon Press, 1982); Fernando Claudin, *The Communist Movement: From Comintern to Cominform*, 2 vols. (New York: Monthly Review Press, 1975); and Paulo Spriano, *Stalin and the European Communists* (London: Verso, 1985)—but these show the development taking place from the late 1920s into the 1940s, in contrast to the earlier period of 1919–1922.

53. Negri, *Factory of Strategy*, 97.

54. Theodore Draper, *American Communism and Soviet Russia* (New York: Viking Press, 1960). Among reminiscences giving a positive sense of the Comintern's early years (1919–23) are those offered in James P. Cannon, *The First Ten Years of American Communism* (New York: Lyle Stuart, 1962); Bertram D. Wolfe, *A Life in Two Centuries* (New York: Stein and Day, 1981), 229; and in the testimony of Jay Lovestone in Paul Le Blanc and Tim Davenport, eds., *The 'American Exceptionalism' of Jay Lovestone and His Comrades, 1928–1940* (Boston and Leiden: Brill, 2015), 612–13, 640–41. These find full corroboration in the

recent, careful scholarship of Jacob Zumoff, *The Communist International and US Communism, 1919–1929* (Boston and Leiden: Brill, 2014); and Bryan Palmer, *James P. Cannon and the Origins of the American Revolutionary Left, 1890–1928* (Urbana, IL: University of Illinois Press, 2007). Among studies massively disproving the "exclusion of African Americans" comment are those of Mark Solomon, *The Cry Was Unity: Communists and African Americans, 1917–1936* (Jackson: University Press of Mississippi, 1998); Mark Naison, *Communists in Harlem during the Depression* (Urbana: University of Illinois Press, 2005); Robin D. G. Kelley, *Hammer and Hoe: Alabama Communists during the Depression* (Chapel Hill: University of North Carolina Press, 1990).

55. See John Riddell, ed., *Founding the Communist International: Proceedings and Documents of the First Congress March 1919* (New York: Pathfinder Press, 1987); John Riddell, ed., *Workers of the World and Oppressed Peoples, Unite! Proceedings and Documents of the Second Congress, 1920*, 2 vols. (New York: Pathfinder Press, 1991); John Riddell, ed., *To the Masses: Proceedings of the Communist International, 1921* (Leiden and Boston: Brill, 2015); John Riddell, ed., *Toward the United Front: Proceedings of the Fourth Congress of the Communist International, 1922* (Leiden and Boston: Brill, 2012). Also part of this series are valuable works dealing with developments leading up to the Communist International—John Riddell, ed., *Lenin's Struggle for a Revolutionary International, Documents: 1907–1916, The Preparatory Years* (New York: Pathfinder Press, 1984), John Riddell, ed., *The German Revolution and the Debate on Soviet Power, Documents 1918–1919, Preparing the Founding Congress* (New York: Pathfinder Press, 1986); John Riddell, ed., *To See the Dawn: Baku, 1920 First Congress of the Peoples of the East* (New York: Pathfinder Press, 1993).

56. David Fernbach, ed., *In the Steps of Rosa Luxemburg: Selected Writings of Paul Levi* (Leiden/Boston: Brill, 2011); and Riddell, ed., *To the Masses*, 14–44, 403–561, 1036–38, 1090–96, 1097, 1099, 1104–5, 1108–152, 1174, 1177, 1178, 1179; also see Riddell, ed. *Toward the United Front*, 1157–59, 1164–73.

57. Riddell, ed., *To the Masses*, 978–1006. An excellent summary of the matter is provided in John Riddell, "Party Democracy in Lenin's Comintern—and Small Marxist Groups Today," *Links: International Journal of Socialist renewal*, February 20, 2013.

58. Riddell, ed., *To the Masses*, 1101–4.

59. Riddell, ed., *To the Masses*, 978.

60. Riddell, ed., *To the Masses*, 979.

61. Riddell, ed., *To the Masses*, 986.

62. Riddell, ed., *To the Masses*, 979.

63. Riddell, ed., *To the Masses*, 979.

64. Riddell, ed., *To the Masses*, 999.

65. Riddell, ed., *Toward the United Front*, 293.

66. Riddell, ed., *Toward the United Front*, 304–5.

67. Krausz, *Reconstructing Lenin*, 118–19.

68. Negri, *Factory of Strategy*, 9.

2. Bolshevism as a Revolutionary Collective

1. For an extensive introductory survey of Marxism, with a sampling of writings from prominent figures associated with it, see Paul Le Blanc, *From Marx to Gramsci: A Reader in Revolutionary Marxist Politics* (Chicago: Haymarket Books, 2016).

2. Raphael Abramovitch, *The Soviet Revolution 1917–1939* (New York: International Universities Press, 1962), 214.

3. V. I. Lenin, "Two Tactics of Social Democracy in the Democratic Revolution," in *Collected Works*, vol. 9 (Moscow: Progress Publishers, 1962), 48.

4. V. I. Lenin, "Social Democracy's Attitude Toward the Peasant Movement," in *Collected Works*, vol. 9, 236–37. Trotsky's theory of permanent revolution is summarized in Le Blanc, *From Marx to Gramsci*, 46–47, 94–96.

5. V. I. Lenin, "Socialism and War," in *Revolution, Democracy, Socialism: Selected Writings*, ed. Paul Le Blanc (London: Pluto Press, 2008), 227.

6. N. K. Krupskaya, *Reminiscences of Lenin* (New York: International Publishers, 1970), 328.

7. Krupskaya, *Reminiscences of Lenin*, 328–29.

8. Paul Le Blanc, *Lenin and the Revolutionary Party* (Chicago: Haymarket Books, 2015), 48.

9. Max Eastman, *Marx, Lenin and the Science of Revolution* (London: George Allen and Unwin, 1926), 159–60.

10. Outstanding sources presenting an array of prominent Bolsheviks can be found in Anatoly Vasilievich Lunacharsky, *Revolutionary Silhouettes* (New York: Hill and Wang, 1968) and Georges Haupt and Jean-Jacques Marie, *Makers of the Russian Revolution: Biographies of Bolshevik Leaders* (Ithaca, NY: Cornell University Press, 1974). Efforts which focus on presenting Lenin in his actual context can be found in Lars Lih, *Lenin* (London: Reaktion Books, 2011), Paul Le Blanc, *Unfinished Leninism: The Rise and Return of a Revolutionary Doctrine* (Chicago: Haymarket Books, 2014), especially 25–75, and Tariq Ali, *The Dilemmas of Lenin: Terrorism, War, Empire, Love, Revolution* (London: Verso, 2017).

11. On Krupskaya and Kollontai, in addition to Haupt and Marie, *Makers of the Russian Revolution*, 156–58 and 353–60, see Robert H. McNeil, *Bride of the Revolution: Krupskaya and Lenin* (London: Victor Gollancz, 1973) and Cathy Porter, *Alexandra Kollontai, A Biography*, Updated Edition (Chicago: Haymarket Books, 2014). Also see Barbara Evans Clements, *Bolshevik Women* (Cambridge: Cambridge University Press,1997) and Jane McDermid and Anna Hillyar, *Midwives of the Revolution: Female Bolsheviks and Women Workers in 1917* (Athens, OH: Ohio University Press, 1999).

12. On Kamenev, in addition to Haupt and Marie, *Makers of the Russian Revolution*, 41–47 and 100–106, see Leon Trotsky, *Portraits Personal and Political* (New York: Pathfinder Press, 1977), 164–73, 179, 180; on Trotsky, see Paul Le Blanc, *Leon Trotsky* (London: Reaktion Books, 2015).

13. Gregory Zinoviev, *History of the Bolshevik Party from the Beginnings to February 1917: A Popular Outline* (London: New Park, 1973) remains a valuable source on the history and nature of Bolshevism. On Zinoviev, in addition to Haupt and Marie, *Makers of the Russian Revolution*, 95–106, and Lunacharsky, *Revolutionary*

Silhouettes, 75–82, see Lars T. Lih, "Zinoviev: Populist Leninist," in Ben Lewis and Lars T. Lih, eds., *Zinoviev and Martov: Head to Head in Halle* (London: November Publications, 2011), 39–60. On Bukharin, in addition to Haupt and Marie, *Makers of the Russian Revolution*, 31–40, see Stephen F. Cohen, *Bukharin and the Bolshevik Revolution: A Political Biography, 1988–1938* (New York: Vintage Books, 1975).

14. On Shlyapnikov, in addition Haupt and Marie, *Makers of the Russian Revolution*, 212–21, see Barbara C. Allen, *Alexander Shlyapnikov, 1885–1937: Life of an Old Bolshevik* (Chicago: Haymarket Books, 2016). On Stalin, in addition to Haupt and Marie, *Makers of the Russian Revolution*, 65–75, see Robert C. Tucker, *Stalin as Revolutionary, 1879–1929* (New York: W. W. Norton, 1974).

15. Lenin, "Letter to American Workers," in *Revolution, Democracy, Socialism*, 299–300.

16. Ypsilon [Jules Humbert-Droz and Karl Volk], *Pattern for World Revolution*, (Chicago: Ziff-Davis, 1947), 19.

17. Alfred Rosmer, *Lenin's Moscow* (Chicago: Haymarket Books 2016), 46.

3. The Unoriginality of Leon Trotsky

1. Paul Le Blanc, *Leon Trotsky* (London: Reaction Books, 2015), 13–14. Two expressions of the criticism can be found in generally friendly reviews by Jeff Mackler, "Leon Trotsky, Revolutionary Fighter," *Socialist Action*, October 15, 2015; and by Michael Löwy, "A Most Intelligent and Insightful Presentation of Trotsky's Thought and Historical Action," *International Viewpoint*, May 3, 2015.

2. Paul Le Blanc, *From Marx to Gramsci: A Reader in Revolutionary Marxist Politics* (Chicago: Haymarket Books, 2016), the elaboration of the common ground and continuity being made in the book's long introductory essay, 3–145.

3. A representative collection of Trotsky's writings in this later period is offered in Kunal Chattopadhay and Paul LeBlanc, eds., *Leon Trotsky: Writings in Exile* (London: Pluto Press, 2012). One should note that Gramsci died only three years earlier than Trotsky, and his analysis of fascism definitely influenced Trotsky's, but his restricted circumstances of fascist imprisonment precluded the development of the kinds of theorizations which Trotsky was able to offer.

4. Leon Trotsky, *Stalin: An Appraisal of the Man and His Influence*, eds. Alan Woods and Robert Sewell (Chicago: Haymarket Books, 2019), 725, 726, 735.

5. This is demonstrated—massively and well—in the seven-volume work of John Riddell and his collaborators on the early years of the Communist International, five published by Pathfinder Press and two published by Haymarket Books. Also see additional writings on the Communist International by John Riddell, available at his website *John Riddell: Marxist Essays and Commentary*, accessed July 22, 2021, https://johnriddell.wordpress.com/.

6. *The Case of Leon Trotsky: Report of Hearings on the Charges Made Against Him in the Moscow Trials* (New York: Merit Publishers, 1968), 319.

7. For Trotsky's account, see "Three Concepts of the Russian Revolution" in *Stalin*, 765–82.

8. Michael Löwy, *The Politics of Combined and Uneven Development: The Theory of*

Permanent Revolution (Chicago: Haymarket Books, 2010), 43. Documentation on common ground between Trotsky and others can be found in Richard B. Day and Daniel Gaido, eds., *Witnesses to Permanent Revolution: The Documentary Record* (Leiden and Boston: Brill, 2009), and in Teodor Shanin, *Late Marx and the Russian Road: Marx and "The Peripheries of Capitalism"* (New York: Monthly Review Press, 1983). On Lenin, see Löwy, *The Politics of Combined and Uneven Development*, 34–36, and Paul Le Blanc, "Lenin and the Revolutionary Party: A Revolutionary Collective," *Links: International Journal for Socialist Renewal*, July 10, 2018.

9. Löwy, *The Politics of Combined and Uneven Development*, 40. Löwy's interpretation is powerfully and capably reemphasized in the first part of an article (coauthored with me; I was responsible for the second part of that article) entitled, "Lenin and Trotsky" in Norman Levine and Thomas Rockmore, eds., *The Palgrave Handbook of Leninist Philosophy* (New York: Palgrave Macmillan, 2018).

10. Isaac Deutscher, Introduction," in *The Age of Permanent Revolution: A Trotsky Reader* (New York: Dell, 1964), 18.

11. Leon Trotsky, *The Permanent Revolution and Results and Prospects* (New York: Pathfinder Press, 1978), 279.

12. For more on the nature of Stalinist theory, practice, and sources, see Paul Le Blanc, "Reflections on the Meaning of Stalinism," *Crisis and Critique* 3, no. 1 (March 29, 2016).

13. Thomas M. Twiss, *Trotsky and the Problem of Soviet Bureaucracy* (Chicago: Haymarket Books, 2015).

14. Leon Trotsky, "What Next? Vital Questions for the German Proletariat" (January 27, 1932), in Leon Trotsky, *The Struggle against German Fascism*, ed. George Breitman and Merry Maisel (New York: Pathfinder Press, 1971), 213. The most complete and rounded analysis can be found in Leon Trotsky, *The Revolution Betrayed* (New York: Doubleday Doran, 1937), which is consistent with the excerpt quoted here.

15. See analyses of fascism in Antonio Gramsci, *An Antonio Gramsci Reader: Selected Writings 1916–1935*, ed. David Forgacs (New York: Schocken Books, 1988), 135–85, and in Clara Zetkin, *Fighting Fascism: How to Struggle and How to Win*, ed. Mike Taber and John Riddell (Chicago: Haymarket Books, 2017).

16. It has been shown that Nikolai Bukharin, briefly Stalin's ally, played a key role in this "third period" theorization, but Stalin and those closest to him utilized it in far more extreme and destructive ways—see Nicholas N. Kozlov and Eric D. Weitz, "Reflections on the Origins of the 'Third Period': Bukharin, the Comintern, and the Political Economy of Weimar Germany," *Journal of Contemporary History* 24, no. 3 (July 1989); also Georg Jungclas, "The Tragedy of the German Proletariat," in *Fifty Years of World Revolution, 1917–1967: An International Symposium*, ed. Ernest Mandel (New York: Merit Publishers, 1967); and Theodore Draper, "The Ghost of Social Fascism," *Commentary*, February 1967.

17. E. H. Carr, *Foundations of a Planned Economy, 1926–1929*, vol. 3, part II (London: Macmillan Press, 1976), 638–43; C. L. R. James, *World Revolution 1917–1936: The Rise and Fall of the Communist International*, ed. Christian Høgsbjerg (Durham: Duke University Press, 2017), 306–48; Allan Merson, *Communist*

Resistance in Nazi Germany (London: Lawrence and Wishart, 1985), 19–22, 71–72.

18. Trotsky, "What Next?" in *The Struggle against German Fascism*, 254.

19. Georgi Dimitroff, *The United Front: The Struggle Against Fascism and War* (New York: International Publishers, 1938), 110; E. H. Carr, *The Twilight of the Comintern, 1930–1935* (New York: Pantheon Books, 1982), 419, 426.

20. "Latin American Problems: A Transcript, November 4, 1938," in *Writings of Leon Trotsky: Supplement 1934–40*, ed. George Breitman (New York: Pathfinder Press, 1979), 782, 783, 784.

21. "The Social Composition of the Party," in *Writings of Leon Trotsky, 1936–37*, ed George Breitman (New York: Pathfinder Press, 1978), 489, 490. See also Dianne Feeley, Paul Le Blanc, and Thomas Twiss, *Leon Trotsky and the Organizational Principles of the Revolutionary Party* (Chicago: Haymarket Books, 2014).

22. Leon Trotsky, *The Transitional Program for Socialist Revolution* (New York: Pathfinder Press, 1974), 75.

23. Daniel Bensaïd, *Strategies of Resistance and "Who Are the Trotskyists?"* (London: Resistance Books, 2009), 23.

24. Rosa Luxemburg, "Reform or Revolution," in *Socialism or Barbarism: The Selected Writings of Rosa Luxemburg*, eds. Paul Le Blanc and Helen C. Scott (London: Pluto Press, 2010), 48.

4. Learning from Bogdanov

1. Alexander Bogdanov, *Red Star: The First Bolshevik Utopia* (Bloomington: Indiana University Press, 1984). An initial examination, from the late 1980s, of the Bogdanov legacy can be found in Paul Le Blanc, *Lenin and the Revolutionary Party* (Chicago: Haymarket Books, 2015), 129–52.

2. Evgeni V. Pavlov, "Nikolai Bukharin on the life of A. A. Bogdanov," *Platypus Review* 5 (June 2013).

3. Alexander Bogdanov Library, accessed July 21, 2021, https://bogdanovlibrary.org/.

4. Tova Yedlin, *Maxim Gorky: A Political Biography* (Westport: Praeger, 1999), 85.

5. Lars Lih, *Rediscovering Lenin: What Is to Be Done? in Context* (Chicago: Haymarket Books, 2008). This and related matters are discussed in Paul Le Blanc, *Unfinished Leninism: The Rise and Return of a Revolutionary Doctrine* (Chicago: Haymarket Books, 2014), 13–14, 53–76.

6. James D. White, *Red Hamlet: The Life and Ideas of Alexander Bogdanov* (Chicago: Haymarket Books, 2019), 463.

7. V. I. Lenin, "Review: A. Bogdanov," in *Collected Works*, vol. 4 (Moscow: Progress Publishers, 1977), 46, 48.

8. Alexander Bogdanov, *A Short Course of Economic Science* (London: Communist Party of Great Britain, 1923), v.

9. Alexander Bogdanov, *The Philosophy of Living Experience: Popular Outlines* (Chicago: Haymarket Books, 2019), 52, 54, 100, 101, 137.

10. In 1915 Einstein noted that "the theory of relativity suggests itself in positivism," and specifically Mach's "line of thought had a great influence on my efforts."

Yet by 1931 he had shifted to a non-Machian formulation: "Belief in an external world independent of perceiving is the basis of all natural science." Walter Isaacson, *Einstein: His Life and Universe* (New York: Simon and Schuster, 2007), 82, 349). While this corresponds to criticisms of Mach posed by Plekhanov, Lenin, and others, Bogdanov argued that it is a "gross misunderstanding" to identify Mach's position with the notion that material reality is nothing more than human perceptions. According to Bogdanov, physical realities (an interconnected series of elements) exist independently of human perceptions (a different interconnected series of elements), and human perceptions do not flawlessly grasp the physical realities being perceived. He saw his approach as sifting out flawed perceptions in order to advance the collective comprehension and alteration of reality. Bogdanov, *The Philosophy of Living Experience*, 132–36.

11. White, *Red Hamlet*, 93.
12. White, *Red Hamlet*, 93–94.
13. White, *Red Hamlet*, 143–44.
14. White, *Red Hamlet*, 288–89. Also see Arran Gare, "Aleksandr Bogdanov and Systems Theory," *Democracy and Nature* 6, no. 3 (2000).
15. White, *Red Hamlet*, 289.
16. White, *Red Hamlet*, 318.
17. White, *Red Hamlet*, 459.
18. White, *Red Hamlet*, 244.
19. White, *Red Hamlet*, 85.
20. White, *Red Hamlet*, 103, 108. Contrary to White's suggestion, the initial belief that there were "no insuperable" differences between Bolsheviks and Mensheviks was also Lenin's view—see LeBlanc, *Lenin and the Revolutionary Party*, 65–66.
21. White, *Red Hamlet*, 114, 117.
22. White, *Red Hamlet*, 109.
23. V. I. Lenin, "To the Party," in *Collected Works*, vol. 7 (Moscow: Progress Publishers, 1977), 453, 456, 459.
24. White, *Red Hamlet*, 88–89.
25. White, *Red Hamlet*, 126, 129, 166, 418.
26. Le Blanc, *Lenin and the Revolutionary Party*, 115–28.
27. White, *Red Hamlet*, 131, 114, 115.
28. White, *Red Hamlet*, 128.
29. White, *Red Hamlet*, 142.
30. N. K. Krupskaya, *Reminiscences of Lenin* (New York: International Publishers, 1970), 153, 156.
31. White, *Red Hamlet*, 342; Krupskaya, *Reminiscences of Lenin*, 193.
32. Zenovia Sochor, *Revolution and Culture: The Bogdanov-Lenin Controversy* (Ithaca, NY: Cornell University Press, 1988), 4, 7.
33. White, *Red Hamlet*, 180–81.
34. White, *Red Hamlet*, 250, 251. For a clear summary, see August H. Nimtz, *The Ballot, the Streets—or Both? From Marx and Engels to Lenin and the October Revolution* (Chicago: Haymarket Books, 2019), 221–25.
35. M. N. Pokrovskii, *Russia in World History: Selected Essays* (Ann Arbor: University of Michigan Press, 1970), 190.

36. Krupskaya, *Reminiscences of Lenin*, 167.
37. V. I. Lenin, "Preface to the Collection *Twelve Years*," in *Collected Works*, vol. 13 (Moscow: Progress Publishers, 1978), 104–5.
38. See LeBlanc, *Lenin and the Revolutionary Party*, 139‒41; and Geoffrey Swain, *Russian Social Democracy and the Legal Labor Movement: 1906–14* (London: Macmillan Press, 1983).
39. LeBlanc, *Lenin and the Revolutionary Party*, 137; Bogdanov, "Letter to All Comrades," in Robert V. Daniels, ed., *A Documentary History of Communism*, vol. 1 (New York: Vintage Books, 1962), 62, 63.
40. White, *Red Hamlet*, 281.
41. White, *Red Hamlet*, 245.
42. Geoffrey Swain, "Editor's Introduction," in *Protokoly Soveshaniya Rasshirennoi Redaktsil "Proletariya" Iyun' 1909* (Proceedings of the Meeting of the Expanded Editorial Board of Proletarii June 1909) (Milwood, NY: Kraus International Publications, 1982), xx.
43. Le Blanc, *Lenin and the Revolutionary Party*, 148–49; Robert C. Tucker, *Stalin as Revolutionary 1879–1929* (New York: W. W. Norton, 1973), 149; Robert C. Williams, "Collective Immortality: The Syndicalist Origins of Proletarian Culture, 1905–1910," *Slavic Review* 39, no. 3 (September 1980): 398–99. In more recent scholarship, a somewhat different balance is struck—Stalin being seen as being "very close to Lenin," although having views that "were far more accommodating to Mach and Bogdanov than were Lenin's, less intransigent about compromise, and more open to working something out with Bogdanov." See Ronald Grigor Suny, *Stalin: Passage to Revolution* (Princeton: Princeton University Press, 2020), 418.
44. White, *Red Hamlet*, 215–16.
45. White, *Red Hamlet*, 362–63.
46. White, *Red Hamlet*, 243.
47. White, *Red Hamlet*, 250. Vilinov composed a philosophical essay which Bogdanov cited at length in 1913, after Vilinov's death (see Alexander Bogdanov, *The Philosophy of Living Experience: Popular Outlines* (Chicago: Haymarket Books, 2019), 191, 8–9, 11–12). For more on Vilinov, see Jutta Scherrer, "The Relationship Between the Intelligentsia and the Workers: The Case of the Party Schools in Capri and Bologna," in *Workers and Intelligentsia in Late Imperial Russia*, ed. Reginald E. Zelnik (Berkeley: University of California Press, 1999), 179–82.
48. White, *Red Hamlet*, 14, 208–9.
49. White, *Red Hamlet*, 226.
50. White, *Red Hamlet*, 250.
51. White, *Red Hamlet*, 251–53. Similar complaints about Bogdanov's alleged "paternalism" would surface in 1920 within the Proletcult movement—see John Biggart, "Bogdanov's Sociology of the Arts," in *Culture as Organization in Early Soviet Thought: Bogdanov, Eisenstein and the Proletkul*, ed. Pia Tikka (Helsinki: Tangential Points Publication Series, 2016), 18.
52. White, *Red Hamlet*, 372.
53. White, *Red Hamlet*, 265.
54. White, *Red Hamlet*, 298.

55. White, *Red Hamlet*, 299.

56. White, *Red Hamlet*, 299.

57. White, *Red Hamlet*, 300, 302.

58. White, *Red Hamlet*, 337.

59. Vladimir Nevsky, "Dialectical Materialism and the Philosophy of Dead Reaction (1920)," Libcom.org, accessed July 8, 2021, https://libcom.org/library/dialectical-materialism-philosophy-dead-reaction-vladimir-nevsky> White, *Red Hamlet*, 408.

60. See Lynn Mally, *Culture of the Future: The Proletkult Movement in Revolutionary Russia* (Berkeley: University of California Press, 1990); and Sheila Fitzpatrick, *The Commissariat of Enlightenment: Soviet Organization of Education and the Arts under Lunacharsky, October 1917–1921* (Cambridge: Cambridge University Press, 1971) for valuable information on Proletcult and related matters.

61. Mally, *Culture of the Future*, 107, 384.

62. Mally, *Culture of the Future*, xxiii–xxiv.

63. White, *Red Hamlet*, 384.

64. White, *Red Hamlet*, 419–29.

65. White, *Red Hamlet*, 431; Victor Serge, *Memoirs of a Revolutionary* (New York: New York Review of Books, 2012), 157.

66. Gerda and Hermann Weber, *Lenin: Life and Works* (London: Macmillan Press, 1980), 197; White, *Red Hamlet*, 429–31.

67. White, *Red Hamlet*, 370–71. Some of Bogdanov's thoughts correspond to material presented in Paul Le Blanc, *October Song: Bolshevik Triumph, Communist Tragedy 1917–1924* (Chicago: Haymarket Books, 2017).

68. White, *Red Hamlet*, 373–74.

69. White, *Red Hamlet*, 418–19.

70. Nikolai Krementsov, *A Martian Stranded on Earth: Alexander Bogdanov, Blood Transfusions, and Proletarian Science* (Chicago: University of Chicago Press, 2011), 12.

71. White, *Red Hamlet*, 455–56.

72. White, *Red Hamlet*, 456. John Biggart notes that, in discussing their old comrade in the late 1920s, Lunarcharsky reflected that "in the philosophical dispute between Bogdanov and Lenin it was too soon to say where the line between orthodoxy and heresy should be drawn," while Pokrovsky insisted that the value of Bogdanov's thought would become "apparent once the period 1905–1917 could be seen in perspective." John Biggart, "Anti-Leninist Bolshevism: the Forward Group of the RSDRP," *Canadian Slavonic Papers/Revue Canadienne des Slavistes* 23, no. 2 (1981): 151.

73. V. I. Lenin, *Materialism and Empirio-Criticism: Critical Comments on a Reactionary Philosophy* (New York: International Publishers, 1970), 337; Dominique Lecourt, *Proletarian Science? The Case of Lysenko* (London: New Left Books, 1977), 143. It should be noted that Karl Kautsky (at the time a strong influence on both Lenin and Bogdanov) spoke of "proletarian science" in writings of 1906 and 1908—see Karl Kautsky, *Ethics and the Materialist Conception of History* (Chicago: Charles H. Kerr, 1918), 116–19, and Karl Kautsky, *The Historic Accomplishment of Karl Marx* (Cosmonaut Press, 2020), 7, 10–11, 20, 32, 38, 43–44, 45.

74. K. M. Jensen, *Beyond Marx and Mach: Aleksandr Bogdanov's "Philosophy of Living Experience"* (Dordrecht: D. Reidel Publishing 1978), 14.

75. A foretaste of what will surely be a wave of new efforts making use of Bogdanov can be found in Paul Mason, *Postcapitalism: A Guide to Our Future* (New York: Farrar, Straus and Giroux, 2015), 219–21; and McKenzie Wark, *Molecular Red: Theory for the Anthropocene* (London: Verso, 2016), xvii, 3–61, 224–25.

5. Spider and Fly: The Leninist Philosophy of Georg Lukács

1. Rosa Leviné-Meyer, *Leviné: The Life of a Revolutionary* (Farnborough, Hampshire, England: Saxon House, 1973), 71.

2. Contained in Georg Lukács, *A Defence of History and Class Consciousness: Tailism and the Dialectic* (London: Verso, 2000), which includes the text plus an informative introduction by John Rees and a stimulating postface by Slavoj Žižek.

3. Such a version of Lukács's story circulated within the Communist movement, as reflected in Franz Borkenau, *World Communism: A History of the Communist International* (Ann Arbor: University of Michigan Press, 1962), 172–74, and Ypsilon [Jules Humbert-Droz and Karl Volk], *Pattern for World Revolution* (Chicago: Ziff-Davis, 1947), 152–59. More modern versions of the story can be found in George Lichtheim, *George Lukács* (New York: Viking Press, 1971); Leszek Kolakowski, *Main Currents of Marxism*, vol. 3 (Oxford: Oxford University Press, 1978), 253–307; and Arpad Kadarkay, *Georg Lukács: Life, Thought, and Politics* (Cambridge, MA: Basil Blackwell, 1991).

4. Georg Lukács, *Tactics and Ethics: Political Essays, 1919–1929*, ed. Rodney Livingston (New York: Harper and Row, 1972), 8.

5. "Bolshevism as a Moral Problem (1918)," in *Georg Lukács's Revolution and Counter Revolution, 1918–1921*, ed. Victor Zitta (Mexico: Hear Talleres Grafricos, 1991), 40, 41.

6. "The Moral Mission of the Communist Party," in Lukács, *Tactics and Ethics*, 69.

7. John Rees, *The Algebra of Revolution: The Dialectic and the Classical Marxist Tradition* (London: Routledge, 1998), 202, 210; István Mészáros, *The Power of Ideology* (New York: New York University Press, 1989), 250. The interpretation by Rees—part of an outstanding larger study of Marxist dialectics—is consistent with that presented here.

8. Georg Lukács, *Record of a Life: An Autobiography*, ed. István Eorsi (London: Verso, 1983), 160, 161.

9. Borkenau, *World Communism*, 124, see also 108–133, 171–75; Georg Lukács, *History and Class Consciousness: Studies in Marxist Dialectics*, (Cambridge, MA: MIT Press, 1971), xv; Lukács, *Record of a Life*, 75; also see Miklos Molnar, *A Short History of the Hungarian Communist Party* (Boulder: Westview Press, 1978), 10–30, and Agnes Szabo, "The Hungarian Party of Communists on the Social Relationships of the Counter-Revolutionary Regime, 1919–1933," in *Studies on the History of the Hungarian Working-Class Movement, 1867–1966*, ed. Henrik Vass (Budapest: Akademiai Kiado,1975), 155–84.

10. Lukács. *Record of a Life*, 74, 7.

11. Eva Fekete and Eva Karadi, eds., *Gyorgy Lukács: His Life in Pictures and Documents* (Budapest: Corvina Kiado, 1981), 119.

12. Kadarkay, *Georg Lukács*, 262, 292; Fekete and Karadi, *Gyorgy Lukács*, 141. Such a simple description was a tell-tale identification of Lukács regardless of underground precautions. He was "a man whose powerful intellect was matched only by his lack of physical substance," Ernst Fischer wrote many years later. "It was as though his mind had constructed this tough and delicate frame with the utmost economy so that only the minimum worldly provision would have to be made for it, and all else could be requisitioned for thought." Ernest Fischer, *An Opposing Man* (New York: Liveright, 1974), 404. Hungarian comrades of the 1940s and '50s recalled: "Gyorgy Lukács always had a cigar in his mouth. Whenever he entered the door of Party headquarters, the Academy of Sciences, the University, or the Writers' Association, the inevitable cigar was always there, clamped between his lips. . . . He was a shortish man, wrinkled and restless of face. He was over sixty, but his eyes frequently sparkled with childish pleasure and excitement—usually when he was explaining something." Tamas Aczél and Tibor Meray, *The Revolt of the Mind: A Case History of Intellectual Resistance Behind the Iron Curtain* (New York: Frederick A. Praeger, 1959), 57–58.

13. Kadarkay, *Georg Lukács*, 286–87. It is bizarre that Lukács's biographer likens efforts at gaining detailed information of working-class life to spying by the USSR's secret police.

14. Lukács, *History and Class Consciousness*, xxviii; Kardakay, *Georg Lukács*, 28.

15. Lukács, *Record of a Life*, 76.

16. Quoted in Paul Le Blanc, *Lenin and the Revolutionary Party* (Chicago: Haymarket Books, 2015), 248. For a slightly different translation, see V. I. Lenin, "Speech in Defense of the Tactics of the Communist International," in *Collected Works*, vol. 32 (Moscow: Progress Publishers, 1973), 474–75.

17. Lukács, *Record of a Life*, 98.

18. Leon Trotsky, *The First Five Years of the Communist International*, vol. 1 (New York: Pathfinder Press, 1972), 295.

19. Lukács, *Record of a Life*, 79, 80; István Mészáros, *Lukács's Concept of Dialectic* (London: Merlin Press, 1972), 136.

20. E. H. Carr, *Twilight of the Comintern, 1930–1935* (New York: Pantheon Books, 1982).

21. Discussion of the Hitler-Stalin Pact of 1939 (background, details, repercussions) can be found in Robert C. Tucker, *Stalin in Power: The Revolution from Above, 1928-1941* (New York: W. W. Norton, 1992), 585–619, and Wolfgang Leonhard, *Betrayal: The Hitler-Stalin Pact of 1939* (New York: St. Martin's Press, 1989).

22. Georgi Dimitroff, *The United Front: The Struggle Against Fascism and War* (New York: International Publishers, 1938), 110.

23. "Blum Theses" in Lukács, *Tactics and Ethics*, 251.

24. Lukács, *Tactics and Ethics*, 243–44. For a discussion of corporatism consistent with this usage, see Ralph Miliband, *Divided Societies: Class Struggle in Contemporary Capitalism* (Oxford: Oxford University Press, 1971), 127–30.

25. Lukács, *Tactics and Ethics*, 244–45. What Lukács calls the US "model of fascism" corresponds to what US historian William Appleman Williams refers

to (somewhat idiosyncratically) as "American syndicalism" in his *The Contours of American History* (London: Verso, 2011), elaborated especially on pages 345–450. Also relevant is William Appleman Williams, *The Tragedy of American Diplomacy*, Fiftieth Anniversary Edition (New York: W. W. Norton, 2009).

26. Lukács, *Tactics and Ethics*, 251.

27. Carr, *Twilight of the Comintern*, 426. The importance of Stalin's behind-the-scenes involvement in the development of the new line is clear from his correspondence with his lieutenant V. M. Molotov, which refers—in regard to the 1935 Seventh Comintern Congress—to "spending a lot of time with the Comintern members," makes positive reference to the reports by Dimitrov and Togliatti, and concludes that "the draft resolutions came out pretty well." See Lars T. Lih, Oleg V. Naumov, and Oleg V. Khlevniuk, eds., *Stalin's Letters to Molotov* (New Haven: Yale University Press, 1995), 237.

28. Indispensable for the serious scholar and activist seeking to comprehend Lukács is Michael Löwy, *Georg Lukács: From Romanticism to Bolshevism* (London: New Left Books, 1979), with a fine discussion of *History and Class Consciousness* on 168–92. A thoughtful appreciation of Lukács's achievement is Stephen Perkins, *Marxism and the Proletariat: A Lukácsian Perspective* (London: Pluto Press, 1993). An incredibly rich and detailed textual analysis is provided in István Mészáros, *Beyond Capital: Towards a Theory of Transition* (New York: Monthly Review Press, 1995), 282–422. Also see István Mészáros, ed. *Aspects of Class Consciousness* (London: Routledge and Kegan Paul, 1971).

29. See E. H. Carr, *The Interregnum, 1923–1925* (Baltimore: Penguin Books, 1969); Russell Block, ed., *Lenin's Fight Against Stalinism* (New York: Pathfinder Press, 1975); Leon Trotsky, *The Challenge of the Left Opposition, 1923–1925*, ed. Naomi Allen (New York: Pathfinder Press, 1975).

30. Löwy, *Georg Lukács*, 168–89.

31. István Mészáros, *The Power of Ideology* (New York: New York University Press, 1989), 312.

32. Lukács, *Tailism and the Dialectic*, 66–67.

33. Lukács, *Tailism and the Dialectic*, 66, 67, 68.

34. Lukács, *Tailism and the Dialectic*, 68–69, 70.

35. Lukács, *Tailism and the Dialectic*, 101, 50–51.

36. Lukács, *Tailism and the Dialectic*, 52, 55.

37. Lukács, *Tailism and the Dialectic*, 56–57, 58.

38. Lukács, *Tailism and the Dialectic*, 60, 61–62.

39. Lukács, *Tailism and the Dialectic*, 71–72.

40. Lukács, *Tailism and the Dialectic*, 72.

41. Lukács, *Tailism and the Dialectic*, 73–74, 77.

42. Kolakowski, *Main Currents of Marxism*, 282, 282. The 1930s Lukács quote is from Lichtheim, *George Lukács*, 104.

43. Lukács, *Tailism and the Dialectic*, 78; Georg Lukács, *Lenin: A Study on the Unity of His Thought* (Cambridge, MA: MIT Press, 1971), 37–38.

44. Lukács, *Tailism and the Dialectic*, 81–82.

45. Lukács, *Tailism and the Dialectic*, 82.

46. Lukács, *Tailism and the Dialectic*, 82.

47. Franz Jacobowski, *Ideology and Superstructure in Historical Materialism* (London: Pluto Press, 1990), 121. For more on Marx and Engels "learning from the proletariat," see Goran Therborn, *Science, Class and Society: On the Formation of Sociology and Historical Materialism* (London: New Left Books, 1976), 326–35.

48. Lukács *Tailism and the Dialectic*, 83.

49. Lukács, *Tailism and the Dialectic*, 84, 85–86.

50. Lukács, *History and Class Consciousness*, 336, 337.

51. This is discussed and documented in a number of works, including: Le Blanc, *Lenin and the Revolutionary Party*; Alexander Rabinowitch, *The Bolsheviks Come to Power* (New York: W. W. Norton, 1976); Stephen Cohen, *Bukharin and the Bolshevik Revolution: A Political Biography, 1888–1938* (New York: Vintage Books, 1975); Leon Trotsky, *The Third International After Lenin* (New York: Pathfinder Press, 1970); Boris Souvarine, *Stalin: A Critical Study of Bolshevism* (New York: Longmans, Green and Co., 1939); Ernest Mandel, *From Stalinism to Eurocommunism* (London: New Left Books, 1978); Roy Medvedev, *Let History Judge: The Origins and Consequences of Stalinism* (New York: Columbia University Press, 1989).

52. Carr, *Twilight of the Comintern*, vii, 427.

53. Georg Lukács, *The Process of Democratization* (Albany: State University of New York Press, 1991), 128, 129, 131, 152. For corroboration compare William Henry Chamberlin, *The Russian Revolution, 1917–1921*, 2 vols. (Princeton: Princeton University Press, 1987 [1935]) with William Henry Chamberlin, *Russia's Iron Age* (Boston: Little, Brown, and Co. 1934); and see Kevin Murphy, *Revolution and Counterrevolution: Class Struggle in a Moscow Metal Factory* (Chicago: Haymarket Books, 2007).

54. Lukács, *The Process of Democratization*, 158; Georg Lukács, *The Ontology of Social Being*, vol. 2, *Marx* (London: Merlin Press, 1978), 157.

55. Lukács, *The Process of Democratization*, 68, 125.

56. Lukács, *The Process of Democratization*, 99.

57. Lukács, *The Process of Democratization*, 165.

6. Antonio Gramsci and the Modern Prince

1. On Lukács, see chapter 5 in this volume. Discussions of Lenin's approach consistent with the point being made here can be found in Tamás Krausz, *Reconstructing Lenin: An Intellectual Biography* (New York: Monthly Review Press, 2014); Alan Shandro, *Lenin and the Logic of Hegemony: Political Practice and Theory in the Class Struggle* (Chicago: Haymarket Books, 2015), and Paul Le Blanc, *Lenin and the Revolutionary Party* (Chicago: Haymarket Books, 2015). Also relevant are two works by Lars T. Lih, *Lenin Rediscovered: "What Is to Be Done?" in Context* (Chicago: Haymarket Books, 2008) and *Lenin* (London: Reaktion Books, 2011), plus August H. Nimtz's *The Ballot, the Streets—or Both: From Marx and Engels to Lenin and the October Revolution* (Chicago: Haymarket Books, 2019). A more general work arguing that—despite meaningful differences—Gramsci shares a basic revolutionary theoretical and strategic framework with Marx, Engels, Luxemburg, Lenin, and Trotsky can be found in

Paul Le Blanc, *From Marx to Gramsci: A Reader in Revolutionary Marxist Politics*, second edition (Chicago: Haymarket Books, 2016).

2. Perry Anderson, *Considerations on Western Marxism* (London: Verso, 1979), 31.

3. Carl Marzani put it well: "Gramsci is the analyst of the superstructure, par excellence. In area after area—sociology, politics, mass psychology, literature, etc.—he deepened Marxism, sometimes going further than Lenin, for in many areas Lenin acted as a Marxist but did not write and develop the lessons of his experiences." Carl Marzani, *The Open Marxism of Antonio Gramsci* (New York: Cameron Associates, 1957), 7. The same can be said of the 1920s contributions of Lukács.

4. Frank Rosengarten makes the same point in his excellent collection of essays *The Revolutionary Marxism of Antonio Gramsci* (Chicago: Haymarket Books, 2015), 15–16.

5. Dante Germino, *Antonio Gramsci: Architect of a New Politics* (Baton Rouge: Louisiana State University Press, 1990), 1; Giuseppe Fiori, *Antonio Gramsci: Life of a Revolutionary* (New York: Schocken Books, 1973), 19.

6. John M. Cammett, *Antonio Gramsci and the Origins of Italian Communism* (Stanford: Stanford University Press, 1967), 11–12; Fiori, *Antonio Gramsci*, 22; Germino, *Antonio Gramsci*, xv.

7. Lynne Lawner, introduction to *Letters from Prison* by Antonio Gramsci, (New York: Harper and Row, 1973), 11; Antonio Gramsci, *A Great and Terrible World: The Pre-Prison Letters, 1908–1926*, ed. Derek Boothman (Chicago: Haymarket Books, 2014), 131, 132, 247.

8. Alastair Davidson, *Antonio Gramsci: Towards an Intellectual Biography* (London: Merlin Press, 1977), 32, 34, 38; Fiori, *Antonio Gramsci*, 53; Germino, *Antonio Gramsci*, 5.

9. Germino, *Antonio Gramsci*, 11.

10. An outstanding work on this period remains Gwyn A. Williams, *Proletarian Order: Antonio Gramsci: Factory Councils and the Origins of Communism in Italy, 1911–1921* (London: Pluto Press, 1975).

11. Victor Serge, *Memoirs of a Revolutionary* (New York: New York Review of Books, 2012), 218–19.

12. Cammett, *Antonio Gramsci and the Origins of Italian Communism*, 138, 182.

13. Peter D. Thomas, *The Gramscian Moment: Philosophy, Hegemony and Marxism* (Chicago: Haymarket Books, 2010), 230–32; Fiori, *Antonio Gramsci*, 212–16, 249–58; Davidson, *Antonio Gramsci*, 240; Rosengarten, *The Revolutionary Marxism of Antonio Gramsci*, 22, 116–17; Germino, *Antonio Gramsci*, 146, 184, 257.

14. Marzani, *The Open Marxism of Antonio Gramsci*, 13–14.

15. Anne Showstack Sassoon, *Gramsci's Politics* (Minneapolis: University of Minnesota Press, 1987), 258, 276.

16. Carl Boggs, *Gramsci's Marxism* (London: Pluto Press, 1976), 108–9. It is interesting that Carl Marzani, in later years, was inclined to make a similar distinction, as he explained his decision to ease out of Communist Party membership in the 1940s. Contrasting New York state chairman Israel Amter's rigidity, characteristic of higher circles in the US Communist Party, with his own more open and free-wheeling approach as a lower-level organizer on New York's

Lower East Side, Marzani later reflected: "He was a stickler for Party discipline, and, in his eyes, I was defying it. Neither of us knew it [then], but he was a Leninist and I was a Gramscian." See Carl Marzani, *The Education of a Reluctant Radical*, vol. 4, *From Pentagon to Penitentiary* (New York: Topical Books, 1995), 50–51, 55. Yet Amter's organizational approach represented a Stalinist mode of functioning that both Amter and Marzani interpreted, in the 1940s, as "Leninism." It would have been impossible for Amter to hold his high position in the Communist Party if he had thought or functioned otherwise. Similarly—but in stark contrast—it would have been impossible for Gramsci to be General Secretary of the Italian Communist Party in the 1920s if he had not been the kind of genuine Leninist that he was. Obviously, Leninism of that time tended to be far more open, critical-minded, creative (more "Gramscian") than would be permissible after Stalin's ascendancy.

17. Davidson, *Antonio Gramsci*, 91, 236, 237.

18. Thomas, *The Gramscian Moment*, 208, 212. This is consistent with sources cited in note 1 above.

19. "Theses on the Organizational Structure of the Communist Parties and the Methods and Content of Their Work," in *To the Masses: Proceedings of the Third Congress of the Communist International, 1921*, ed. John Riddell (Chicago: Haymarket Books, 2016), 978–1006; Paul Le Blanc, *Unfinished Leninism: The Rise and Return of a Revolutionary Doctrine* (Chicago: Haymarket Books, 2014), 85; Le Blanc, *Lenin and the Revolutionary Party*, 285–86.

20. Antonio Gramsci, "The Modern Prince," in *Selections from the Prison Notebooks*, ed. Quintin Hoare and Geoffrey Nowell Smith (New York: International Publishers, 1971), 135. See also Quentin Skinner, *Machiavelli: A Very Short Introduction* (Oxford and New York: Oxford University Press, 2000).

21. Gramsci, "The Modern Prince," 144.

22. Gramsci, "The Modern Prince," 195.

23. Gramsci, "The Modern Prince," 148, 156.

24. Gramsci, "The Modern Prince," 193.

25. Gramsci, "The Modern Prince," 197; Antonio Gramsci, "Real Dialectics," in *Selections from Political Writings, 1921–1926*, ed. Quintin Hoare (New York: International Publishers, 1978), 15–16.

26. Gramsci, "The Modern Prince," 203–4.

27. Julius Braunthal, *History of the International, 1914–1943* (New York: Frederick A. Praeger, 1967), 199, 208; Williams, *Proletarian Order*, 299; Antonio Gramsci, "Communists and the Elections," in *Selections from Political Writings, 1921–1926*, 34.

28. Marzani, *The Open Marxism of Antonio Gramsci*, 6; Rosengarten, *The Revolutionary Marxism of Antonio Gramsci*, 121.

29. Quoted in Rosengarten, *The Revolutionary Marxism of Antonio Gramsci*, 43.

30. Gramsci, "The Modern Prince," 150–51.

31. Gramsci, "The Modern Prince," 152–53.

32. Gramsci, "The Modern Prince," 196, 198, 200.

33. Gramsci, "The Modern Prince," 188–89.

34. David James Fisher, *Romain Rolland and the Politics of Intellectual Engagement* (Berkeley: University of California Press, 1988), 87–88; Davidson, *Antonio*

Gramsci, 70, 80, 99, 101–2, 247. Rolland's multivolume masterwork, *Jean-Christophe* (New York: Modern Library, 1938), published from 1904 to 1912, about a fictional musical genius who does not compromise with oppressive forces of the status quo, as well as his opposition to the First World War—documented in *Above the Battle* (London: George Allan & Unwin, 1916)—powerfully impacted on other figures in the Marxist movement, including Rosa Luxemburg, Leon Trotsky, Karl Radek, Nikolai Bukharin, Victor Serge—although in later years he would tragically compromise his moral authority through acceptance of Stalin's 1936–1938 purges.

35. Antonio Gramsci, "Address to the Anarchists," in *Selections from Political Writings 1910–1920*, ed. Quintin Hoare (New York: International Publishers, 1977), 188–89.
36. Gramsci, *Letters from Prison*, 158–59.
37.` Romain Rolland, "For Those Dying in Mussolini's Jails. Antonio Gramsci" (1934), in *I Will Not Rest* (New York: Liveright Publishing Corporation, 1937), 310–13.

7. Rosa Luxemburg and the Actuality of Revolution

1. Such critiques include: Hal Draper, "Marxism and Trade Unions" (criticizing her views on trade unions as "monstrous" and un-Marxist), Marxist Internet Archive, accessed July 22, 2021, https://www.marxists.org/archive/draper/1970/tus/index.htm; and Eric Blanc, "The Rosa Luxemburg Myth: A Critique of Luxemburg's Politics in Poland," *Historical Materialism* 25, no. 4 (2017): 3–36.
2. V. I. Lenin, "Notes of a Publicist," in *Collected Works*, vol. 33 (Moscow: Progress Publishers, 1965), 210.
3. Rosa Luxemberg, *The Complete Works of Rosa Luxemburg*, vol. 5, edited by Helen Scott and Paul Le Blanc (London: Verso, forthcoming 2022).
4. Rosa Luxemburg, "Organizational Questions of the Russian Social Democracy," Marxist Internet Archive, accessed July 9, 2021, https://www.marxists.org/archive/luxemburg/1904/questions-rsd/ch02.htm.
5. Rosa Luxemburg. *Reform or Revolution*, Marxist Internet Archive, accessed July 9, 2021, https://www.marxists.org/archive/luxemburg/1900/reform-revolution/intro.htm
6. Rosa Luxemburg, *The Accumulation of Capital* in *The Complete Works of Rosa Luxemburg*, vol. 2, ed. Peter Hudis and Paul Le Blanc (London: Verso, 2015), 267, 270.
7. Luxemberg, *The Complete Works of Rosa Luxemburg*, vol. 5.
8. Luxemberg, *The Complete Works of Rosa Luxemburg*, vol. 5.
9. Georg Lukács, *Lenin: A Study in the Unity of His Thought* (London: Verso, 2009), 11–12.
10. Luxemberg, *The Complete Works of Rosa Luxemburg*, vol. 5.
11. Luxemberg, *The Complete Works of Rosa Luxemburg*, vol. 5.
12. Antonio Gramsci, "The Modern Prince," in *Selections from the Prison Notebooks*, ed. Quinton Hoare and Geoffrey Nowell Smith (New York: International Publishers, 1971), 198–99, 188–89.
13. Luxemberg, *The Complete Works of Rosa Luxemburg*, vol. 5.

14. Karl Kautsky, "Rosa Luxemburg," in *Rosa Luxemburg, Karl Liebknecht, Leo Jogiches: Ihre Bedeutung für deutsche Sozialdemokratie* (1921), 14–20; translated into English, with an introduction, by Rida Vaquas, in *Prometheus*, winter 2020–2021, accessed July 22, 2021, https://www.prometheusjournal.org/2021/01/15/translation-rosa-luxemburg-by-karl-kautsky/.

15. John Riddell, ed., *To the Masses: Proceedings of the Third Congress of the Communist International, 1921* (Chicago: Haymarket Books, 2015), 979.

16. Riddell, ed., *To the Masses*, 980; Luxemburg quoted in F. L. Carsten, "Freedom and Revolution: Rosa Luxemburg," in *Revisionism: Essays on the History of Marxist Ideas*, ed. Leopold Labedz (New York: Frederick A. Praeger, 1962), 65, 66.

17. Carsten, "Freedom and Revolution," 66.

8. The "Anti-Philosophy" of Karl Korsch

1. See Perry Anderson, *Considerations on Western Marxism* (London: Verso, 1979).

2. David Renton, *Dissident Marxism, Past Voices for Present Times* (London: Zed Books, 2004), 80. See also chapter 5 in this volume; and Paul Le Blanc, *From Marx to Gramsci: A Reader in Revolutionary Marxist Politics* (Chicago: Haymarket Books, 2016), 333–78.

3. This draws from Patrick Goode, *Karl Korsch: A Study in Western Marxism* (London: Macmillan Press, 1979); Russell Jacoby, *Dialectic of Defeat: Contours of Western Marxism* (Cambridge: Cambridge University Press, 1981), 92–99, and Douglass Kellner, "Korsch's Revolutionary Marxism," in *Karl Korsch: Revolutionary Theory*, ed. Douglass Kellner (Austin: University of Texas Press, 1977), 3–113. The volume edited by Kellner also contains a good selection of Korsch's "lesser" writings.

4. Karl Korsch, *Marxism and Philosophy* (New York: Monthly Review Press, 1970), 97.

5. Zinoviev, "Report of E.C.C.I.," *Fifth Congress of the Communist International, Abridged Report* (London: Communist Party of Great Britain, 1924), 16–17; Joel Geier, "Zinovievism and the Degeneration of World Communism," *International Socialist Review* 93 (Summer 2014): 41–73. The friend referred to here was Bertolt Brecht.

6. See Paul Mattick, *Anti-Bolshevik Communism* (London: Merlin Press, 1978), and Jacoby *Dialectic of Defeat*, 72–81.

7. Karl Korsch, *Karl Marx* (Leiden and Boston: Brill, 2016), 47, 155.

8. Sidney Hook, *Out of Step: An Unquiet Life in the 20th Century* (New York: Harper and Row, 1987), 111–12. Brecht's comments are quoted from Margot Heinemann, "Karl Korsch" (in response to letter by Geoffrey Minish), *London Review of Books*, September 16, 1982.

9. Korsch, *Karl Marx*, 41, 57, 76, 137.

10. Goode, *Karl Korsch*, 170–87. Brecht quoted from Heinemann, "Karl Korsch."

11. Quoted in Korsch, *Marxism and Philosophy*, 74–75, 95, and in Korsch, *Karl Marx*, 197. Alex Callinicos, *Marxism and Philosophy* (Oxford and New York: Oxford University Press, 1985), 1; Helena Sheehan, *Marxism and the Philosophy of Science: A Critical of History* (Atlantic Highlands, NJ: Humanities Press, 1993), 261.

12. Roy Edgley, "Philosophy," in *Marx: The First 100 Years*, ed. David McLellan (London: Fontana, 1983), 241.

13. Korsch, *Marxism and Philosophy*, 30–31; Korsch, *Karl Marx*, 122, 123.

14. Korsch, *Karl Marx*, 7, 8, 11.

15. Sheehan, *Marxism and the Philosophy of Science*, 261; Leszek Kolakowski, *Main Currents of Marxism*, vol. 3 (New York: Oxford University Press, 1981), 322–23; Korsch, *Karl Marx*, 57.

16. C. Wright Mills, *The Marxists* (New York: Dell Publishing, 1962), 102.

17. Korsch, *Karl Marx*, 56; Korsch, *Marxism and Philosophy*, 35, 97.

18. Sidney Hook, "The Scope of Marxian Theory," in *The Making of Society: An Outline of Sociology*, ed. V. F. Calverton (New York: Random House, 1937), 852. This repeats themes to be found in Hook's classic *Towards the Understanding of Karl Marx* (New York: John Day, 1933), in which he expresses his indebtedness to Korsch for confirmation of his own "hypothesis of the practical-historical axis of Marx's thought" (xii). It is worth pondering that Hook found it impossible to sustain this orientation beyond the 1930s, as did Korsch.

19. Korsch, *Karl Marx*, 12, 28–29.

20. Korsch, *Karl Marx*, 32, 34, 37, 46, 54.

21. Quoted in Korsch, *Karl Marx*, 136.

22. Korsch, *Karl Marx*, 156.

23. Korsch, *Karl Marx*, 90, 101.

24. A discussion of the controversies around the transformation of values into prices can be found in Paul M. Sweezy, *The Theory of Capitalist Development* (New York: Monthly Review Press, 1968), 109–130.

25. Korsch, *Karl Marx*, 109–110.

26. Korsch, *Karl Marx*, 104.

27. Korsch, *Karl Marx*, 105.

9. The Odyssey of James Burnham

1. Gary Dorrien, *The Neo-Conservative Mind: Politics, Culture and the War of Ideology* (Philadelphia, Temple University Press, 1993), 63. For "new leftists" duplicating Burnham's trajectory, see Peter Collier and David Horowitz, eds., *Second Thoughts: Former Radicals Look Back at the Sixties* (Lanham, MD: Madison Books, 1989); also relevant is the collective portrait of slick and secular young conservative publicists—much in the Burnham mold—who have become a power in US politics, sketched in James Atlas, "The Counter-Counterculture," *New York Times Magazine*, February 12, 1995.

2. Several years after this essay was first published, a full-scale biography finally appeared, written from a conservative point of view (though with an understandable lack of familiarity with certain specifics of left-wing history and politics): Daniel Kelley, *James Burnham and the Struggle for the World: A Life* (Wilmington: Intercollegiate Studies Institute, 2002).

3. Alan Wald, *The New York Intellectuals: The Rise and Decline of the Anti-Stalinist Left from the 1930s to the 1980s* (Chapel Hill: University of North Carolina Press, 1987),

176; John P. Diggins, *Up from Communism: Conservative Odysseys in American Intellectual History* (New York: Columbia University Press, 1975), 163, 164.

4. Wald, *The New York Intellectuals*, 176–77; Sidney Hook in "James Burnham, 1905–1987," *National Review*," September 11, 1987, 32. This reminiscence was in a special memorial issue of *National Review* dedicated to Burnham; further citations in these notes to "James Burnham" refer to that issue of *National Review*.

5. Hook, "James Burnham," 32; Wald, *The New York Intellectuals*, 178.

6. Sidney Hook, *Out of Step: An Unquiet Life in the 20th Century* (New York: Harper and Row, 1987), 533. On the democratic nature of Lenin's and Trotsky's thought, see Paul Le Blanc, *Lenin and the Revolutionary Party* (Chicago: Haymarket Books, 2015) and Ernest Mandel, *Trotsky: A Study in the Dynamic of His Thought* (London: New Left Books, 1979); one can argue whether these particular interpretations are "correct," but the point is that they correspond to the manner in which Burnham himself, during his left-wing incarnation, understood Leninism and Trotskyism. See the self-consciously *Leninist* formulations which Sidney Hook employs in his defense of revolutionary democracy in *Towards the Understanding of Karl Marx: A Revolutionary Interpretation* (New York: John Day, 1933), as well as in his essay "On Workers' Democracy." That Burnham intellectually embraced such revolutionary democracy is clear from his writings (e.g., see note 11 below).

7. Information on the American Workers Party can be found in A. J. Muste, "My Experience in the Labor and Radical Struggles of the Thirties," in *As We Saw the Thirties*, ed. Rita James Simon (Urbana: University of Illinois Press, 1967), 123–50; Hook, *Out of Step*, 190–207.

8. Sidney Hook, "On Workers' Democracy," *Modern Monthly*, October 1934, 532, 531; Hook, *Out of Step*, 198–99, 202. Hook's views changed in a manner that also paralleled changes in Burnham's "mature" thought. He later commented self-critically that his workers' democracy essay "suffered from the old illusion that the fundamental conflict was between socialism and capitalism rather than between democracy and totalitarianism." This conceptual shift is related to his later rejection—more or less shared by Burnham—of the Marxist view that "the mode of economic production determines politics," a notion he felt had been "decisively refuted" by historical experience, Sidney Hook, *Marxism and Beyond* (Totowa, NJ: Rowman & Littlefield, 1983), 31. There is an important link here with more radical post-Marxists of recent years. Applauding Hook's "trenchant and prescient . . . critique of historical materialism's traditional failure to recognize the disjuncture between the economic infrastructure and the forms of political rule," radical post-Marxist Stanley Aronowitz (in an explication of the ideas of Ernesto Laclau and Chantal Mouffe) concludes: "Thus, if the political level is autonomous, just as the economic and the ideological, then the *centrality* of class and class struggle in the Marxist paradigm must be denied." Aronowitz, *The Politics of Identity* (New York: Routledge, 1992), 181–82. This "depriviledging" of economics and class constitutes a theoretical link with the post-Marxism of Hook and Burnham.

9. On the US Trotskyist movement, see: Robert J. Alexander, *International Trotskyism, 1929–1985: A Documented Analysis of the Movement* (Durham: University of North Carolina Press, 1991), 751–952, and entries by Paul Le Blanc

on "Socialist Workers Party" and Tim Wohlforth on "Trotskyism" in Mari Jo
Buhle, Paul Buhle, and Dan Georgakas, eds., *Encyclopedia of the American Left*
(Urbana: University of Illinois Press, 1992). Also see George Breitman, Paul Le
Blanc, and Alan Wald, eds., *Trotskyism in the United States: Historical Essays and
Reconsiderations* (Chicago: Haymarket Books, 2016). Various issues related to
Marxism are also dealt with succinctly in Tom Bottomore, Laurence Harris, V. G.
Kiernan, and Ralph Miliband, eds., *A Dictionary of Marxist Thought* (Cambridge,
MA: Harvard University Press, 1983).

10. Diggins, *Up from Communism*, 161.

11. Hook in "James Burnham," 33.

12. Diggins, *Up from Communism*, 161; James P. Cannon, *The Struggle for a
Proletarian Party* (New York: Pathfinder Press, 1970), 29. Also see Burnham's
The People's Front: The New Betrayal (New York, 1937), a sophisticated left-wing
analysis which has held up well over time—as suggested by an examination
of E. H. Carr, *The Twilight of the Comintern, 1930–1935* (New York: Pantheon
Books, 1982). In his pamphlet *Let the People Vote on War!* (New York: Pioneer
Publishers, 1938), Burnham argued that "war has become, in our day,
totalitarian," that it "dominates and controls the total life and activities of the
totality of the people," and that "it would seem wise and proper for us to try to
decide ourselves what to do, and not to turn ourselves blindly over to the hands
of others." Calling for a mobilization of the American people (through "rallies,
petitions, speeches, meetings, canvassings") to push through a law requiring
a popular referendum whenever the question of war was posed, he concluded:
"Before the assembled might of the people, the secret diplomats, the star-
chamber heroes, the war-mongers and their fellow conspirators, will be routed
into the open and compelled to give their accounting. Let *the people* decide!" (*Let
the People Vote on War!*, 5, 14.) The slogan with which Burnham concluded this
pamphlet was, in the 1960s, popularized by the "new left" activists of Students
for a Democratic Society, whose conception of "participatory democracy"
harmonized with Burnham's views of the 1930s. See James Miller, *"Democracy is
in the Streets": From Port Huron to the Siege of Chicago* (Cambridge, MA: Harvard
University Press, 1994), 141–54.

13. Wald, *The New York Intellectuals*, 178.

14. George Novack, "My Philosophical Itinerary: An Autobiographical Forward," in
Polemics in Marxist Philosophy (New York: Pathfinder Press, 1978), 21; Diggins,
Up from Communism, 162; Cannon, *The Struggle for a Proletarian Party*, 22–31.
In addition to confessing such deeper doubts, Burnham represented at the
1938 founding of the Socialist Workers Party—along with Joseph Carter and
Hal Draper—a minority arguing that the USSR was no longer a workers' state
but instead was "bureaucratic collectivist," and also urging what they saw as a
more democratic understanding of Leninist organizational norms. See George
Breitman, ed., *The Founding of the Socialist Workers Party* (New York: Pathfinder
Press, 1981), 28.

15. James Burnham and Max Shachtman, "Intellectuals in Retreat," *New
International*, January 1939, 18, 15. In this article, however, the authors indicated
that dialectics—which Burnham himself rejected—had little relevance to

practical politics, which brought a sharp protest from Trotsky, who held that Marxism without dialectics is like "a clock without a spring." See Leon Trotsky, *In Defense of Marxism* (New York: Pathfinder Press, 1970), 43 and see also 48–54 for Trotsky's explanation of this view.

16. This is based on the scholarship of the late George Breitman, presented in "The Liberating Influence of the Transitional Program," in *Trotskyism in the United States*, eds. Breitman, Le Blanc, and Wald.

17. George Clarke, "The Truth About the Auto Crisis," in *Background to "The Struggle for a Proletarian Party,"* ed. Fred Feldman (New York: Education for Socialists Bulletin, Socialist Workers Party, 1979), 24–29, 32. Also see Robert J. Alexander, *The Right Opposition: The Lovestoneites and the International Communist Opposition of the 1930s* (Westport, CT: Greenwood Press, 1981), 56–59; Benjamin Stolberg, *The Story of the CIO* (New York: 1938); Victor G. Reuther, *The Brothers Reuther and the Story of the UAW: A Memoir* (Boston: Houghton Mifflin Co., 1979), 181–92; Irving Bernstein, *Turbulent Years: A History of the American Worker 1933–1941* (Boston, 1971), 554–69.

18. George Clarke, "The Truth About the Auto Crisis," 32.

19. Clarke, "The Truth About the Auto Crisis," 33. This incident suggests a contradiction between revolutionary-democratic theory and elitist practice, which Burnham would soon resolve through the abandonment of the former.

20. Louis Cassel, "The Secret Life of James Burnham," *New International*, February 1948, 62; Trotsky, *In Defense of Marxism*, contains the resignation letter, see 207.

21. James Burnham, *The Managerial Revolution* (Bloomington: Indiana University Press, 1962), 55; for Burnham, Marxism was like "a clock without a spring," as Trotsky had put it (see footnote 15, above). Different evaluations than Burnham's on the relevance of Marxism in the light of later historical, anthropological, and other research are offered in Bertell Ollman and Edward Vernoff, eds., *The Left Academy: Marxist Scholarship on American Campuses* (New York, 1982). Also see Ernest Mandel, *The Place of Marxism in History* (Atlantic Highlands, NJ: Humanities Press, 1994). Of interest as well is Paul Sweezy's 1942 essay, "The Illusion of the Managerial Revolution," republished in *The Present as History* (New York: Monthly Review Press, 1953), 39–66—one of the earliest serious attempts at a Marxist critique of Burnham's book (along with that by Albert Glotzer cited in footnote 42, below).

22. Burnham, *The Managerial Revolution*, ix–x.

23. Burnham, *The Managerial Revolution*, 42, 46–47, 49–54. For studies of these matters, see Wolfgang Abendroth, *A Short History of the European Working Class* (New York: Monthly Review Press, 1972); Perry Anderson, *Considerations on Western Marxism* (London: Verso, 1979); Warren Lerner, *A History of Socialism and Communism in Modern Times: Theorists, Activists, and Humanists* (Englewood Cliffs, NJ: Prentice-Hall, 1982).

24. Burnham, *The Managerial Revolution*, 56.

25. Various points that Burnham makes here can be found in the later work of such sociologists as Daniel Bell in *The End of Ideology* (New York: The Free Press, 1960) and C. Wright Mills in *The Marxists* (New York: Dell Publishers, 1962); such historical studies as Leonard Schapiro's *The Rise of Communist Autocracy*

(Cambridge, MA: Harvard University Press, 1956) and Carmen Sirianni's *Workers' Control and Socialist Democracy* (London: Verso, 1982); in some of the themes and reflections to be found in Robin Blackburn, ed., *After the Fall: The Failure of Communism and the Future of Socialism* (London: Verso, 1991); and in numerous articles in a magazine that has become the beacon of contemporary post-Marxism, *Telos*.

26. John Kenneth Galbraith, *The New Industrial State* (New York: New American Library, 1971), 115; John Kenneth Galbraith in "James Burnham," 35; Alfred Kazin, *New York Jew* (New York: Vintage Books, 1979), 92; C. Wright Mills, "A Marx for Managers," in *Power, Politics and People: The Collected Essays of C. Wright Mills*, ed. Irving Louis Horowitz (New York: Ballantine Books, 1963), 53–71; Burnham, *The Managerial Revolution*, 71, 72. Since the appearance of *The Managerial Revolution*, prominent social critics and scholars keep returning to critical and often searching discussions of Burnham's contribution—see Lewis Corey, *The Unfinished Task: Economic Reconstruction for Democracy* (New York: Viking Press, 1942), 140–41, 202, 304; T. B. Bottomore, *Elites and Society* (Harmondsworth, England: Penguin Books, 1966), 77–82; Daniel Bell, *The Coming of Post-Industrial Society* (New York: Basic Books, 1976), 90–94; and Christopher Lasch, *The True and Only Heaven: Progress and Its Critics* (New York: W. W. Norton, 1991), 509–12, 568–69. The positive evaluation of Burnham's work by the liberal economist Galbraith became unusual after Burnham associated himself with political conservatism. Even before that, Burnham's suggestion that Stalinism and fascism had something important in common with the modern liberal corporate-capitalist order seemed too bizarre or disturbing a notion for many. A common opinion, articulated from the crossroads of liberalism and socialism by Michael Harrington, is that "the dangers inherent in the kind of sweeping historical generalizations that James Burnham learned during his years in the Trotskyist movement . . . are apparent in the *Managerial Revolution*," but that, "impressionistic and sloppy as his insight was, Burnham was talking about an important trend in the world economy." See Harrington, *The Twilight of Capitalism* (New York: Simon and Schuster, 1976), 390, 215.

27. Burnham, *The Managerial Revolution*, 272, x.

28. Max Nomad, *A Skeptic's Political Dictionary* (New York: Bookman Associates, 1953), 69. Nomad's first US article on "managerialism" can be found in "White Collars and Horny Hands," *Modern Quarterly* (Autumn 1932), 68–76. Another partial predecessor to Burnham's perspective (especially related to the belief in the inability of the working class to bring about socialism) is Selig Perlman, A *Theory of the Labor Movement* (New York: Macmillan, 1928).

29. Burnham, *The Managerial Revolution*, viii, ix. Introducing Bruno Rizzi's *The Bureaucratization of the World* (New York: Free Press, 1985), Adam Westoby shows Burnham did not plagiarize from the 1939 work of this eccentric Italian radical (20–26).

30. A. L. Riesch Owen, ed., *Selig Perlman's Lectures on Capitalism and Socialism* (Madison: University of Wisconsin Press, 1976), 134, 147; T. B. Bottomore, *Sociology: A Guide to Problems and Literature* (New York: Vintage Books,

1972), l4l; Tom Bottomore, "The Capitalist Class," in *The Capitalist Class: An International Study*, eds. Tom Bottomore and Roben J. Brym (New York: New York University Press, 1989), 5–6.

31. Brian Crozier, Joseph Sobran in "James Burnham," 36, 46; Brian Crozier, *The Masters of Power* (Boston: Little Brown,1969), 335. Like more than one agent for British and US intelligence services engaged in what he calls "the secret war for people's minds," Crozier considered Burnham his mentor. See Crozier, *Free Agent: The Unseen War 1941–1991* (New York: HarperCollins, 1993), xii, xiii, 7–8, 13, 15, 17.

32. James Burnham, The *Machiavellians: Defenders of Freedom* (New York: John Day, 1943), 236, 162, 247, 253–44. Influential "democratic theorists" of later years accepted Burnham's critique of democracy but simply redefined the term "democracy" so that, rather than meaning *rule by the people*, it would be consistent with rule by competing elite factions as described by Burnham. See, for example, Henry B. Mayo's explicit mention of and adaptation to Burnham in his *Introduction to Democratic Theory* (Oxford and New York: Oxford University Press, 1960), 270–71, 286–87. This general phenomenon is explored in Peter Bachrach, *The Theory of Democratic Elitism: A Critique* (Boston: Little Brown, 1967), and in Philip Green, ed., *Democracy* (Atlantic Highlands, NJ: Humanities Press, 1993).

33. Burnham, *The Machiavellians*, 243–44, 246, 254. Burnham later repeated and elaborated on these perspectives, while focusing on US political institutions, in *Congress end the American Political Tradition* (Chicago: Regnery, 1954), 34–44, 281–352. In this book he grudgingly accepted the common use of the term "democracy" to describe the form of elite rule he favored, labeling as *democratism* the "pure" definition of democracy.

34. Burnham, *The Machiavellians*, 270.

35. Jeanne Wacker in "James Burnham," 33–34; Dwight Macdonald, "The Future of Democratic Values," *Partisan Review* (July-August 1943), 336. It was not long before Burnham publicly proclaimed that the totalitarian order of Stalin was the genuine continuation of the Bolshevik Revolution, and perhaps the wave of the future, in "Lenin's Heir," *Partisan Review* (Winter 1945), 61–72, a much-misunderstood essay which marked a deepening of his anti-Communism. To this Macdonald offered a spirited defense of revolutionary socialist perspectives, "Beat Me, Daddy," *Partisan Review* (Spring 1945), 181–87. Burnham scornfully responded that Macdonald "is busily occupied with the defense of revolution in one psyche," an irresponsible program of sentimental dilettantism "which shouts for the causes of totalitarianism [i.e., socialist revolution] without the totalitarian result" in "Politics for the Nursery Set," *Partisan Review* (Spring 1945), 188–90). Richard H. Pells places this debate in its broader context in *The Liberal Mind in a Conservative Age: American Intellectuals in the 1940s and 1950s* (New York: HarperCollins 1985), 76–83.

36. James Burnham, *The Struggle for the World* (New York: John Day, 1947), 55. In "The Double Crisis (a dialogue)"—a transcribed discussion with André Malraux appearing in *Partisan Review* (April 1948)—Burnham relates this global power struggle to the "long-term crisis [of] the transition from one dominant form of

society to another: from traditional capitalism to what I have called in my books 'managerial society,' though the name itself is not important. Superimposed on the long-term crisis, like a wind-driven wave added to the deeper ground swell, is a shorter but still more acute crisis." This second crisis is described as "the struggle for leadership in the organization of a world political order between Communism, directed from its Soviet inner fortress, and Western Civilization, basing itself necessarily, in terms of material power, first of all on the United States" (407).

37. W. A. Swanberg, *Luce and His Empire* (New York: Scribner, 1972), 254; James P. Cannon, *Notebook of an Agitator* (New York: Pioneer Publishers, 1958), 160; Burnham's comment that "socialism is a moral ideal which men choose through a moral act" can be found in his polemic "Science and Style," in Trotsky, *In Defense of Marxism*, 205.

38. Miles Copeland in "James Burnham," 36–37; George H. Nash, *The Conservative Intellectual Movement in America Since 1945* (New York: Basic Books, 1979), 96–97; Diggins, *Up from Communism*, 321–22, 12. In *Blowback: America's Recruitment of Nazis and Its Effects on the Cold War* (New York: Weidenfield and Nicholson, 1988), 276, Christopher Simpson argues that in this period Burnham's political outlook was influenced by "his work with exiles during the early years of the [CIA-sponsored] American Committee for Liberation, Radio Liberation from Bolshevism, and similar projects that enlisted numerous Nazi collaborators among that generation of 'freedom fighters.'" Varying perspectives on the larger context of US foreign policy can be found in Frank J. Merli and Theodore A. Wilson, eds., *Makers of American Diplomacy: From Theodore Roosevelt to Henry Kissinger* (New York: Scribner, 1974). Also see Walter LaFeber, *America, Russia, and the Cold War, 1945–1980* (New York: Wiley, 1980).

39. Daniel Kelley, *James Burnham and the Struggle for the World: A Life* (Wilmington, DL: Intercollegiate Studies Institute Books, 2002), 183–84.

40. Christopher Lasch, "The Cultural Cold War: A Short History of the Congress for Cultural Freedom," *The Agony of the American Left* (New York: Vintage Books, 1969), 64, 76, 82. Lasch comments (84, 67–68) that "the student of these events is struck by the way in which ex-communists seem always to have retained the worst of Marx and Lenin and to have discarded the best," and elaborates: "Elitism was one of the things that attracted intellectuals to Leninism in the first place (more than to orthodox Marxism); and even after they had dissociated themselves from its materialist content, they clung to the congenial view of intellectuals as the vanguard of history and to the crude and simplified dialectic (of which Borkenau's speech is an excellent example, and James Burnham's *The Managerial Revolution* another) which passed for Marxism in left-wing circles of the thirties." An extensive defense of these two organizations by a leading participant can be found in Sidney Hook's *Out of Step*, 420–60.

41. James B. Burnham recounts the destruction of his father's Trotsky correspondence in "James Burnham," 51. The rise of liberal anti-Communism in the Cold War period, which Burnham did so much to shape, is charted in Mary Sperling McAuliffe, *Crisis on the Left: Cold War Politics and American Liberals, 1947–1954* (Amherst, MA: University of Massachusetts Press, 1978), and

William O'Neill, *A Better World: The Great Schism—Stalinism and the American Intellectuals* (New York: Simon and Schuster, 1982). Burnham's Congressional testimony can be found in Eric Bentley, ed., *Thirty Years of Treason: Excerpts from Hearings before the House Committee on Un-American Activities, 1938–1968* (New York: Viking, 1970), his comment on Communism being right-wing rather than left-wing on 277. Burnham's break with the "non-Communist Left" represented by *Partisan Review* is described in James B. Gilbert, *Writers and Partisans: A History of Literary Radicalism in America* (New York: Columbia University Press, 1968), 273; his more general break with liberalism and departure from the CIA are described in John B. Judis, *William F. Buckley, Jr.: Patron Saint of the Conservatives* (New York: Simon and Schuster, 1988), 122–23. Burnham's *The Web of Subversion* (New York: John Day, 1954) is worth examining as one of the more articulate examples of the red-scare genre of the 1950s. More recent studies helping us contextualize Burnham's writings and actions in this period include: Richard H. Pells, *The Liberal Mind in a Conservative Age*; Allen J. Matusow, ed., *Joseph R. McCarthy* (Englewood Cliffs, NJ: Prentice Hall, 1970); Ellen Schrecker, *The Age of McCarthyism: A Brief History with Documents* (Boston: St. Martin's Press, 1994); and David Caute, *The Great Fear: The Anti-Communist Purge under Truman and Eisenhower* (New York: Simon and Schuster, 1978). Even after his departure from the CIA, Burnham was inclined (by his own admission) to remain an uncritical apologist for it—though late in life he expressed alarm that "innumerable bureaucratic protuberances" were making the US intelligence community unwieldy as well as increasingly beyond the realm of accountability or control (in his article "Too Much Intelligence," *National Review*, July 4, 1975, 711).

42. Diggins, *Up from Communism*, 13; Wald, *The New York Intellectuals*, 189–92; Tim Wohlforth, *The Prophet's Children: Travels on the American Left* (Atlantic Highlands, NJ: Humanities Press, 1994), 47. Wohlforth claims "Shachtman was the original theorist of the Evil Empire," yet the concept popularized by Ronald Reagan, was first advanced, it would seem, by Burnham. Also see Paul Buhle, ed., *The Legacy of the Workers Party, 1940–1949: Recollections and Reflections* (New York, 1985); and Peter Drucker, *Max Shachtman and His Left: A Socialist's Odyssey Through the "American Century"* (Atlantic Highlands, NJ: Humanities Press, 1993). Incisive critiques of Burnham's antisocialist and antidemocratic perspectives by his erstwhile Shachtmanite comrades can be found in Albert Gates [Glotzer], "Burnham and His Managers," *New International*, July 1941, 144–48, and R. Fahan [Irving Howe], "Machiavelli and Modern Thought: A Critique of James Burnham's Book," *New International*, December 1943, 334–37; January 1944, 24–28; February 1944, 50–54.

43. Burnham and Malraux, "The Double Crisis," 434, 42.

44. Burnham and Malraux, "The Double Crisis," 408.

45. William F. Buckley Jr. in "James Burnham," 31; Garry Wills, *Confessions of a Conservative* (Harmondsworth: Penguin Books, 1980), 35; Judis, *William F. Buckley, Jr.*, 440. According to Gary Dorrien in *The Neo-Conservative Mind* (58), it was Burnham who recruited Buckley to the CIA in 1951.

46. James Gilbert, *Designing the Industrial State: The Intellectual Pursuit of Collectivism*

in America, 1880–1940 (Chicago: Quadrangle Books, 1972), 284; James Burnham, *The Suicide of the West* (New York: John Day, 1964), 278, 283, 289–90. Burnham is appropriately placed in the context of American conservatism in William F. Buckley, ed., *American Conservative Thought in the Twentieth Century* (Indianapolis: Bobbs-Merrill, 1970). Peter Viereck's relatively centrist historical survey *Conservatism* (Princeton, NJ: Van Nostrad, 1956) also is useful.

47. These quotations, from articles published in *National Review*, are presented in a sympathetic study, Samuel T. Francis, *Power and History: The Political Thought of James Burnham* (Lanham, MD: University Press of America, 1984), 124–25.

48. James Burnham, *The War We Are In: The Last Decade and the Next* (New Rochelle, NY: Arlington House, 1967), 13. For the authoritarian/totalitarian distinction, see James Burnham, "The Alternatives to Democracy," *National Review*, October 25, 1975, 1225, and "Distinctions Within Distinctions," *National Review*, January 17, 1975, 27—which concludes that "democracy's defects lead toward its replacement by despotism," and that despotism of the Right is preferable to that of the Left. As Gary Dorrien shows (*The Neoconservative Mind*, 370–72), elements of Burnham's perspective were held in common with sectors of "the anti-Stalinist Old Left" (such as his old comrade Max Shachtman) as well as with Hannah Arendt's 1951 classic *The Origins of Totalitarianism*. It can be argued, however, that it was Burnham's version that was most faithfully reflected in neoconservative Jeane Kirkpatrick's "Dictatorships and Double Standards," *Commentary*, November 1979, 34–45, consequently permeating the foreign policy of the Reagan-Bush administrations.

49. Burnham, *The War We Are In*, 13–14, 320, 321. Dorrien notes that Burnham was an early and consistent proponent of "the domino theory" (*The Neoconservative Mind*, 60–61), which mirrors Marxism's revolutionary internationalism. Journalist Sidney Blumenthal has suggested that Burnham's variant of Cold War anti-Communism represented a perverse utilization of elements in the Trotskyist orientation—transforming Trotsky's theory of permanent revolution into a policy of "permanent counter-revolution." See Sidney Blumenthal, "The Reagan Doctrine's Strange History," *Washington Post*, June 29, 1986, cited in Simpson, *Blowback*, 276.

50. C. Wright Mills, "The Conservative Mood," in *Power, Politics, and People*, 220; C. Wright Mills, *The Marxists* (New York: Dell Publishing, 1962), 16; Dwight Macdonald, *Politics Past* (New York: Viking, 1970), 342, 335.

51. Nash, *The Conservative Intellectual Movement in America Since 1945*, 153, iv; Judis, *William F. Buckley, Jr.*, 425–26.

52. Medal of Freedom Citation, in "James Burnham," 53. Also see Simpson, *Blowback*, 276.

53. Irving Howe, *Steady Work: Essays in the Politics of Democratic Radicalism, 1953–1966* (New York: Harcourt, Brace and World, 1966), 253; Jeffrey Hart, "James Burnham," 44.

54. C. H. Simonds, Linda Bridges in "James Burnham," 52, 48.

55. Author's interview with Morris Lewit, December 19, 1993, tape in author's possession. Lewit, a plumber by trade, had been a teenage participant in the Russian Revolution, later becoming active in the American Communist

movement; a founder of the Communist League of America and an early translator of Trotsky's works into English, Lewit was a sometime member of the Political Committee of the Socialist Workers Party; his party-name was Morris Stein. A useful introductory study of "the workers" who were the source of Burnham's idealization and disappointment can be found in James R. Green, *The World of the Worker: Labor in Twentieth-Century America* (New York: Farrar, Strauss and Giroux, 1980). Also see George Lipsitz, *Rainbow at Midnight: Labor and Culture in the 1940s* (Urbana: University of Illinois Press, 1994).

56. Priscilla Buckley, "James Burnham," 47.

57. Wills, *Confessions of a Conservative*, 46; Sobran in "James Burnham," 46. Also see Irving Howe, ed., *Orwell's Nineteen Eighty-Four: Text, Sources, Criticism* (New York: Harcourt, Brace and World, 1963).

58. Paul Siegel, *Revolution and the 20th-Century Novel* (New York: Pathfinder Press, 1979), 150–60; George Orwell, "James Burnham and the Managerial Revolution," *Collected Essays, Journalism and Letters*, vol. 4 (New York: Mariner, 1968), 165. A powerful alternative to Burnham's orientations is the approach which can be traced in the writings of one of his cothinkers of earlier years, Hal Draper, *Socialism from Below*, ed. E. Haberkern (Atlantic Highlands, NJ: Humanities Press, 1992); also Hal Draper, "The Secret Weapon: Political Warfare," *New Politics* 2, no. 3 (Summer 1963): 111–20.

10. Dennis Brutus: Poet as Revolutionary (1924–2009)

1. Portions of this essay previously appeared, during Dennis's life, in a review appearing in the journal *Against the Current*, July-August 2007.

2. Dennis Brutus, *Leafdrift*, ed. Lamont B. Steptoe (Camden, NJ: Whirlwind Press, 2005); Dennis Brutus, *Poetry and Protest: A Dennis Brutus Reader*, eds. Lee Sustar and Aisha Karim (Chicago: Haymarket Books, 2006).

3. Brutus, *Poetry and Protest*, 95–96.

4. Brutus, *Leafdrift*, 50–51.

5. Brutus, *Poetry and Protest*, 274.

6. Brutus, *Poetry and Protest*, 393.

7. Aspects of the antiapartheid struggle, and what happened after the ANC victory, are traced in an account which Dennis influenced—Paul Le Blanc, "South Africa: Race, Class, Vanguard," *Revolutionary Studies: Essays in Plain Marxism* (Chicago: Haymarket Books, 2017), 181–203.

8. Brutus, *Leafdrift*, 87.

9. Dennis Brutus, foreword to *Marx, Lenin and the Revolutionary Experience: Studies of Communism and Radicalism in the Age of Globalization* by Paul Le Blanc (New York and London: Routledge, 2006), x–xi.

10. Nadine Gordimer, "Tribute to Dennis Brutus: Brighter Than Their Searchlights," *Illuminations* 20 (August 2004): 34–35.

11. Brutus, *Leafdrift*, 204.

12. Dennis Brutus, *China Poems* (Austin: University of Texas, 1975), 35.

13. Brutus, *China Poems*, 36.

14. Brutus, *Leafdrift*, 208.
15. Also see Alan Wieder, *Ruth First and Joe Slovo in the War Against Apartheid* (New York: Monthly Review Press, 2013), 91–92; and Joe Slovo, *Slovo: The Unfinished Biography of ANC Leader Joe Slovo* (Melbourne: Ocean Press, 1997), 130–32.
16. Dennis Brutus, *Airs and Tributes* (Camden, NJ: Whirlwind Press, 1989), 13.

11. Revolutionary Patience: Daniel Bensaïd

1. Daniel Bensaïd, *An Impatient Life: A Memoir* (London: Verso, 2013), 18. Hereafter referred to parenthetically in the main text.
2. The decisive experience for "the generation of '68" is described in the classic by Daniel Singer, *Prelude to Revolution: France in May 1968* (Chicago: Haymarket Books, 2013).
3. Information and analyses on the history of the Fourth International can be found in Pierre Frank, *The Long March of the Trotskyists: Contributions to the History of the Fourth International*, with contributions by Daniel Bensaïd and Ernest Mandel (London: Resistance Books, 2010); and Robert J. Alexander, *International Trotskyism: A Documented Analysis of the Movement, 1929–1985* (Durham: University of North Carolina Press, 1991).
4. The post-World War II evolution of the Fourth International in Europe, in which these developments took place, is covered by Livio Maitan, *Memoirs of a Critical Communist: Towards a History of the Fourth International* (London: Merlin Press, 2020).
5. Hansen's polemics can be found in *The Leninist Strategy of Party Building: The Debate on Guerrilla Warfare in Latin America* (New York: Pathfinder Press, 1979) and online in the Marxist Internet Archive: https://www.marxists.org/archive/hansen/1971/indef.htm. His political background and context are explicated in George Breitman, Paul Le Blanc, and Alan Wald, eds., *Trotskyism in the United States: Historical Essays and Reconsiderations*, 2nd edition (Chicago: Haymarket Books, 2016).
6. See Willem Stutje, *Ernest Mandel: A Rebel's Dream Deferred* (London: Verso, 2009), as well as the Ernest Mandel Internet Archive, https://www.ernestmandel.org/en/.
7. See Daniel Bensaïd, Alda Sousa, Alan Thornett, and others, *New Parties of the Left: Experiences from Europe* (London: Resistance Books, 2011).
8. Daniel Bensaïd, *Marx for Our Times: Adventures and Misadventures of a Critique* (London: Verso, 2002), xv. More information about and writings of Bensaïd can be found within the Marxist Internet Archive (https://www.marxists.org/archive/bensaid/index.htm) and Le Site de Daniel Bensaïd (https://danielbensaid.org/Welcome-to-the-Daniel-Bensaid-website?lang=fr). Also see Daniel Bensaïd, *Recorded Fragments: Twelve Reflections on the 20ᵗʰ Century* (London: Resistance Books, 2020); on the projected publication of *Politics as a Strategic Art: Selected Writings of Daniel Bensaïd*, see: https://www.toledotranslationfund.org/daniel_bensaid.

12. Conclusions on Coherence and Comradeship

1. Friends directly influencing the crystallization of the current draft of reflections presented here include Michael Löwy, Eleni Varikis, Pierre Rousset, Helen Scott, John Riddell, Joost Kircz, Peter Boyle, and Tamás Krausz. It should not be assumed that any of them necessarily agree with all that is said here.

2. Some of these have, of course, continued to exist as shells or fragments of their former selves. In some cases they would continue in reinvented forms, generally with new and quite different leaders, but (from what I can see) generally without the earlier vibrancy, effectiveness, and impact.

3. All of this is in his all-too-commonly-denounced 1902 polemic *What Is to Be Done?*—for the excerpts cited here, see V. I. Lenin, *Revolution, Democracy, Socialism: Selected Writings*, ed. Paul Le Blanc (London: Pluto Press, 2008), 140–44.

4. George Breitman, "The Current Radicalization Compared with Those of the Past," in Jack Barnes, George Breitman, Derrick Morrison, Barry Sheppard, and Mary-Alice Waters, *Towards an American Socialist Revolution: A Strategy for the 1970s* (New York: Pathfinder Press, 1971), 101.

5. The relevant passage can be found in Lenin, *Revolution, Democracy, Socialism*, 306.

INDEX

"Passim" (literally "scattered") indicates intermittent discussion of a topic over a cluster of pages.

ABOUT HAYMARKET BOOKS

Haymarket Books is a radical, independent, nonprofit book publisher based in Chicago. Our mission is to publish books that contribute to struggles for social and economic justice. We strive to make our books a vibrant and organic part of social movements and the education and development of a critical, engaged, international left.

We take inspiration and courage from our namesakes, the Haymarket martyrs, who gave their lives fighting for a better world. Their 1886 struggle for the eight-hour day—which gave us May Day, the international workers' holiday—reminds workers around the world that ordinary people can organize and struggle for their own liberation. These struggles continue today across the globe—struggles against oppression, exploitation, poverty, and war.

Since our founding in 2001, Haymarket Books has published more than five hundred titles. Radically independent, we seek to drive a wedge into the risk-averse world of corporate book publishing. Our authors include Noam Chomsky, Arundhati Roy, Rebecca Solnit, Angela Y. Davis, Howard Zinn, Amy Goodman, Wallace Shawn, Mike Davis, Winona LaDuke, Ilan Pappé, Richard Wolff, Dave Zirin, Keeanga-Yamahtta Taylor, Nick Turse, Dahr Jamail, David Barsamian, Elizabeth Laird, Amira Hass, Mark Steel, Avi Lewis, Naomi Klein, and Neil Davidson. We are also the trade publishers of the acclaimed Historical Materialism Book Series and of Dispatch Books.

ALSO AVAILABLE FROM HAYMARKET BOOKS

The American Exceptionalism of Jay Lovestone and His Comrades, 1929-1940: Dissident Marxism in the United States: Volume 1
Edited by Tim Davenport and Paul Le Blanc

Black Liberation and the American Dream: The Struggle for Racial and Economic Justice | Edited by Paul Le Blanc

C. L. R. James and Revolutionary Marxism: Selected Writings of C.L.R. James 1939-1949 | Edited by Paul Le Blanc and Scott McLemee

From Marx to Gramsci: A Reader in Revolutionary Marxist Politics
Edited by Paul Le Blanc

Left Americana: The Radical Heart of US History | Paul Le Blanc

Lenin and the Revolutionary Party | Paul Le Blanc

The Living Flame: The Revolutionary Passion of Rosa Luxemburg
Paul Le Blanc

October Song: Bolshevik Triumph, Communist Tragey, 1917–1924
Paul Le Blanc

Revolutionary Studies: Theory, History, People | Paul Le Blanc

A Short History of the U.S. Working Class: From Colonial Times to the Twenty-First Century | Paul Le Blanc

Trotskyism in the United States: Historical Essays and Reconsiderations
Edited by George Breitman, Paul Le Blanc, and Alan Wald

Unfinished Leninism: The Rise and Return of a Revolutionary Doctrine
Paul Le Blanc

ABOUT THE AUTHOR

Paul Le Blanc, long-time activist and professor of history at La Roche College, is the author of a number of widely read studies, including *Lenin and the Revolutionary Party*, *From Marx to Gramsci*, and *Marx, Lenin, and the Revolutionary Experience*. With Michael Yates, he has written the widely acclaimed *A Freedom Budget for All Americans*. He has also written and spoken extensively on the politics and legacy of Rosa Luxemburg.